Unclean Lips

THE GOLDSTEIN-GOREN SERIES IN AMERICAN JEWISH HISTORY
General editor: Hasia R. Diner

We Remember with Reverence and Love: American Jews and the Myth of Silence after the Holocaust, 1945–1962
Hasia R. Diner

Is Diss a System? A Milt Gross Comic Reader
Edited by Ari Y. Kelman

All Together Different: Yiddish Socialists, Garment Workers, and the Labor Roots of Multiculturalism
Daniel Katz

Jews and Booze: Becoming American in the Age of Prohibition
Marni Davis

Jewish Radicals: A Documentary History
Tony Michels

1929: Mapping the Jewish World
Edited by Hasia R. Diner and Gennady Estraikh

An Unusual Relationship: Evangelical Christians and Jews
Yaakov Ariel

Unclean Lips: Obscenity, Jews, and American Culture
Josh Lambert

Unclean Lips

Obscenity, Jews, and American Culture

JOSH LAMBERT

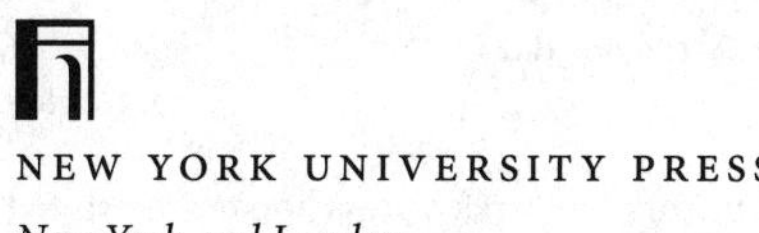

NEW YORK UNIVERSITY PRESS
New York and London

NEW YORK UNIVERSITY PRESS
New York and London
www.nyupress.org

LIBRARY OF CONGRESS CATALOGING-IN-PUBLICATION DATA
Lambert, Joshua N.
Unclean lips : obscenity, Jews, and American culture / Josh Lambert.
pages cm
Includes bibliographical references and index.
ISBN 978-1-4798-7643-3 (cloth : alk. paper)
1. Pornography—Social aspects—United States. 2. Erotic comic books, strips, etc.—United States—History and criticism. 3. Obscenity (Law)—United States. 4. Censorship—United States. 5. Words, Obscene—Humor. 6. American fiction—20th century—History and criticism. 7. American fiction—Jewish authors—History and criticism. I. Title.
HQ471.L225 2013
363.4'70973—dc23
2013019860

New York University Press books are printed on acid-free paper, and their binding materials are chosen for strength and durability. We strive to use environmentally responsible suppliers and materials to the greatest extent possible in publishing our books.

Manufactured in the United States of America

10 9 8 7 6 5 4 3 2 1

Also available as an ebook

For Sara

CONTENTS

ACKNOWLEDGMENTS

This book has benefited from the support of many institutions, colleagues, and friends.

At the University of Michigan, where the project began, I had the privilege of studying with a remarkable group of scholars and teachers. Jonathan Freedman, Anita Norich, Deborah Dash Moore, Julian Levinson, and June Howard in particular continue to serve as mentors, models, and inspiration. Hasia Diner was generous in bringing me to New York University and was an ideally supportive colleague during my time there, not least in connecting this book with its editor and publisher. The collegiality of Lawrence Shiffman, Jeffrey Rubinstein, David Engel, Gennady Estraikh, Yael Feldman, Micah Gottlieb, and others in the Skirball Department of Hebrew and Judaic Studies helped to make my years as a Dorot Assistant Professor and Faculty Fellow at NYU not only productive but also, unwaveringly, a pleasure. Recently, as I have taken on new roles at the Yiddish Book Center and the University of Massachusetts, Amherst, the support of Aaron Lansky, Susan Bronson, James Young, and Joseph Bartolomeo has made it possible to bring this project to a close while beginning a handful of new ones.

Many other scholars offered me suggestions, opportunities to speak, and encouragement during the time I researched and wrote the book. They include Amy Adler, Nehama Ashkenazy, Murray Baumgarten, Sara Blair, Joanna Brooks, Justin Cammy, Beatrice Caplan, Marc Caplan, Mark Cohen, June Cummins-Lewis, Jeremy Dauber, Morris Dickstein, Jonathan Elukin, Esther Frank, Richard Freund, Jay Gertzman, Loren Glass, Dagmar Herzog, Amy Hungerford, Samuel Kassow, Ellen Kellman, Ari Y. Kelman, Michael P. Kramer, Mikhail Krutikov, Louis Menand, Tony Michels, Alan Mintz, Dan Miron, Kenneth Moss, Edna Nahshon, Elisa New, Ranen Omer-Sherman, Eileen Pollack, Eddy Portnoy, Riv-Ellen Prell, Leah Price,

David Rosen, Laurence Roth, Adam Rovner, Rachel Rubinstein, Jonathan Sarna, Raymond Scheindlin, Esther Schor, Jeffrey Shandler, Adam Shear, Mark Shechner, David Shneer, Steven W. Siegel z"l, Ilan Stavans, Michaël Taugis, Alan Wald, Donald Weber, Hana Wirth-Nesher, and Ruth Wisse.

The project received financial support from the Mark Uveleer Dissertation Scholarship of the Memorial Foundation for Jewish Culture, a summer fellowship from the Feinstein Center at Temple University, the Dr. Sophie Bookhalter Fellowship in Jewish Culture at the Center for Jewish History, and a handful of other grants and fellowships from both the Rackham Graduate School and Frankel Center for Judaic Studies at the University of Michigan.

Editors at *Tablet* magazine, the *Forward*, the *Los Angeles Times*, and the *Los Angeles Review of Books* worked with me on reviews and essays related to my research for this book, and I appreciate their editorial suggestions and their willingness to publish my writing. Carolyn Hessel and her staff at the Jewish Book Council have helped me to connect with audiences across the country and with many contemporary writers. I am grateful to Brukhe Lang Caplan, Vera Szabo, David Braun, and Esther Frank for teaching me Yiddish, and I appreciate the intellectual and professional support of many junior scholars and friends, including Ari Ariel, Daniel Belasco, Amos Bitzan, Lia Brozgal, Greg Cohen, Rachel Gordan, Jessica Hammerman, Lori Harrison-Kahan, Warren Hoffman, Sonia Isard, David Koffman, Avinoam Patt, Benjamin Pollak, Lara Rabinovitch, Andrew Romig, Kerry Wallach, Loren Wolfe, and Paul Zakrzewski. Kevan Choset's generosity as a reader saved me from too many errors to count.

Material from this book has been presented as conference papers and invited talks at the Center for Jewish History, Columbia University, Trinity College, McGill University, and conferences organized by Post45, the Modern Languages Association, and the Association for Jewish Studies. The project has been strengthened by the responses of audience members, respondents, and copanelists. In substantially different form, a portion of chapter 2 appeared in *The Jewish Graphic Novel: Critical Approaches* (Piscataway: Rutgers University Press, 2008), edited by Ranen Omer-Sherman and Samantha Baskind, and parts of chapter 4 appeared in *Choosing Yiddish: Studies in Yiddish Literature,*

Culture, and History (Detroit: Wayne State University Press, 2012), edited by Lara Rabinovitch, Hannah Pressman, and Shiri Goren.

No one could ask for a more committed editor than Jennifer Hammer, and I am grateful to her colleagues at New York University Press for the effort they have poured into this project.

Many years of support from my family, Lamberts and Kippurs both, made this book possible.

And Sara and Asher? What else can I say but that I owe you both so fucking much?

Introduction

In late October 1961, the police chief of Mount Prospect, a Chicago suburb, took action against what he perceived to be a disturbing threat to his community: a paperback edition of Henry Miller's notorious 1934 novel *Tropic of Cancer*. Visiting six drugstores that sold paperbacks, he succeeded in having all copies of the book pulled from the shelves.[1] He could do this, the First Amendment notwithstanding, because Miller's novel included what the law regarded as obscenity: obscenity defined, that is, in words with which U.S. Postmaster General Arthur Summerfield characterized Miller's novel, as "descriptions in minute detail of sexual acts" and the use of "filthy, offensive and degrading words and terms."[2] By then, a long series of legal precedents had established that obscenity, like libel and "fighting words," did not merit First Amendment protection.

A few weeks later, a Northwestern University professor named Franklyn Haiman, acting with the support of the American Civil Liberties Union, sued the local police for infringing on what he considered his right to read Miller's novel. The book's American publisher, Barney Rosset of Grove Press, described the resulting trial as "the most dramatic" of sixty such legal cases nationwide that contested the suppression of Miller's *Tropic of Cancer*. Edward de Grazia, a lawyer and legal historian, singles out that Chicago trial as "one of the best examples" of how lawyers and judges together transformed a few statements from a 1957 Supreme Court obscenity decision, *Roth v. United States*, into a widely applicable First Amendment defense of so-called dirty books, a defense that had profound consequences for the representation of sex in American literature and culture.[3]

What goes unmentioned in accounts of this crucial trial is the prominence of Jews among the advocates for Miller's novel. Haiman, the plaintiff who initiated the suit, was Jewish, and so was his lawyer, the veteran First Amendment advocate Elmer Gertz. The book's publisher, Rosset, considered himself half Jewish. The paperback of Miller's book contained an introduction by the poet Karl Shapiro, whose most recent collection of verse was titled *Poems of a Jew*. Gertz called as the first expert witness to testify on behalf of the novel Northwestern University literary scholar and James Joyce biographer Richard Ellmann, son of Jewish immigrants from Romania and Ukraine. The presiding judge, Samuel B. Epstein—who referred to Miller's novel as "filth" but ultimately decided the case in favor of Haiman's "freedom to read"—was, like Ellmann, a first-generation American, whose father had trained at the famed Slobodka yeshiva in Lithuania and had come to Chicago in 1911 to lead one of the nation's largest Orthodox Jewish communities.[4]

Should the Jewishness of Haiman, Gertz, Rosset, Shapiro, Ellmann, and Epstein matter to literary historians interested in the legal defense of *Tropic of Cancer*? Miller, a German American whose forebears were Catholics, did consider Jewishness relevant to his literary project and to the issue of American treatments of obscenity. In *Tropic of Cancer*, Miller's autobiographical narrator almost prophesizes the events of the Chicago trial when he notes that "the first people to turn to when you're down and out are the Jews." Even more pointedly, the narrator, aware that his monologues constitute criminal obscenity under the American laws of his time, remarks that he might as well "become a Jew" himself: "Why not?" he wonders, on the book's third page. "I already speak like a Jew."[5]

* * *

We cannot, of course, blithely accept the implication of Miller's narrator's remark. It would be a mistake to explain the participation of Haiman, Gertz, Rosset, Shapiro, Ellmann, and Epstein in the defense of *Tropic of Cancer* by saying that as Jews they were predisposed to favor obscene language. That would mean endorsing a venerable, deplorable, and ignorant anti-Semitic tradition that has understood Jewish speech and writing as obscene. Indeed, the concept of obscenity evolved in American legal discourse in the late 19th century as a response to fears about the speech and behavior of Jews and others suspected of being insufficiently American and Christian. The idea of Jews as differing sexually from Christians had a long history by then: in the ancient Mediterranean, Jews had been called an "obscene people," who were "prone to lust," and "indisputably carnal" by Romans and early Christians who repudiated the Jewish practices of circumcision and polygamy.[6] Such fantasies about Jews' abnormal sexuality persisted in the centuries that followed, though not always as explicitly.[7] They resurfaced forcefully, however, in the panics arising from the democratization of the mass media in the decades after the Civil War, when the new European anti-Semitism, which frequently linked Jewish greed with lust, found its way to the United States.[8] A leading French anti-Semite, Édouard Drumont, fumed in 1886 about a "pornographic war" being waged by avaricious Jews against Christian France, and his American counterpart, Telemachus Timayenis, repeated and enlarged such claims in English-language publications.[9] In *The Original Mr. Jacobs* (1888)—which was not very "original" but largely a plagiarism-in-translation of Drumont's *La France juive*—Timayenis claimed,

> Nearly all obscene publications are the work of the Jews. . . . The historian of the future who shall attempt to describe the catalogue of the filthy publications issued by the Jews during the last ten years will scarcely believe the evidence of his own eyes. Scenes of gross debauchery, representing drunken monks in the society of girls, priests lashing nude women, filthy groups, and other outrageous pictures, are displayed on all sides, with Jewish effrontery, in the windows and stores.[10]

Adding a detail peculiar to the American scene, Timayenis ventured to hope that "Anthony Comstock . . . would try to bring to justice the Jew editors that disgrace public morals by their filthy articles."[11] Comstock was, of course, the architect of American obscenity law—the 1873 federal statutes regulating obscenity in the mail have always been referred to as the Comstock laws. In fact, by the time Timayenis published his condemnation of the "filthy publications issued by Jews," Comstock had already been devoting considerable energy to regulating the activities of American Jews.

Comstock first gained institutional support from the New York City YMCA in the wake of an 1871 scandal in which a Polish Jewish immigrant, Jacob Rosensweig, was convicted for the accidental death of a young woman during an attempted abortion in New York City. In the years that followed, as Comstock arrested scores of people—frequently, the sociologist Nicola Beisel has shown, women and immigrants—for distributing contraceptive devices and obscene texts, he explicitly identified a number of his targets, including Moses Jacoby and Morris Bass, as Jews.[12] Comstock did not regard these Jews as acting as individuals but as conspiring with other Jews: in the case of Bass, a news report quoted a director of the New York Society for the Suppression of Vice (NYSSV), Comstock's organization, to the effect that Comstock believed that a district attorney and judge had corruptly colluded to place onto the jury six "Dutch Jews . . . who were opposed to [the] society," thus winning the case for Bass, who "was a Dutch Jew, too."[13] Comstock's speeches regularly emphasized a commitment to Christian virtue, at times in contrast, at least symbolically, to Jewish sinfulness. In an address to a gathering of evangelical Christians at the 1893 Chicago World Exposition, Comstock declared, "as we contemplate the foes of moral purity and the harvest of their seed-sowing, we cry out in the words of the prophet of old in his lamentation over the sins of the Jews," and then he cited a verse from Jeremiah.[14]

As it turned out, Comstock's greatest legal triumph in the regulation of printed obscenity would be the Supreme Court's upholding of the conviction of one "Jew editor" in 1896, in a judicial decision that defined obscenity in American constitutional law for half a century. Comstock deliberately and cunningly pursued this editor, whose name was Lew Rosen. Under a false name, Comstock dispatched a letter in April 1893 to the magazine Rosen edited, *Broadway*, a "witty New York society journal," complaining that he had received the recent issue but that "some boy or printer's devil has been playing a joke on you, as the paper on three pages is marred with a black substance marked over them."[15] "There has been no practical joke played on you at all," one of Rosen's employees quickly replied, following instructions from the editor. "It is only lamp black . . . and is easily removed with a piece of bread."[16] When Comstock scrubbed away the grease, he discovered beneath it what the court later referred to as "pictures of females, in different attitudes of indecency." Comstock testified against Rosen, and the latter was convicted and sentenced to thirteen months at hard labor for sending obscenity through the mail. Rosen appealed his conviction all the way up the judicial ladder, but the Supreme Court finally upheld his sentence, condemning Rosen to jail because his aim had been, as Justice John Marshall Harlan wrote, "of course, to excite a curiosity to know what was thus concealed."[17]

Unlike many of the other targets of Comstock's attention, Jewish or not, Rosen was neither an immigrant nor a pauper. Born Lewis Rosenthal in Baltimore, Maryland, on September 10, 1856, he had graduated from Dartmouth College in 1877 and then relocated to Paris, where he tutored an American diplomat's son and contributed to English-language newspapers. He published his first book, *America and France: The Influence of the United States in France in the Eighteenth Century*, with Henry Holt & Company in 1882.[18] Back in the United States, he published a novella titled *Grisette: A Tale of Paris and New York* in 1889 and that same year began to contribute regular, chatty columns of theatrical gossip to the popular *National Police Gazette*.[19] While these later publications were somewhat frivolous, Rosen was more or less respected: a Boston magazine described him in 1889 as "a short, stoutly-built man, with a Boulanger beard," who was "very unassuming and a pleasant conversationalist" and who kept, "in his apartments on Broadway, a magnificent collection of sketches by the artists of to-day."[20] Like a few other American-born, college-educated Jews of his generation, Rosen seems to have eagerly embraced cosmopolitan culture while still unselfconsciously identifying as Jewish. He allowed himself to be listed in a social directory of American Jews in 1888, at least, and in one of his *National Police Gazette* columns he mocked "actors and actresses [who are] ashamed of their beginnings," noting the absurdity of an actress who claimed Scotch descent "while . . . her maiden name, Roth, plainly indicated her German origins" and the silliness of another actor "who was of Jewish descent and denied it."[21] This suggests that Rosen changed his own name not to hide his "Jewish descent" but for the sake of showbiz snappiness—indeed, if the former had been his goal, "Lew Rosen" was a rather clumsy choice.

As comfortable and cultured an American Jew as Rosen may have been, his background made him vulnerable to Comstock. At one point in Rosen's first trial, a prosecutor asked one of the *Broadway* employees, "Didn't Mr. Rosen and yourself get the idea of blacking [the magazine's pages] from the system of press censorship in Russia?"[22] Though the judge sustained Rosen's lawyer's objection to this question—and though nothing in Rosen's background indicates that he had any special interest in Russian periodicals—the implication is clear: despite being a native-born, college-educated American, Rosen, as a Jew, was perceived by his accusers as suspiciously foreign and thus vulnerable to prosecution. In the following half century, other prosecutors would regularly employ the same tactic, raising doubts in court about the American citizenship or legal residence in the United States of Jews accused of obscenity.[23] Rosen seems to have known the courts would not side with him, even if his journalistic colleagues would support him: he avoided jail by relocating to Europe before the Supreme Court considered his case; he resettled in London and earned his keep writing a weekly gossip column for the *Washington Post*.[24] In his absence, a publishing-industry magazine implicitly acknowledged the arbitrariness of Comstock's pursuit of editors who could be smeared as non-Christian and un-American, explaining in 1897 that "several gentlemen are walking the streets of New York who are more guilty of the charge of publishing filthy reading matter than Rosen."[25]

Rosen's case has had an especially high profile as a precedent, but it was hardly atypical for Comstock.[26] According to figures tabulated by the literary historian Jay Gertzman, Comstock's New York Society for the Suppression of Vice throughout its history brought charges against Jews more frequently than against Catholics and Protestants combined. In 1887, nine out of nineteen (47%) of the people arrested for obscenity whose religion was noted in the society's records were Jewish. The proportion hovered between 50% and 60% in the following decades, and in the 1930s it often topped 90%.[27] It is in this context, with Jewish publishers and entrepreneurs being regularly arrested on obscenity charges in New York City, that Miller's narrator's remark about "speak[ing] like a Jew" can be understood. The first publisher of *Tropic of Cancer*, Jack Kahane, was a Manchester-born dandy and one of a few Anglophone Jews who had immigrated to France in the 1920s and begun to publish

English-language books there that were unpublishable in the United States and England because of Comstock and his British counterparts.[28] Miller, then, understood himself as uneasily allied with Jews committed to the publication of what U.S. law deemed obscenity, though he could not have predicted that it would be American Jewish lawyers, editors, and judges who would free his novel from censorship in the 1960s.

In the decade leading up to Rosset's republication of *Tropic of Cancer*, and in the decade that followed it, many of the defendants in crucial, precedent-setting Supreme Court obscenity cases were Jewish men, specifically in *Burstyn v. Wilson* (1952), *Roth v. United States* (1957), *Freedman v. Maryland* (1965), *Mishkin v. New York* (1966), *Ginzburg v. United States* (1966), *Ginsberg v. New York* (1968), *Cohen v. California* (1971), and *Miller v. California* (1973).[29] As conventional and mail-order publishers, editors, film distributors, newsdealers, and social protesters, the men named in these cases tested the limits of the American law of obscenity and of the First Amendment. As in Rosen's case, decisions in several of these cases—particularly *Roth*, *Ginzburg*, *Ginsberg*, and *Miller*—affirmed the defendants' sentences and prison terms while redefining the concept of obscenity in American legal discourse and dramatically transforming the horizon of possibility for American cultural production.

As the Chicago trial of Miller's novel illustrates, American Jews played crucial roles in obscenity controversies not just as defendants but also as lawyers, judges, and witnesses. Jewish lawyers were often willing to defend people accused of obscenity even when their liberal non-Jewish colleagues were not. The American Civil Liberties Union furnishes an example. It was founded after World War I by liberal Protestants who were eager to distance themselves from the anarchists, atheists, and radicals in the Free Speech League who had been the first organized opponents of Comstock's deployment of obscenity law in the late 19th century. As such, the ACLU refused to take up obscenity cases in its first decade. The acting director of the organization pointedly wrote to a Boston librarian in 1927, "We cannot go into the 'anti-obscenity' campaign. . . . That is a phase of free speech we have kept clear of . . . to avoid complicating our main issues." Yet the three prominent Jewish lawyers associated with the group at the time—Harry Weinberger, Arthur Garfield Hays, and Morris Ernst—defended the work of

Sholem Asch, H. L. Mencken, Theodore Dreiser, and James Joyce in a series of crucial obscenity cases in the 1920s and early 1930s.[30] As late as the early 1950s, an ACLU official could remark that the organization did not "believe that the obscenity laws are interfering with freedom of the press in any way."[31] It was another Jewish lawyer, Ernst's protégé Harriet Pilpel, who eventually convinced the ACLU to defend other civil rights threatened by obscenity law, including the sexual rights of gays and lesbians and women's rights to contraception.[32] In the postwar decades, many of the most influential lawyers who took on obscenity cases were also Jewish: Charles Rembar advised his cousin Norman Mailer to bowdlerize "fuck" to "fug" in *The Naked and the Dead* (1948) and served as lead counsel for Rosset's Grove Press; Jake Ehrlich famously defended Allen Ginsberg's *Howl* in San Francisco; Stanley Fleishman was the most prominent First Amendment lawyer in Los Angeles for several decades; and Ephraim London argued key film-censorship cases in front of the Supreme Court. In addition to their legal work, these lawyers also wrote or edited books and essays for popular audiences in which they agitated against the suppression of literature and art, presenting the relevant arguments to authors, publishers, and general audiences who were unlikely to consult articles in legal journals.[33]

Some Jewish judges also exerted substantial influence on the development of the law of obscenity. For example, in 1933, Benjamin Greenspan, a founder of the Wall Street Synagogue, ruled against the suppression of Erskine Caldwell's novel *God's Little Acre*.[34] In the 1940s, the single written opinion to emerge from all four trials of Edmund Wilson's *Memoirs of Hecate County*, the suppression of which was upheld by the Supreme Court, was a dissent by a Polish Jewish immigrant and former congressman, Nathan D. Perlman, who presided along with two other judges over the book's first trial in New York.[35] In the 1950s, it was a thoughtful dissent by a Jewish judge, Jerome Frank, in a case involving a Zionist-poet-turned-literary-pirate-and-pornographer, Samuel Roth, that inspired the Supreme Court to reexamine the law of obscenity.[36] In Chicago in 1960, Judge Julius Hoffman, who was to infamously preside over the trial of Abbie Hoffman and the Chicago Seven later in the decade, acknowledged the consequences of the *Roth* decision in a case about *Big Table*, the literary journal that had been founded by Irving Rosenthal and Paul Carroll, with the help of Allen Ginsberg, after the

University of Chicago refused to let them print pieces by Jack Kerouac and William S. Burroughs in the *Chicago Review*.[37]

These Jewish lower-court judges were hardly alone in countering the suppression of literature under the charge of obscenity and in laying the groundwork in precedent and legal theory for a First Amendment defense of the representation of sexuality in literature and art. Non-Jewish judges including Learned Hand, Augustus Hand, and John Woolsey also contributed influentially to this tradition, as did non-Jewish legal scholars including Theodore Schroeder, Zechariah Chafee, Jr., and Harry Kalven, Jr. Moreover, Jewish judges were hardly of one mind on the question of obscenity. The role of Jewish Supreme Court justices, and particularly of Abe Fortas, in decriminalizing pornography in the 1960s has been strategically overstated by these judges' political opponents, with unfortunate political consequences. The justice with the most influence over the Supreme Court's treatment of obscenity in the postwar decades was not Felix Frankfurter, Arthur Goldberg, or Fortas but a Catholic, William J. Brennan, Jr., and the justices most consistently and most fervently committed to the protection of freedom of expression during the 1950s and 1960s, Hugo Black and William O. Douglas, were also not Jewish.[38] Still, the Jewish lower-court judges mentioned earlier, and a handful of others, contributed progressive decisions that helped lead to the freeing of virtually all literature and most film from obscenity prosecutions by the mid-1960s.

This brief survey of American Jews' interventions in debates about obscenity law hardly exhausts its subject. Many of the American Jews who produced or distributed materials legally classified as obscene, or who worked in the pornography industry, have not left their names on legal landmarks, and the preceding survey also neglects Jewish literary critics and sexologists who either testified at trials or whose insights influenced lawyers, judges, and pornographers themselves.[39] The question remains, too, whether and how the Jewishness of participants in these debates matters.

Certainly one cannot assume that an individual American Jew, simply because he or she is Jewish, will favor laxity in obscenity laws. On the contrary, any number of American Jews have staunchly and influentially opposed the relaxation of obscenity prohibitions, from many Reform rabbis before World War I to Harry Kahan, an operative of the

NYSSV; to Henry Loeb, a Memphis mayor (and convert to Episcopalianism and outspoken segregationist) who mounted a campaign to suppress Philip Roth's novel *Portnoy's Complaint* in the late 1960s; to Irving Kristol, who articulated the neoconservative case for the censorship of pornography in 1971; to Andrea Dworkin, a leader of the antipornography feminist movement in the 1980s; to Judith Reisman, who has more recently attacked Alfred Kinsey as a pervert and advocated for censorship.[40] It seems likely that at least one of the witnesses who testified against *Tropic of Cancer* in that celebrated Chicago trial, a Skokie neuropsychiatrist named Samuel Irving Stein, was also Jewish.[41] There is little evidence, moreover, that any of the half dozen Jewish men who met in that 1960s Chicago courtroom to defend *Tropic of Cancer* considered it important that any of the others were Jews or that any single one of them acted as he did on the basis of a shared Jewish idea or value. Without endorsing and repeating the pernicious anti-Semitic claims of Timayenis and his ilk—for whom Jews will always be an "obscene people," "indisputably carnal," and disturbingly "prone to lust"—how, then, can Jewishness be productively understood as relevant to the interventions of individual Americans in 20th-century debates about obscenity?

* * *

Cultural and legal historians and literary scholars who have studied literary obscenity in the United States and England have tended to avoid the question of the relationship of Jewishness to their subject.[42] Not wanting to reproduce the nativist anti-Semitism of Comstock and other antivice crusaders or to provide support for the racist claims about Jewish sexuality trumpeted by avowed anti-Semites, serious scholars of American law and culture tend not to dwell on the Jewishness of so many of the figures who played key roles in the history of obscenity and pornography in the United States, even while these same scholars do attend scrupulously to the religious and ethnic affiliations of Protestants and Catholics.[43] Jewishness is typically mentioned in the finest books on this subject only when it is raised unavoidably by the participants themselves, and scholars then typically eschew any commentary. Edward de Grazia's massive history of obscenity and American law, for one example, quotes Edmund Wilson's remark that the only judge to write "a highly intelligent opinion" in the original trial of his suppressed collection of short stories, *Memoirs of Hecate County* (1946), was "the Jewish one, Perlman"—but de Grazia does not address the question of why Wilson considered Perlman's Jewishness to be relevant or whether there was any merit in that observation.[44]

The role of Jews in the history of obscenity in 20th-century American culture offers an extraordinary case, then, of what the intellectual historian David Hollinger has identified as the "booster-bigot trap," which "tempts the scholar" interested in the contributions of a minority group to an industry or area of cultural endeavor—the role of Jews in the institutional developments of physics or of free-market capitalism or of the Hollywood studio system, or the role of Italians in the construction industry or in organized crime, or of African Americans in the development of American basketball or jazz—"to choose between the uncritical celebration of '[that group's] contributions' and the malevolent complaint about '[that group's] influence.'"[45] As Hollinger would predict, boosters and bigots on the subject of Jews and obscenity abound. A handful of observers, journalists, and popular writers have proffered generalized, "uncritical celebration[s]" of Jews' support of sexual expression: Hugh Hefner, a lifelong non-Jewish philo-Semite, asserted admiringly in the 1960s, for example, that "American Jews—while not nearly as sexually permissive as the Hebrews of the Old Testament—are more liberal than either American Catholics or the main stream of American Protestantism,"[46] while the Jewish celebrity sexologist Dr. Ruth Westheimer has more recently claimed that "Judaism is intensely sexual" and that "sex, in and of itself, has never been a sin for Jews, or something not to discuss."[47] Their good intentions notwithstanding, such approaches rely on essentialist visions of Jewishness that mirror those of anti-Semites. Thus, these statements can easily be exploited by people with unsavory aims: when, in 2004, Nathan Abrams, a scholar of American Jewish culture, published an article arguing that "secular Jews have played (and still continue to play) a disproportionate role throughout the adult film industry in America," almost immediately anti-Semitic websites seized on the story and folded it into hoary accusations about an "international Jewish child porn/murder operation" that grimly evokes false accusations that, as we will see, circulated in Europe and the United States in the late 19th and early 20th centuries.[48]

This helps to explain why the most sophisticated studies of obscenity in American law and culture to date have remained silent on the subject of participants' Jewishness. As Hollinger notes, most often the way that Americanist scholars "avoid both boosterism and bigotry" around the question of Jews' influence in a particular industry or area of cultural endeavor is simply "to avoid talking about Jews."[49] The unintended consequence of such understandable reticence has been the neglect by scholars of American culture of some of the key dynamics through which concerns about ethnicity, religion, and sexuality intertwined in the literary and cultural history of the United States.

* * *

The alternative to the booster-bigot trap should not come as a methodological surprise to scholars working in ethnic and cultural studies. As Hollinger phrases it, the solution is to insist on a resolute antiessentialism that recognizes "the internal diversity of ethnoracial groups and the contingent, historically specific character of the culture these communities present to the larger society at any given moment."[50] One cannot responsibly make general, transhistorical claims about Asian American musical culture or homosexuals' attitudes toward religion—or, for that matter, about "the Jews" (as both anti-Semites and philo-Semites regularly do)—because ethnic, racial, and sexual identities and affiliations are almost never tidy or stable enough to pin such generalizations on. This point would seem to be so widely agreed on by contemporary scholars, at least, that it hardly needs restating. Yet for the sake of the coherence of their analyses, and in service to identitarianism, scholars do continue to slip back into essentialism—which, when pressed, they can defend as "strategic"—all too regularly.[51]

A wave of recent studies of Jews and sexuality have emphasized both the internal diversity and historically specific nature of Jews' sexual behavior and attitudes.[52] One excellent entry in this literature, David Biale's synoptic *Eros and the Jews*, emphasizes the "tensions, contradictions, and conflicts" that characterize Jewish attitudes toward sex across thousands of years of history—a project he framed in the early 1990s as part of the scholarly effort of "deconstructing Judaism."[53] This makes it all the more noticeable when Biale slips into reductive essentialism in his chapter on Jews and sexuality in the United States, generalizing that the variety of American Jews' treatments of sexuality are "all dedicated to a common struggle: to harmonize the Jewish experience with American culture and thus to negotiate the integration of Jews in American society." This claim is, at best, partially true.[54] To posit a desire for Jewish American harmony at the center of all American Jewish representations of sexuality—another instance of what Jonathan Sarna has perceptively diagnosed as a "cult of synthesis" in the writing of American Jewish history[55]—does not adequately account for the usefulness of obscenity to those American Jews who wished to reject their own Jewish heritage or for the vehemence with which some Jews battled against the U.S. government's regulation of expression.[56] As inconvenient as it may be for the cultural historian, there simply is no unifying dynamic that can explain the variety of Jews' engagements with obscenity: American Jews who have engaged with obscenity from the late 19th century to the present are simply too diverse, too subject to historical contingency, too unpredictable to fit *any* single generalization. It should be self-evident that even meaningful analytical concepts, such as those of the "pariah capitalist" and "middleman minority," which Jay Gertzman valuably brings to bear on the American Jewish erotica dealers of the 1920s and 1930s, cannot sensibly be applied to all American Jews throughout history.[57] However well these categories apply to poor, relatively marginalized mail-order book dealers such as Esar Levine and Benjamin Rebhuhn, they do not shed much light on the six Jewish men—a prize-winning poet, two university professors, an eminent lawyer, a wealthy banker's-son-turned-publisher, and an appointed judge—whose combined efforts resulted in the freeing of Miller's *Tropic of Cancer* from censorship in Illinois in early 1962.[58]

This book builds on the studies that have analyzed Jews' sexual representations and activities in the United States, such as Biale's and Gertzman's, while insisting that no single explanatory paradigm adequately accounts for the range of phenomena it addresses. It takes its title from a traditional rabbinic text that adduces such antiessentialism in a discussion about Jews and sinful speech. In Isaiah 6:5, the prophet refers to himself as "a man of unclean lips" who dwells among "a people of unclean lips"—a moment Henry Roth relates to "dirty words" in his novel *Call It Sleep*. It is the Babylonian Talmud's trenchant critique of the prophet's remark that resonates most with the method of the current study: Isaiah's calling *himself* unclean is tolerable enough, the rabbis of the Talmud suggest, but it was egregious on his part that he went on to generalize about all Jews on the evidence of a single individual.[59] Like the authors of that statement, if in a radically different context and for entirely different reasons, this book refuses to accept broad generalizations about Jews and obscenity.

It must be acknowledged, moreover, that American Jews often engaged with obscenity—produced it, defended it, wrote about it—for precisely the same reasons that many of their Protestant, Catholic, and nonreligious peers did so: to make money, to seek sexual gratification, to express antisocial rage. None of these motivations is any more Jewish than it is non-Jewish. Take the first, as an example. Since antiquity, it has been obvious to just about everyone (except perhaps self-appointed moralists) that suppressed literature has tremendous sales potential: as the linguists Keith Allan and Kate Burridge point out, Tacitus remarked as early as the 2nd century CE that "banned writings are eagerly sought and read."[60] It is a non-Jewish publicist to whom the quintessential, if apocryphal, anecdote about this dynamic, as it applies to the modern United States, is attributed: the legendary public-relations pioneer Harry Reichenbach claimed that when he was hired to promote the sale of lithographs of Paul Chabas's painting *September Morn* by a New York store owner who had purchased thousands of copies of the print, Reichenbach cannily posted the print in a shop window, hired a group of young children to ogle it, and then anonymously informed Anthony Comstock of the situation. According to the mythical anecdote, Comstock arrested the store owner, newspapers reported the event, and the print sold like hotcakes forever after.[61] Jewish erotica dealers certainly used similar tactics: in 1930, Esar Levine suggested to the wife of a cash-strapped author, "Have a French printer set up the . . . volume of short stories. Have it 'privately printed' by the author. . . . If you do this, the public will buy hundreds of copies. . . . You have no idea . . . what a magic effect 'privately printed' on the title page of a book of snappy stories would have!"[62] Yet in sources of information about Jews who produced and defended obscenity in the modern United States, I have not been able to discover anything that makes their interest in the financial rewards of these endeavors distinct from the financial interests of

American non-Jews. On the contrary, when Jews talk about making a fortune by selling pornography, they sound the same notes as do Americans of other ethnic and religious backgrounds, such as Larry Flynt and Gerard Damiano, for whom obscenity held the same promise.[63]

Similarly, some American Jews have embraced obscenity as a means for obtaining sexual gratification, or for expressing anger about their individual lives, in ways that do not seem to have any particular stakes or resonances for them as members of a religious, social, or other group. Such embraces of obscenity as transgression for its own sake, for the pleasure of catharsis, tend to implicitly, if not explicitly, acknowledge their own lack of instrumentality. The shouting of a taboo word in a moment of sudden pain does not mean anything more or different for an American Jew than it does for anyone else.[64] Al Goldstein, publisher of *Screw* and host of *Midnight Blue*, furnishes a colorful example of such motivation for engagements with obscenity. While Goldstein invokes his own Jewishness regularly, his signature concern has been his implacable rage. "What motivates me is not love, but hatred," Goldstein remarks in his autobiography. "*Screw* was always fueled by anger. Unlike others who reach success, I was not warmed or tempered by it. I remained angry and only got crazier."[65] Decades earlier, Philip Roth captured this aspect of Goldstein's motivation when he ventriloquized him in *The Anatomy Lesson* (1983): "With me money is not the paramount issue," Roth's Goldstein-stand-in insists. "The defiance is. The hatred is. The outrage is."[66]

Of course, even in Goldstein's case, one can hardly distinguish the use of obscenity as personal, apolitical rage from its use for political, social, or aesthetic ends.[67] Dickering over whether "redeeming value" inheres in a particular allegedly obscene text or act has often made American judges look ridiculous. An apposite case occurred in March 1965 in Berkeley, where the insistence of a few students that "free speech" included obscenity troubled the leaders of the Berkeley Free Speech Movement (FSM). When an aspiring poet from New York wrote the word "fuck" on a piece of paper and sat on the corner of Bancroft Way and Telegraph Avenue, at the edge of campus, a police officer arrested him. A graduate student in education named Art Goldberg organized a rally in which students asserted their right to use the word *fuck* as much as they liked. Nine of the participants were arrested; Goldberg was arrested, impressively, twice on a single day.[68] Goldberg's cause was not sympathetic to the majority of the Free Speech Movement's leaders, because the defense of obscene speech did not seem a sufficiently worthy issue. As a historian of the movement explains, "most FSM veterans, prudish as dedicated politicos often are, were dismayed" by what came to be dubbed as the Filthy Speech Movement. Mario Savio, a leader of the FSM, recalled that "somehow the issue seemed too abstract to people. People didn't want to associate themselves with the problem of obscenity."[69] Goldberg received a sentence of ninety days in jail and was expelled from the university, and the FSM did not protest. A few years later, the U.S. Supreme Court declared in its ruling in *Cohen v. California* (1971) that "the State may not . . . make the simple public display here involved of this single four-letter expletive a criminal offense," speaking to the facts of Goldberg's case almost directly and effacing the distinction that the FSM leaders made between what might be called abstract obscenity—the use of taboo words outside a meaningful context—and obscenity for patently political or aesthetic ends.[70] Cohen had worn a jacket reading "Fuck the Draft" into a courthouse, but the court went beyond the defense of his right to political protest, legitimizing the "simple public display" of a taboo word, whether or not that display is obviously political. Was Goldberg's rally on behalf of the word *fuck* apolitical and Cohen's jacket political? On some level, the distinction is moot, as David Goines argues from an absolutist perspective in his memoir of participation in the Free Speech Movement, as "all forms of speech become political when they are restricted or forbidden."[71] In this sense, government efforts to suppress obscene speech mean that all obscenity, however abstract or apolitical it may seem, constitutes a putatively political act.

Still, this book considers obscenity such as Goldberg's and Goldstein's—obscenity that appears to be produced for thrills or catharsis, or simply as a rejection of the law for the sake of rejecting the law, irrespective of its contents—as obeying such universal human urges that, like obscenity motivated exclusively by profit, they are not of central concern to a consideration of the relations between Jewishness and obscenity in American culture. Jewishness is simply not relevant to every engagement with obscenity by a Jew, so this book focuses on cases, and on cultural dynamics, through which obscenity has been specifically meaningful to American Jews *as* Jews.[72] No motivations for engagement with obscenity have applied uniquely to American Jews, of course, nor can any such motivations be said to have applied to all Jews in the United States. Nor did factors operate in isolation. They regularly intertwined, in unexpected ways, in the cases of individual artists, legal professionals, and cultural agents, with many other social factors and with these people's broader interests.

This book argues, nonetheless, that Jewishness served as a crucial factor in the decisions made by many of the participants in the long, strange history of American obscenity, especially because of the complexity of the roles Jews played in American publishing and literary culture. Each chapter that follows concentrates on one aspect of obscenity that made debates about sexual representation specifically meaningful for American Jews and selects a set of sample cases that most strikingly demonstrate that particular link. Though these are not cases in which a single motivating factor operates in isolation, they have been selected because they seem somewhat less bewilderingly overdetermined by a dozen competing factors than other cases one might examine. This volume intentionally does not offer a comprehensive accounting of cases in which American Jews intervened in obscenity debates or a chronological historical survey of such interventions. The dynamics around Jewishness in the American film and theater industries' engagements with obscenity law, mentioned mostly in passing here, deserve complete studies of their own. The most famous cases are not always emphasized here, either: the comedian Lenny Bruce, for example, is discussed but not nearly in as much depth as some readers might expect. For reasons both disciplinary and practical, this book focuses most often on literary texts and devotes its attention to surprising and critically neglected examples that most clearly substantiate the argument that Jewishness could and did matter to many Americans, Jewish or not, in their engagements with the question of obscenity.

Broadly, the first two chapters emphasize the effects of widely held anti-Jewish sentiments and resulting policies on the relationship between obscenity and Jewishness in the United States. The first chapter surveys the embrace of obscenity as a means of refuting accusations made by anti-Semites about Jewish sexual abnormality, which, as noted earlier, circulated widely in the late 19th and early 20th centuries and spurred Comstock's moral activism and the development of the American law of obscenity itself. Accusations of Jewish lechery appeared in anti-Semitic tracts and medical textbooks and also surfaced in popular and prestigious realist and naturalist literature by the likes of H. Rider Haggard, Émile Zola, and Edith Wharton. As a response to such texts, and inspired by the sexological theories of Sigmund Freud, literary modernists including James Joyce and Theodore Dreiser rejected the idea of Jewish sexual deviance by positioning nonnormatively sexual Jews at the center of their narratives. In so doing, they simultaneously acknowledged the range of sexual behaviors engaged in by all humans and asserted that Jews were no more "prone to lust" than were non-Jews. American Jewish authors, beginning with Ludwig Lewisohn, intensified this approach, representing Jewish perspectives on sex as uniquely healthy alternatives to American puritanism. By the 1940s, Americans began to figure the rise of Nazism as a symptom of sexual repression and rapacity that could be countered through frank and open discussions of sexual desires; in texts from Ka-Tzetnik's *House of Dolls* (1955) to Edward Lewis Wallant's *The Pawnbroker* (1961) and beyond, writers insisted on explicit sexual representation as necessary for a complete accounting of the Nazis' crimes. At the same time, American lawyers began to frame obscenity as a crucial test of the government's support of the minority rights that had been infamously abrogated by the Nazi regime. The dynamic traced throughout the chapter—the explicit representation of sexuality as countering the spread of sexual anti-Semitism—reaches its apotheosis in Robert Rimmer's *The Harrad Experiment* (1966), a best-selling novel that distilled anti-anti-Semitic sexological theory into a mass-market fiction of sexual utopia. While it is by no means clear, in retrospect, that the explicit discussion of sex actually mitigates sexual anti-Semitism, this chapter argues that the *perception* that it might do so shaped key developments in literary modernism and, especially, in the liberalization of obscenity law in the postwar United States.

While the first chapter takes up a specific and rather consistently articulated set of anti-Semitic images, the second chapter examines how changes in the social and cultural positioning of Jews in the United States could transform the meaning of obscenity for them. In the heyday of literary modernism after World War I, obscenity served as an effective medium of exchange through which Americans could transform financial resources or even social marginality into literary prestige (or, as the sociologist and theorist Pierre Bourdieu calls it, cultural capital)—and, in the 1920s, this was something wealthy Jews needed, because other avenues to respectability had been barred to them. The career of Horace Liveright exemplifies how this dynamic operated for many American Jewish publishers. Liveright transformed himself from a ridiculed parvenu to the most respected of American publishers, with a list that included Dreiser, Sherwood Anderson, T. S. Eliot, Ezra Pound, Djuna Barnes, Jean Toomer, Ernest Hemingway, and William Faulkner. He achieved this by fighting censorship in courts and in the press. His struggle against the New York Clean Books League bill in 1923, in particular, earned him the gratitude of modernist tastemakers. The case of Henry Roth demonstrates that obscenity could function similarly for an author: while acknowledged as a classic of American fiction, Roth's *Call It Sleep* (1935) includes all the taboo words that resulted in the novels of James Joyce and D. H. Lawrence being suppressed. Attention to the precise contexts of that novel's publication helps to explain why Roth, a poor immigrant with none of the cultural stature of Joyce or Lawrence and none of the financial resources of Liveright, would have had the temerity to thrust himself into the debate about literary obscenity. The chapter insists that the power of an engagement with obscenity to earn a Jew cultural prestige was the contingent product of the positioning of Jews and obscenity in American culture at a particular historical moment, and so it concludes with a contrasting discussion of the use of obscenity by American Jews in the late 1970s and early 1980s in their efforts to imbue a discredited cultural form, the so-called graphic novel, with literary prestige. This demonstrates just how much had changed, for obscenity and for Jewishness, in American literary culture in half a century.

These first two chapters demonstrate that anti-Semitism, both sexual and genteel, has made obscenity seem meaningful and useful, even necessary, to some American Jews. The third and fourth chapters turn to ways in which tropes from the Jewish literary tradition and debates in contemporary Jewish thought have produced similar results for other Jews, at other moments. American obscenity law developed out of linked anxieties about textual and sexual reproduction: the Comstock laws in one breath prohibited textual representations of sexuality and the circulation of information about contraception. Jewish textual traditions have a rich, complex discourse about reproduction, and over the course of the 20th century, as Jewish demographics in the United States changed—from the beginning of the century, when immigrant Jews lived in one of the poorest and most overpopulated neighborhoods in the world, to the postwar decades, when journalists and social scientists worried that American Jews were "vanishing"—reproduction recurred as a tense and fascinating subject. Obscenity mattered, then, in a different way, whenever American Jews wrote and thought about reproduction, whether they were Yiddish anarchists and prominent doctors advocating for birth control in the 1910s or novelists taking up the question of intermarriage as a threat to cultural reproduction in the 1960s. The chapter examines the stakes of early birth control debates for Jewish entrepreneurs, lawyers, doctors, and writers and then turns to a discussion of how the language of obscenity, once it became available in the mid-1960s, could be used, by such writers as Philip Roth and Adele Wiseman, to engage and renew traditional allegories of reproduction from the Jewish textual tradition. This chapter demonstrates, then, that graphic representations of sexuality, among their many other uses, enable innovative literary examinations and exhibitions of American and Jewish communal politics.

The other key area of traditional Jewish discourse that impinges on the questions raised by obscenity in the 20th-century United States is that of modesty and appropriate speech. How different is *nivul peh*, the rabbinic category of foul-mouthed language, from American obscenity? The fourth chapter answers this question by focusing on differences between standards for sexual representation as established with or without state authority—and by presenting Yiddish literature in America as an example of the latter. Unlike Yiddish literature in Russia or Hebrew literature in Israel, Yiddish literature in America was almost never subject to legal regulation but only to what Yiddish critics called *tsnies* (modesty): limits imposed by publishers, authors, and reading communities, rather than by state and legal authorities. Since *Memoirs v. Massachusetts* (1966), the situation of American novelists writing in English has come to resemble the situation of Yiddish American writers in the first half of the century, in the sense that the representation of sexuality in their works is no longer regulated by the state but instead by the metaphorical censorships described by Freud and Bourdieu. Fittingly, the 1980s and 1990s saw the rise of a new discourse of modesty in American culture that is by no means exclusively Jewish but that has often been promulgated by Orthodox Jewish writers and critics such as Wendy Shalit and Shmuely Boteach. The chapter demonstrates how this emergent model of literary modesty reflects the transformation of American literature, for better and worse, into a symbolically diasporic one: a literature, in other words, unthreatened by and nonthreatening to legal and political authorities. The example of Yiddish American literature, then, in addition to its own aesthetic and historical importance, provides a sense of the stakes of the American turn from obscenity regulated by law to modesty regulated by participants in the literary system.

These chapters treat a wide swath of texts, from canonical modern and postmodern literature to mass-market fiction and hard-core pornography, and they do so with attention to a variety of historical circumstances. Together they provide four complementary lenses through which we can view obscenity debates as mattering to American Jews, as Jews: because of their opposition to sexual anti-Semitism, their pursuit of cultural capital, their anxieties about reproduction, and their concerns about modesty. One could point to dozens of other texts and cases, not discussed in detail here, in which ideas about obscenity and about Jewishness became meaningfully intertwined in the United States during the 20th century. This book cannot possibly offer an exhaustive accounting of all of those, but my hope is that the approaches demonstrated here may illuminate many of those other cases, too, and also serve as a model for the kind of study that can be produced on the way religious, ethnic, and racial affiliations influence authors, publishers, lawyers, and pornographers as they engage with obscenity. The focus on Jews and Jewishness in this book should not be understood as implying that there are not equally important studies still to be done on other American groups and their engagements with legal and literary obscenity—the question of obscenity is crucial in African American literary history, for one clear example[73]—but what this volume hopes to accomplish through its concentration on one particular minority group is, first, to fill an unnecessary, gaping, literary-historiographical gap and, second, to model an approach to American Jewish literary studies that attends to the full and complex range of Jews' contributions to American literary history, not just as celebrated authors but also throughout the publishing industry and in a variety of contiguous fields.

* * *

Which of the four issues treated in the chapters that follow, one might ask, explains the role of Jews in the Chicago trial of *Tropic of Cancer* with which we began? It should now be clear that there can be no single or simple answer to any question of this sort. One can, at best, consider the players as individuals. In the Chicago trial, the plaintiff and his lawyers at the ACLU framed the trial as concerning individual rights, while Judge Epstein's remark that "recent history has proven the evil of an attempt at controlling the utterances and thoughts of our population"[74] suggests that he understood the case in relation to anti-Semitic fascism as well as McCarthyism. The lawyer Elmer Gertz suggested how present the Holocaust might have been in his mind when he approvingly quoted a bookseller who, questioned about the suppression of Miller's novel, asked, "Why did we fight the Nazis if we are now imitating them?"[75] It is telling, along the same lines, that among the critical letters Epstein received in the wake of his decision, "some were anti-Semitic," including one screed that invoked hoary anti-Semitic rhetoric worthy of Timayenis: "I am certain . . . the Elders of Zion smiled in whole-hearted approval at your ingrained method of dispensing Pharasaic justice, as it met all the specifications regarding the letter of their perverted laws and rulings."[76] Rosset, the publisher of Grove Press who started it all, seems to have been motivated to publish Miller's novel, in part, by his hope of establishing himself as a celebrated publisher and cultural icon, while Karl Shapiro's introduction to *Tropic of Cancer* references Wilhelm Reich but also calls Miller "a holy man" and "a prophet of doom," suggesting Shapiro's appreciation of Miller's rewriting of Biblical tropes; Gertz, too, compared Miller's work to the Song of Songs.[77] A more detailed study of these individuals and their participation in this trial might yield insight into how, or if, their contributions were inflected by their sense of being Jewish. Given enough evidence, the influence of any individual's Jewishness on his or her participation in an obscenity controversy is likely to be richly overdetermined, conditioned by a welter of factors difficult to tease out from one another.

Rather than positing a single explanatory paradigm that explains the many fascinating and unpredictable engagements of American Jews in obscenity controversies, then, this book offers a heuristic framework for exploring such controversies, along with a series of case studies that demonstrate how to make sense of such engagements without relying on perniciously reductive essentialisms or bolstering boosters' and bigots' simplistic claims about "Jewish sexuality"—and yet also without effacing or understating the roles played by Jews in the institutional and ideological development of American literature from the late 19th century to the present. American Jews did not produce or defend literary obscenity for any consistent or simple reasons, but they did so in ways that transformed American literature and culture; and in the cases examined in this book, they did so in dynamic interplay with their understandings of themselves as connected to Jewish culture or tradition. Their interventions, which this book is committed to recovering, remain crucial not only to the history of American literature but also for understanding how law, sexuality, religion, and ethnicity intersect.

1

Sexual Anti-Semitism and Pornotopia

Theodore Dreiser, Ludwig Lewisohn, and The Harrad Experiment

One Friday night in 1917, Theodore Dreiser accompanied Irwin Granich, a young Jewish playwright associated with the Provincetown Players, to the apartment on Chrystie Street, on New York's Lower East Side, where Granich and his mother lived.[1] Dreiser wanted atmospheric details for a play he had been writing about poor tenement dwellers. Though he had written about immigrant Jews as a journalist and had included Jews as minor characters in some of his fiction, this play was to be the only one of his literary works in which a Jewish character figured as the protagonist.[2]

When Dreiser had finished a draft of the four-act play, he sent it over to H. L. Mencken. Mencken was a supporter of free speech and of Dreiser's work; he had lately campaigned on behalf of Dreiser's novel *The "Genius,"* which had been suppressed as obscene in 1916 by John Sumner, Anthony Comstock's successor at the NYSSV. Yet, having read Dreiser's Jewish play, Mencken reacted unequivocally: "Put the ms. behind the clock," he wrote, "and thank me and God for saving you from a mess."[3] Horace Liveright—the newly established Jewish publisher who was so eager to add Dreiser to his list in 1917 that he offered the celebrated author an unusually generous 25% royalty rate—felt similarly. According to the publisher's biographer, despite Liveright's general enthusiasm for Dreiser's work, he had no desire to see this particular play in print, and, after first demurring, Liveright finally "agreed to publish the play solely to retain Dreiser as an author."[4] When Liveright eventually did publish it, in the fall of 1919, as *The Hand of the Potter*, many critics agreed with Mencken's and Liveright's initial assessments. One reviewer in Chicago expressed her disgust emphatically: "Ugh! It's a horrible thing," she wrote. "If I were a censor I would bar 'The Hand of the Potter' from circulation and turn Mr. Dreiser over to the psychiatric ward."[5]

It is not difficult to guess what all these readers found objectionable: *The Hand of the Potter* focuses on Isadore Berchansky, a young Jewish man who, as the play opens, is a convicted child rapist who has just returned from two years at the state penitentiary to his parents' apartment in East Harlem.[6] His time away has not dampened his unhealthy desires: "It's their faces an' their nice make-ups an' the way they do their hair," he says, describing the lure of young women on the street. "That's what's the matter with me. It's their stockin's an' their open shirtwaists an' their shoulders an' arms. I can't stand it no more. I can't seem to think of nothin' else" (34). Isadore's "uncontrolled and unnatural sex-interest" (42) so overwhelms him that he even makes overtures to his own younger sister (36). Dreiser's stage directions have him stare at an eleven-year-old neighbor in a "a greedy, savage, half-insane way" (49), and these adjectives link Isadore's uncontrollable lusts to the stereotypes of Jewish avariciousness, primitiveness, and mental illness that were common during the fin de siècle.[7] The drama's first act ends with Isadore raping and killing the eleven-year-old neighbor, offstage, and the remaining acts detail the police investigation and Isadore's suicide. Combining sexual accusations that surfaced during the 1910s around the Leo Frank trial (Jewish perversion leading to child rape and then murder) and, a few decades earlier, during the Jack the Ripper scandal in England (the notion that the murderer's poor Jewish peers shielded him from the police)[8] and folding these in with conventional trappings of literary representations of Jews in the period, including plenty of Jewish dialect speech and a reference to a "*mezuze*," *The Hand of the Potter* seems to collect in a single literary work just about all the sexual anti-Semitic discourse that had been circulating in Europe and America since the mid-19th century. No wonder, then, that some Jewish critics have lambasted the play as purveying the most egregious racist stereotypes: the theater scholar Ellen Schiff, for example, characterizes *The Hand of the Potter* as "one of the few blatantly anti-Semitic works in the American repertory."[9]

Yet Dreiser understood his play not as a work of hateful anti-Semitic propaganda but, on the contrary, as evidence of the depth of his sympathy for American Jews. What is more, authoritative Jewish critics of the period—Abraham Cahan and Ludwig Lewisohn among them—agreed with him.[10] To understand why Dreiser, Cahan, and Lewisohn felt that publishing and staging a dramatization of a Jewish man's uncontrollable pedophilia could be an act of support for and friendship with the American Jewish community, it is necessary to attend in more detail to the claims that had been made about Jewish sexuality in anti-Semitic propaganda, as well as in popular and highbrow literature, in Europe and the United States since the 1880s and how such claims were refuted by the sexological theory on which Dreiser relied for his understanding of sexual abnormality.

Reading Dreiser's play as a response to anti-Semitic discourse—particularly in its insistence on the relevance of the explicit representation of sex to sexological theory—allows us to understand it as a crucial example of one way in which obscenity mattered to American Jews. It also helps to explain, as this chapter goes on to explore, why, in the decades after World War II, writers began to understand the explicit representation of sexuality and the embrace of sexual pleasure as effective strategies to counter the grievous anti-Semitism and other hatreds on the march in America and Europe—such that, by the 1960s, a best-selling, mass-market novel by a non-Jewish writer, billed as "the sex manifesto of the free love generation," could figure pornography, group marriage, and other facets of sexual radicalism as solutions to the persisting problem of "indirect" American anti-Semitism.

Sexual Anti-Semitism in the Fin de Siècle

The sexual anti-Semitism that circulated in Europe and America in the late 19th and early 20th centuries concentrated not only on the "Jew editors" discussed in the introduction but also on Jews in other sexually threatening roles, especially those of pimp, prostitute, and pedophile. One of the main tenets of the international "white-slavery panic," for example, was the accusation that Jewish pimps sold non-Jewish young women into sexual slavery. Such claims did not spring up from nowhere but had their basis in the rhetorical excesses of scientific studies of prostitution that began to proliferate in the mid-19th century: indeed, "The Jews" were the subject of the very first chapter of the book that Walter Kendrick characterizes as marking the U.S. arrival of "hygienic pornography," that is, writing (*graphos*) about prostitutes (*porne*) with the goal of social and medical reform.[11]

At the outset of that book, *The History of Prostitution* (1858), Dr. William W. Sanger notes that "prostitution is coeval with society," but he emphasizes first and foremost that "prostitutes were common among Jews in the eighteenth century before Christ." Sanger's readings of the Bible suggests that though Moses commanded his people not to prostitute their daughters, the lawgiver "appears to have connived at the intercourse of [the Jews'] young men with foreign prostitutes," having taken "an Egyptian concubine himself." Sanger presents prostitution as widespread and generally accepted among ancient Jews: it was "legally domiciled in Judaea at a very early period and never lost the foothold it had gained," and it "continued to be practiced generally and openly until the destruction of the old Jewish nation." The Israelites were not just pioneers of prostitution, according to this view, but also excessive in their patronage and legal toleration of it: "it may be questioned whether it ever assumed more revoltingly public forms in any other country," Sanger declares.[12]

These descriptions of ancient Jewish prostitution could neatly be aligned with reports of Jewish pimping in the present so as to produce broad, transhistorical claims about Jewish sexuality. Another hygienic pornographer echoed Sanger's claims in an American medical journal in 1895, noting that "the Hebrew people were one of the agents in propagating syphilis and prostitution in times of antiquity" and that "prostitution enjoyed the greatest liberty among the Israelites, and was not even considered infamous." Yet this was the heyday of white-slavery panic, and the author, a French doctor, went further than Sanger, quoting an unnamed source to the effect that "the plague of prostitution always remained attached like leprosy to the Jewish nation"[13]—a statement that, with its metaphor of prostitution as contagious disease, could be interpreted as asserting that whether ancient or contemporary, Jews "always" carried the germ of prostitution—and that they involved themselves in the practice in modern times just as excessively as their ancestors did. In fact, in the publications that fomented the white-slavery panic, modern Jews were, at times, explicitly linked to their Biblical ancestors: George Kibbe Turner's "The Daughters of the Poor," an infamous muckraking exposé printed in *McClure's* in 1909, uses the word "ancient" repeatedly to refer to the contemporary Jewish pimp, describing him, for example, as distinguished by "his long beard—the badge of his ancient faith."[14] Moreover, as the historian Edward Bristow notes in his excellent study of Jews and the white-slavery panics, anti-Semites often neglected to mention that most of the women victimized by Jewish procurers and traffickers were themselves Jewish, an omission that thereby fomented fears about Jews preying on Christian women and also echoed Sanger's description of the ancient Israelites' fondness for "foreign prostitutes."[15] As several observers have pointed out, such claims about Jewish pimps resonated with more general ideas about Jewish difference, greed, and sexual immorality.[16]

An even purer expression of the sexual anti-Semitism of the period was the claim, echoing Tacitus's contention that Jews are "prone to lust," that Jewish men—just like Dreiser's Isadore Berchansky—harbor intense, uncontrollable sexual desires. Timayenis led the hateful charge, as usual, proclaiming in *The American Jew* (1888), "Next to his lust for money, the strongest passion in the Jew is his licentiousness." He closes his chapter on "the licentious Jew" suggesting that "such is the insatiability of [the Jew's] carnal appetites, and to such an extent does he give rein to his lasciviousness, that his debauches only too frequently exceed the ordinary limits of lust."[17] In other words, Timayenis suggests, hypertrophied Jewish sexuality leads inevitably to rape, child abuse, and murder. In this vision, a stereotypical Jewish economic exploiter, the sweatshop owner, could quickly be transformed into a sexual criminal: "Not long ago," Timayenis claimed, "in New York, the officers of the Society for the Prevention of Cruelty to Children neatly trapped a Jew employer who was in the habit of inducing little girls under fourteen to remain after work-hours, and debauching them."[18] Two decades later, in a well-known case with uncannily similar details, Leo Frank, the superintendent of the National Pencil Factory in Atlanta, Georgia, was accused of killing one of his thirteen-year-old employees, a girl named Mary Phagan. The suggestion that Frank was a sexual deviant, possibly a homosexual, whose lust for girls had led him to rape and murder Phagan, constituted a major tenet of his accusers' case and of his unjust conviction and then played a part in the organization of a mob of Atlanta residents to kidnap and lynch him after he was granted clemency by the governor.[19]

Such visions of Jews as sexual predators and child molesters appeared not only in the rantings of populist anti-Semitic demagogues and mobs but also in popular and literary fiction written by European and American authors during the same period. H. Rider Haggard's adventure tale *Benita: An African Romance* (1906) features a German Jew, Jacob Meyer, whose "insane passions" for riches and for the heroine's body drive the novel's plot. Like Svengali, the frightening Jewish antagonist of the wildly popular *Trilby* (1894), Meyer practices mind control that could gain him access to the body of the vulnerable heroine, Benita. "In the beginning," she explains fearfully to her father, "Mr. Meyer only wanted the gold. Now he wants more, me as well as the gold. . . . I have read a good deal about this mesmerism, and seen it once or twice, and who knows? If once I allowed his mind to master my mind, although I hate him so much, I might become his slave."[20] Linking visions of Jewish greed, lust, and mind control even more explicitly to the international white-slavery panic, Reginald Wright Kauffman's muckraking novel *House of Bondage* (1910) begins with a Hungarian Jew who sexually exploits an innocent non-Jewish American girl. In the book's first chapter, Max Crossman ("not my real name," he says, "because I vas born in Hungary an' nobody could say my real name ofer here") lures a sixteen-year-old American girl named Mary Denbigh away from her parents' small-town home with promises of urban luxury and then promptly sells her as a sexual "slave" to a brothel keeper.[21]

In the more prestigious literary culture of the period, similar Jewish sexual excesses tended to be more subtly represented or simply implied. This was not only a matter of delicacy or subtlety on the part of the writers, of course, but also an imposition of obscenity laws that reigned in the representation of sexuality. Still, many celebrated novels featured Jews who, like Haggard's and Kauffman's, combine acquisitiveness, vulgarity, and an extraordinary lust, especially directed toward young, non-Jewish women. Émile Zola's *Nana* (1880) features a German Jewish banker, Steiner, whose desire for wealth, and skill for acquiring it, is exceeded only by his insatiable sexual lust:

> The terrible German Jew, the great hatcher of businesses whose hands founded millions, became quite a fool whenever he had a hankering

> after a woman; and he wanted them all. One could never appear at a theatre but he secured her, no matter at what price. The most incredible amounts were mentioned. Twice during his life had his furious appetite for the fair sex ruined him.[22]

Zola does not particularly distinguish Steiner's "*furieux appétit des filles*" from those of other non-Jewish characters entranced by Nana. Other portraits of Jews in Zola's fiction, and his reaction to the Dreyfus affair, exculpate him from any reductive claims of anti-Semitism, but Steiner, a Jew prone to extreme lust, nevertheless reproduces a common stereotype of Jewish sexual deviance.

Other characters followed suit in the naturalist American fiction inspired by Zola's example. Simon Rosedale, the "plump rosy man of the blond Jewish type" in Edith Wharton's *The House of Mirth* (1905), for one familiar case, conflates his economic desires with sexual ones. "If I could get Paul Morpeth to paint [Lily Bart] like that," he is reported to say, almost as if acknowledging the financial possibilities of erotic portraiture, "the picture'd appreciate a hundred per cent in ten years." Of course, Rosedale, unlike Zola's Steiner, finally prioritizes his financial and social aspirations over his sexual desires, agreeing with Lily that his "idea of good friends" would be "making love to [her] without asking [her] to marry [him]."[23] While it must be noted that Zola's and Wharton's multifaceted literary characters can be read in multiple ways, and to dismiss Rosedale or Steiner as anti-Semitic caricatures would be a reductive mistake,[24] it is difficult to deny that these authors traffic in representations of Jewish lust that overlap with the stereotypical characters of Haggard's *Benita*, Kauffman's *House of Bondage*, and even Timayenis's hateful screeds.[25]

Modernist and Sexological Defenses of Jewish Sexuality

Stereotypes of Jewish hypersexuality did not disappear with the ascension of literary modernism in the years after World War I, but the works of celebrated modernist authors repudiated the stereotypes with the assertion, underwritten by attention to current medical authorities and especially Freud, that sexual deviance is not the particular burden of Jews or any single demographic group. Many prominent European medical experts of the period, including Freud's teacher Jean-Martin Charcot, had understood Jews as prone to "degeneracy," which, as historian John Efron notes, "perhaps, most frequently . . . was applied in popular and medical usage to describe the sexual deviant."[26] Yet, as another medical historian, Toby Gelfand, phrases it, "for Freud, what was true for the Jew became true for everybody."[27]

One very prominent literary example of how charges against Jews could be reframed as universal problems affecting people in general, underwritten by modern sexology, can be found in James Joyce's *Ulysses*, which, as scholars have often discussed, presents Leopold Bloom's nominal Jewishness with considerable sympathy, if also with characteristic ambivalence. Joyce's identification with Jews throughout his life, and with Bloom as a character, suggests that far from a despised sexual deviant, the masturbating, cuckolded, fantasizing quasi-Jew whose sexuality is represented explicitly and controversially in the novel constitutes Joyce's thoughtful portrait of what Judge Woolsey referred to as an "*homme moyen sensuel*"—that is, a person with average sex instincts—in his decision decriminalizing *Ulysses*.[28] As the literary scholar Neil Davidson puts it, "in Bloom, one of the era's most prevalent stereotypes—'the degenerate Jew'—has been transformed into the great paradigm of complete characterization."[29] Joyce's election of Bloom as the exemplar of modern sexuality is itself a subtle argument that Jews are no more or less lustful, or "degenerate," than anyone else.[30]

Dreiser's *The Hand of the Potter* aims, more directly than this, to exculpate its Jewish protagonist from anti-Semitic claims about his sexuality through reference to recent developments in the science of sexuality. The model for Isadore Berchansky was Nathan Swarz, a young Jewish resident of New York who was accused of murdering a fourteen-year-old girl named Julia Connors in the summer of 1912. The tale of the police search for Swarz and his eventual admission and suicide had been a national sensation; Dreiser drew many details—including the suicide note Berchansky leaves: "I'm guilty, and I'm insane, caused by the beautiful make-ups of girls that has set me very passionate" (*Hand of the Potter*, 183)—directly from newspaper accounts of Swartz's case.[31] For Dreiser, sexual perversion of this type must be understood as a medical illness to be studied and treated by doctors, like any other malady, and not as the degeneration typical of a particular ethnic or racial group. "I've been readin' up on these cases for some time," one of Dreiser's characters remarks about Isadore's crime,

> an' from what I can make out they're no more guilty than any other person with a disease. . . . There's something they've called harmones [i.e., hormones] which the body manufactures . . . which excites us to the m'aning ave beauty an' thim things. . . . Now if a felly is so constituted that he has more ave that an' less ave something' else—something' which balances him a little an' makes his less sensitive to the beauty of women or girls—he's likely to be like that. He can't help it. . . . If ye'd ever made a study ave the passion ave love in the sense that Freud an' some others have ye'd understand it well enough. It's a great force about which we know naathing as yet an' which we're just beginnin' to look into. (193, 200)[32]

Importing into this character's ham-handed speeches an explicitly Freudian perspective on human sexuality, Dreiser insists that Jews are no more "prone to lust" than anybody else. Ascribing Isadore's lust to hormones, rather than to his environment, culture, or heredity, suggests that his problem is a human one, no more likely to befall a Jewish individual than any other—a view also reflected in Dreiser's contemporaneous work.[33] Notwithstanding the reactions of some critics, then, *The Hand of the Potter* was a deliberate attempt to reject anti-Semitic claims about Jews' sexuality by introducing the medical discourse around sexual abnormality into discussions of Swartz's pedophilia.

The novels that Ludwig Lewisohn published in late 1920s and early 1930s expand this exculpation of Jews from anti-Semitic claims of perversion into a claim for the unique healthiness of Jews' sexual expression. Lewisohn, by far the most prominent Jewish writer in interwar America, was on friendly terms with both Joyce and Dreiser and had been briefly analyzed by Freud in Vienna. Given Lewisohn's immersion in German culture, as well as his prominence as an American Jew, he was ideally situated to promulgate a positive view of Jewish sexuality bolstered and informed by sexological theory. Indeed, when the Provincetown Playhouse briefly staged *The Hand of the Potter* in 1921, Lewisohn applauded the performance in print as "courageous and admirable" and particularly praised Dreiser's sympathy for the protagonist:

"It is so easy and final and virile to electrocute the Isadore Berchanskys of the world. It is supremely difficult to understand and compassionate and cure," Lewisohn wrote, framing his review in terms of a choice between the criminalization or medicalization of sexual abnormality.[34] In his own fiction, Lewisohn advocated for the psychoanalytic treatment of sexual dysfunction and positioned Jews as the promulgators of understanding, compassion, and cures. In Lewisohn's *The Island Within* (1928), for example, the protagonist, Arthur Levy, is a psychiatrist who has "read and reread the works of Sigmund Freud."[35] While David Sampson, in *Stephen Escott* (1930), works as a lawyer and not a doctor, he specializes in procuring "freedom" for married couples suffering from a "lack of sexual satisfaction" produced by New York's divorce laws;[36] as a *New York Times* reviewer noted upon the novel's publication, "one gets the effect from the book that [Sampson's] is a firm of psychoanalysts, not a firm of lawyers."[37] In *An Altar in the Field* (1934), the wise adviser to a couple of unhappily married American bohemians is a self-described "up-to-the-minute psychologist," Dr. Weyl, a German Jew and outspoken Zionist.[38]

As Jews, Lewisohn's gurus are deeply knowledgeable about the discourses of modern sexology—Sampson, for one, heard all of Greenwich Village's "libertarian theories . . . years ago expressed in Russian and Yiddish at the old Café Monopole on Second Avenue"[39]—and Lewisohn emphasizes that this sexological theory is, in and of itself, considered obscene by many Americans and Europeans. In his memoir, *Mid-Channel* (1929), he laments that "Christianity . . . calls Freud a dirty fellow," and in *The Island Within*, he has one of Levy's colleagues call psychoanalysis "disgusting" and "immoral," while another opines, "as Americans we couldn't possibly go in for that degenerate, dirty Freudian stuff."[40] None of this was a product of Lewisohn's imagination; antipathy to Freud's writings on sexuality could be intense, and a few attempts had been made to suppress the circulation of psychoanalytic studies of sexuality in the United States. Nathan McHale's history of psychoanalysis in America reports, for example, that "as late as 1917 some of the basic psychoanalytic texts were kept in a guarded room of the New York public library, to be read in a cage only by those with special permission"—the same way pornographic works, such as *Fanny Hill*, were often archived.[41] Rejecting such opposition to Freud's theories as part of the puritanism that bedevils American sexuality and inspires anti-Semitism, Lewisohn insisted on the efficacy of Freudian sexology.

Indeed, Lewisohn proffers, through his gurus, a singular prognosis of the dolorous state of American sexuality. According to them, modern women's feminism and Jews' assimilationism are parallel and similarly misguided pursuits, flawed because they contradict the essential nature of the woman and the Jew. "What ailed Elizabeth," Lewisohn writes of the female protagonist of *The Island Within*, "as it ailed many women of her type and precise period, was not wholly unlike the thing that ailed so many Jews. She had an inferiority complex as a woman."[42] This directly echoes Lewisohn's friend, the Austrian psychoanalyst Otto Rank, whose short essay "The Essence of Judaism" (1905) proclaimed that Jews "are, so to speak, women among the people."[43] An even more direct echo: Dr. Weyl remarks in *An Altar in the Field* that "so-called modern women often remind me of Jews."[44] According to this view, both feminist women and assimilationist Jews, in reaction to the oppression they have each suffered and under the demands of modernity, deny their natures and erode their sexual vitality. In articulating this theory, Lewisohn builds on Freud's influential essay "'Civilized' Sexual Morality and Modern Nervousness" (1908), in which Freud contrasts a healthy primitive sexual instinct to the repressions of "civilization" and "modern society," as well as on Rank's related notion that "the essence of Judaism is its stress on primitive sexuality."[45] For Lewisohn, this "primitive" Jewish "essence" meant that American Jews who embraced their Jewish identity were perfectly positioned to work toward alleviating the suffering caused by the sexual dysfunctions of modern Americans—which, Lewisohn insists, are inseparable from the anti-Semitic tendencies of Jews and non-Jews alike.

Dr. Weyl ventures to hope that if Americans follow his advice, they may be able to "return to the classical forms and loyalties of human life"—that is, to a more "primitive" sexual morality—"without hatred and terror, without Fascist or Nazi atrocities, without lynchings and pogroms, without slavery and the death of all decency and freedom."[46] The mistreatment of Jews is not uniquely a European ("Nazi") phenomenon in Weyl's view, either. "In America we [Jews] identified ourselves by love and loyalty with soil and speech," but "the masters and creators of that soil and speech made us feel in an hundred ways—most of them subtle, a few of them gross—that they did not want our love and loyalty and identification." As if aware that this language might be a bit too abstract to convey the vigor of American anti-Semitism, Lewisohn has Weyl tell a story about his dead son to the novel's non-Jewish protagonist, Dick Belden. Weyl's son "ran away at seventeen to become a sailor on a Pacific freighter" but was hounded by "his fellow-sailors" because of their Judeophobia ("the old mythic folk-malignity") until he "flung himself into the sea." Weyl offers this anecdote not to seek sympathy but with a moral in mind for Belden, who has lately been living with his wife in Paris as alienated, unhappy expatriates. "I can tell you your job, Belden," Weyl says. "It is to go to America and to see to it that your children are more tolerant and civilized"—less anti-Semitic, that is, than the sailors who taunted Weyl's son to his death. The first step on this journey is for Belden to establish newly healthy sexual relations with his wife, which he does by traveling alongside Weyl to the Sahara desert, where the doctor celebrates the uncorrupted natives' primitiveness, their "supreme capacity" to "naturally and satisfactorily [deal] with the constant and changeless elements of human life." These are the grounds, in Lewisohn's imagination, for sexual utopia. In the desert, Belden and his wife, following Weyl's advice ("Let your natural instincts guide you," Belden tells her), share what the novel calls "their first true marriage-bed."[47] As is true throughout Lewisohn's fiction of this period, in *An Altar in the Field*, healthy sexuality—which can be achieved by Americans willing to follow the counsel of Jewish gurus who paraphrase and riff on Freudian notions of civilization and its discontents—coincides exactly with, and contributes to, an overcoming of American tendencies toward anti-Semitism.

The Holocaust and Sexual Anti-Semitism

Though Lewisohn was the most outspoken American promulgator of these ideas in the interwar years, his wooden *romans à thèse* were promptly forgotten in the following decades, and Dreiser's controversial play rejecting sexual anti-Semitism was overshadowed by that author's turn, in the 1930s and 1940s, to disturbing anti-Semitic proclamations.[48] Still, anti-Semitism and frank considerations of sexuality came to be conceptually linked even more vigorously in the United States after 1945 thanks to a couple of complex, interrelated developments. During the Nazis' rise to power and throughout the war, American cultural critics consistently sought out psychosexual explanations for and manifestations of German villainy—in this sense continuing Lewisohn's project—and in doing so they drew on the theories of German Jewish psychoanalysts and theoreticians, some of whom had arrived in the United States as refugees from Nazi-held territories in the 1930s. At the same time, American free-speech advocates, who had always relied on the notion of minority rights, acquired new rhetorical and historical support for the argument that the American Constitution must protect the expressive rights of minorities, given the catastrophic results of the Nazis' abrogation of such rights in Europe. These sometimes competing, often overlapping strains of American anti-Nazism played out in eclectic, often bizarre, and not always progressive ways in American discourse about obscenity and freedom of sexual expression. While this chapter cannot do justice to the myriad of ways that anti-Nazi rhetoric informed American sexual radicalism in the postwar decades, a survey of some of the more compelling manifestations of these trends, as they relate to arguments for unfettered sexual expression, will help to explain part of the place of Jewishness in the increasingly utopian theories of sexual expression that drove the U.S. sexual revolution.[49] In a handful of ways, in short, the association of sex with the Holocaust bolstered arguments that sex must be frankly and publicly discussed.

First, it is crucial to recall that Nazi anti-Semitism built on the vilification of Jews as sexual deviants in 19th-century anti-Semitism. From Hitler's nightmare vision, in *Mein Kampf*, of "the black-haired Jew-boy" who "waits in ambush for the unsuspecting girl whom he defiles with his blood" to mounting critiques in the 1930s of sex educators such as Max Marcuse and Magnus Hirshfeld as "Jewish sex criminals" and of the practice of psychoanalysis as "the Jewish nation's rape of Western culture," Nazi discourse relied on sexual anti-Semitism to dehumanize Jews and to mobilize the party's political base in Germany against them, while also justifying the Nazi government's own radical sexual policies. Whether castigated for being pimps, sexologists, or movie producers, German Jews were routinely blamed by pro-Nazi propagandists for "the poisoning of marital and sexual morality."[50] Since one typical response to sexual anti-Semitism, as we have seen in the work of Dreiser and

Lewisohn, was to insist that sexuality must be discussed openly and rationally and studied scientifically, motivation for Jewish engagements with frank discussions of sex increased as sexual anti-Semitism became enshrined in Nazism. It is not difficult to imagine the relief an American Jew might have felt to read in Alfred Kinsey's 1948 report *Sexual Behavior in the Human Male* that while "sexual propaganda against the Jews as a race was a cornerstone of the Hitlerian attack on that group in Germany," according to Kinsey's research, American Jews exhibited no differences in sexual behavior from that of their peers in other demographic groups.[51] No wonder that while there were a few instances in which American Jews protested the circulation of sexological materials, in the postwar decades many American Jews supported the work of sexual scientists from Kinsey to Masters and Johnson and beyond.[52]

The Nazis also managed to transform the burning of books into an unsympathetic practice in the United States. In the 1930s, John Sumner's NYSSV regularly burned books as a press stunt, and Sumner was photographed in the act of proudly depositing books into a raging furnace. The organization's seal itself at one point featured an image of a dapper top-hatted man adding books to a bonfire. Notwithstanding that anti-obscenity statutes enjoyed broad support and that book burnings have continued to be a feature of American political theater, such images of the destruction of books were obviously much less sympathetic after the widely circulated newsreels of Nazi book burnings became indelibly associated for many Americans with the Nazi crematoria.[53] That many of the Nazis' burned books came from Hirshfeld's Institut für Sexualwissenschaft could only help to cement the association between the suppression of sexology and the dangers of fascism for postwar Americans.

Nazi Sexual Villainy and the Compulsion to Witness

During and after the war, many Americans were entranced by a vision of the Nazis as sexually villainous and of their crimes as partly sexual. For example, in a lecture the German Jewish émigré theorist Herbert Marcuse composed in the early 1940s, while under contract with the U.S. Office of Strategic Services, he described Nazism as excessive in its sexual permissiveness and as exploiting the "abolition of sexual taboos" so as "to intensify the 'Gleichschaltung' [coordination] of individuals into the National Socialist system."[54] Decades later, Lucy Dawidowicz generalized that "lurid sex and violence have traditionally accompanied Nazism."[55] While this notion led Dawidowicz and other observers to oppose the proliferation of pornography, it has also often served precisely to justify the explicit representation of sexuality as part of the documentation of Nazi crimes.[56]

Images of Nazis as sexual criminals, as rapists and defilers of Jewish women, whether based on fact or on fantasy, proliferated in the United States along with the earliest reports of the Holocaust. In one crucial and resonant case, on January 8, 1943, the *New York Times*, which was infamously reticent about reporting details of the Nazi genocide during those years,[57] printed in full the translated text of a Yiddish letter received in New York that purported to tell the story of "ninety-three Jewish girls and young Jewish women" in a Bais Yakov religious school who "chose mass suicide to escape being forced into prostitution by German soldiers" in Krakow in August 1942.[58] Despite doubts about the letter's veracity, the story of this incident spread widely and continues to be retold to this day as fact.[59] Incidents of rape and forced prostitution of Jewish women during the Holocaust have been substantiated by historians, but this particular case has not.[60] The two scholars who have written the most assiduous study of the incident conclude with "serious doubts that it occurred."[61]

Yet the story compelled attention and inspired creativity in the United States. Within months, the ninety-three martyred girls had become the subject of at least two published poems—one written in English, the other translated from Hebrew into English—and one English-language short story.[62] In the postwar years, the story also seems to have partly inspired novels which depict concentration-camp brothels filled with Jewish women: Yehiel Dinur's *House of Dolls*, translated to English and published in the United States in 1955, and Edward Lewis Wallant's *The Pawnbroker* (1961). Historians agree that while rape and forced prostitution of Jewish women and girls occurred under Nazi rule, no brothels filled with Jewish girls existed for the pleasuring of German soldiers on the grounds of concentration camps, as these two novels suggest. Still, the books were widely read and reviewed, and Wallant's was adapted into a celebrated Hollywood film that broke new ground in sexual representation. While the novels dramatize the trauma of being forced to watch sexual degradations and torture, their circulation and reception depends on the idea that it is incumbent on Americans to witness such sexual spectacles because they constitute evidence of Nazi perfidy. In other words, the consumption of explicit representations of sex is transformed, by these texts, from a crime into a responsibility.

In both novels, characters are forced to witness sexual violence against their will. In *House of Dolls*, which follows a young Jewish woman as she is forced to serve in a "Joy Division," a brothel adjacent to an extermination camp, one scene describes the public torture of Jewish prostitutes who have not performed their duties with sufficient enthusiasm. The punishment involves the girls being marched, "nude," into a square where they are strapped to "stools—hands to the forelegs, feet to the rear legs," and then beaten with bludgeons.[63] It is noteworthy that one of the women being punished is described as looking "as though she . . . were stepping thus directly from the Daughters of Jacob [i.e., Bais Yakov] night school" in her hometown, suggesting how directly the mythic tale of the ninety-three Bais Yakov martyrs might have inspired Dinur's vision of forced prostitution. Importantly, the novel frames the scene by aligning the reader with neither the victims nor the perpetrators but with the witnesses: that is, the narrator focuses on a group of other prisoners of the camp who are compelled to observe the punishment. "The prisoners of the Labor Division now clustered in to a huge mass of gaping eyes. . . . Eyes were agape . . . in fear of the kalefactresses' [female guards'] bludgeons: See, they're watching! They're looking! . . . They don't take their eyes off the stools! . . . Won't the kalefactresses see how they're looking there . . . and please not beat them over the head with the clubs!"[64]

Wallant's novel offers an even more pointed scene of forced witnessing of sexual violence. The book centers on a Holocaust survivor, Sol Nazerman, who works as a pawnbroker in Harlem and is haunted by memories of his and his family's persecution under the Nazis.[65] In one crucial flashback to a concentration camp, Nazerman remembers being forced by a club-wielding guard, as in Dinur's book, to observe a concentration-camp brothel where his wife has been imprisoned and forced to have sex with S.S. officers: "*The guard wouldn't let him turn his head from the window, knocked with menacing playfulness on the side of his jaw every time he tried. So he looked in the vast room.*" The novel emphasizes that Nazerman is forced to witness the scene. The Nazi guard insists, "I'm taking you to see for yourself. . . . So look, keep looking, that's what you're here for." "*I couldn't stand to see anymore,*" Nazerman begs, but the guard insists: "*You'll stay and you'll look, once and for all.*" What Nazerman sees, of course, is his wife's forced sexual encounter with a Nazi: "*For a minute or two the SS man handled her breasts and her loins vengefully.*"[66] The reader, as in *House of Dolls*, is aligned with the spectator of sexual violence, forced by the narrative to witness the interaction just as Nazerman is compelled by a Nazi. Nazerman endures what Wallant's narrator refers to as an "obscene experience," and so does the reader, alongside him—a point emphasized by Sidney Lumet's 1964 film adaptation, in which the viewer watches from Nazerman's perspective during the flashback. In the film, the flashback is triggered, in Harlem, by an African American prostitute's revealing her breasts to Nazerman and saying, "Look. Look. That's it, look. Look." It is a contemporary act of sexual display, framed in the language of looking, that summons Nazerman's memory. Then, in the flashback, Nazerman's head is thrust through a window by a Nazi guard—who says "Willst du was sehen? . . . Mach gerne Augen auf" (Do you want to see something? . . . Keep your eyes open)[67]—and he is forced to peer into the brothel, where he and the audience watch two fully clothed Nazis showering a naked woman; then, a naked woman sprawled out on cots; another, covered in a sheet; a third, entertaining a clothed Nazi; and then, finally, Nazerman's wife, naked from the waist up as a Nazi ominously enters her room. Throughout this sequence, which includes intercut shots of Nazerman's face in the present, the soundtrack features the African American prostitute's voice: "Look. It don't cost you nothing to look. Just look. Look. Look."[68] It would be difficult to imagine how a film could insist more emphatically on the fact that its protagonist and audience are being compelled to bear witness to a display of the sexual activities that take place in a Nazi brothel.

The message of these scenes for their readers and viewers should be clear: as distasteful as it is to witness forced prostitution and sexual abuse, there is an ethical imperative to do so when reckoning with the crimes of the Nazis. The novelist Meyer Levin, who had been instrumental in bringing *The Diary of Anne Frank* to the attention of the

American media, suggested as much in his review of *House of Dolls* in the *New York Times*, in which he noted, "there is a common impulse to cry, 'Why read more? We know, we already know.' But 'House of Dolls' shows us that we do not know. . . . Only in knowing such instances of sadistic bestiality can we understand the sublimity of the innocent love that a human being . . . still carried in her heart through every desecration."[69] While Levin implies that sexual explicitness is necessary for a full psychological understanding of the victims, he also relies on an understanding of *House of Dolls* as a factual account. The book was marketed as a "novel based on an authentic diary" and as having "been acclaimed for, . . . above all, its truth," and many readers have taken it as a historical document.[70] A reviewer for the *New York Herald Tribune Book Review* assimilated that claim—"There probably has never appeared in print before, outside official documents, so precise a testimonial to what the Jews had to endure under Nazi Germany"—and echoed Levin's point. The book, the reviewer goes on, though unpleasant, is necessary: "Why should such accounts as these be written? The answer is simple: the truth, no matter how shameless, must be known."[71]

This argument has carried weight in discussion of the appropriateness of sexuality in representations of the Holocaust, even when those works are acknowledged to be fictional. *House of Dolls* included a good deal of taboo language and scenes of sexual torture and was never the subject of censorship controversy. More dramatically, Lumet's film version of *The Pawnbroker* included more nudity than any film previously approved by the Production Code but managed to win approval from the MPAA thanks in part to its subject matter—and managed to play in theaters across the country despite a "Condemned" rating from the Catholic Legion of Decency, which objected to the introduction of "nudity into American films."[72] Decades later, the same argument continued to be effective: considering whether or not *Schindler's List* (1993) could be deemed "indecent" and thus impermissible to air on broadcast television during prime time, the Federal Communications Commission declared in 2000 that "although this airing of *Schindler's List* did contain incidental frontal nudity, the material broadcast depicted a historical view of World War II and wartime atrocities which, viewed in that context, was not presented in a pandering, titillating or vulgar manner or in any way that would be considered patently offensive and, therefore, actionably indecent."[73] Like it or not, this widely accepted, if troubling, argument goes, audiences must confront the Nazis' atrocities, and so the law must permit the circulation of sexual images at least, or especially, in such contexts.[74]

Linking Nazi and American Sexual Suppression

A third tendency in American anti-Nazi discourse likewise viewed Nazis as sexually diseased, but rather than insisting on their sexual excesses, these visions emphasized sexual suppression as a cause of fascism and genocide. The most prominent exponent of this idea was Wilhelm Reich, whose influence the literary scholar Mark Shechner has shown to be crucial for an understanding of American Jewish literature and culture in the decades after World War II.[75] Like Lewisohn's Dr. Weyl, Lewisohn himself, and Marcuse, Reich was an inspired post-Freudian sexological thinker who identified culturally, before the war, as a German. He relocated to the United States in 1939 as a refugee, with a two-year faculty appointment at the New School for Social Research. He began to publish in English in the 1940s, and though he was always controversial, he quickly came to serve as a theoretical source for American sex progressivism and sexual radicalism; he was also taken up vigorously by a number of the Jewish writers who were busy transforming American literature.[76] Particularly relevant to a discussion of how American ideas about sexuality developed in reaction to the Nazi genocide are his books *The Sexual Revolution* and *The Mass Psychology of Fascism*, both of which were written in the 1930s in German and translated into English in the 1940s. In the former, Reich declared that a Nazi, with his "negative sexual structure," could not be "capable of love." In the latter, he argued that "sexual repression strengthens political reaction and makes the individual in the masses passive and nonpolitical" and that "the core of the fascist race theory"—the impetus for the Nazis' "persecution of the Jews"—"is a mortal fear of natural sexuality and of its orgasm function."[77]

Summing up these ideas, Myron Sharaf, a student, patient, and biographer of Reich, remarked that "Reich believed that the only political answer to the distorted 'sex-politics' of Hitler was his own positive sex-politics. One did not answer Hitler's use of the Jews as scapegoats by pointing out the intellectual fallacies of his argument or its function as a diversion from other issues. One countered by directly dealing with the people's sexual longings."[78] The ranks of Reich's American literary followers included Norman Mailer, Paul Goodman, Saul Bellow, Allen Ginsberg, and Isaac Rosenfeld.[79] Rosenfeld in particular exemplified the appeal of Reichian ideas to American Jews in the wake of the Holocaust in a 1949 symposium when he described "anti-Semitism as a symptom of a serious, underlying psycho-sexual disease of epidemic proportion in our society."[80] Cure the sexual ills of America, this argument goes, and one relieves it of its anti-Semitism.

Reich himself, it should be said, concluded on the basis of his analyses of fascism that "any kind of literature which creates sexual anxiety must be prohibited," including "mystery stories," "gruesome fairy tales for children," and "pornography."[81] But others followed his arguments about sexual suppression as a cause of Nazism to different conclusions. In the same year as Rosenfeld's symposium remark, Gershon Legman published *Love & Death: A Study in Censorship*, which incorporated a loosely Reichian perspective into an eccentric analysis of U.S. obscenity law.

Born in Scranton, Pennsylvania, the son of a kosher butcher, Legman went on to a fascinating, unusual career that included a stint as the archivist for the Kinsey Institute and authorship of a massive scholarly examination of dirty jokes. Legman is said to have been conscious, as he composed *Love & Death*, that his extended family in Hungary had perished in the Holocaust.[82] This helps to explain why the Holocaust crops up repeatedly, as one might not expect it to do, in a polemic about sexual censorship in American popular culture. Legman's argument is that the fascination with violence in American culture results from, and feeds, the widespread suppression of sexuality: "Sex being forbidden, violence took its place."[83] In his first chapter, Legman laments the popularity in the United States of murder mystery novels, arguing that they inculcate the habit of mind that is required for genocide: the strategic dehumanization of a particular person or group of people whose torture or murder can then be contemplated, and presumably executed, without guilt. In the murder mystery, that dehumanized target is not the victim whose death initiates the plot but the murderer, whom the detective—and, vicariously, the reader—methodically hunts down and destroys. "By casting one living individual into the character of a murderer," Legman explains, "he is thrown automatically outside the pale of humanity, and neither justice nor mercy need be shown him." Making the Reichian point explicit, Legman notes that "in the same way, Germans were given to understand that Jews are not human and, as such, can properly be gassed, electrocuted, and incinerated wholesale."[84] Readers desire such violent fantasies, moreover, because healthy sexual expression has been denied them: "My dear fellow, it is not easy to take the adolescent's mind off sex," Legman notes, in characteristically inflated deadpan. "It takes death, death, death, and more death. For adults, more still." Legman argues his point inconsistently; so committed is he to the notion that violent culture contributes to mass murder that he has to insist finally, on the last page of his book, that his readers not take him to be making "Milton's mistake—pleading for free speech with one hand, and writing the censor's *damnatur* with the other."[85] There are other uncomfortable elements of Legman's strange screed, including the issue, raised by the intellectual historian Carolyn Dean, of Legman's underlying vision of Nazis not just as sexually repressed but as latent homosexuals.[86] Less relevant here than whether there is any merit in Legman's argument, though, is simply the fact that it derives much of its rhetorical force and impetus from the Holocaust. His stated purpose was to advocate the repeal of American obscenity laws, and the genocide of the Jews motivated him in that project and provided him with useful evidence.

Legman's book, not now widely read, was hardly obscure; two of its chapters were translated and published in Jean-Paul Sartre's *Les temps modernes* in 1948 and 1950, and William Carlos Williams included it on a list of the ten best books of the year in the *New York Times*.[87] The Reichian association of sexual repression with Nazism and fascism, which Legman espoused and adapted, came to be widely accepted by American cultural critics in the following decade.

Nazism, Minority Rights, and Obscenity as Free Speech

The fourth, and in a sense the most direct, discursive tendency through which attention to the Nazis' crimes figured in postwar discussions of freedom of expression was in bolstering the legal discourse that aligned freedom of speech with the rights of political minorities. Long before World War II, legal debates over freedom of speech in America often focused on the question of the degree to which a political majority can impose its values on a minority group or individual.[88] As one legal scholar recently phrased it, "People in the majority are unlikely to encounter legal restrictions on what they can say, [but] people who belong to unpopular social groups, such as ethnic and religious minorities, . . . cannot look with any assurance to majoritarian institutions to protect their right to speak as they wish on matters of great controversy and of great anxiety."[89]

Such reasoning can be observed at the outset of the 20th century, in a treatise written by the American legal theoretician Ernst Freund. An early faculty member at the University of Chicago Law School and widely respected scholar, Freund insisted in *The Police Power* (1904) that "the idea of a public welfare bought at the cost of suppressing individual liberty and right is . . . inadmissible."[90] Following this principle, Freund asserted that legitimate scientific and artistic expression should not be subject to censorship, noting that "moral, intellectual and political movements, in which our constitutions proclaim the principle of individual liberty," must be "exempt" from "police power."[91] Following the same principle, Freund, who was Jewish, opposed a Louisiana court's ruling denying Jews the right to work on Sundays, pursuant to the Sunday laws that generally prohibited work on that day, if they observe their Sabbath on Saturdays. He remarked that "such a prohibition creates a special burden" for Jews: under the Louisiana ruling, Jews who observed the Sabbath would have to close their businesses for two days each week, rather than the one day of their Christian competitors, at a significant loss of income. Freund felt that "all laws should scrupulously respect the principle of religious equality," which "should be recognized as a constitutional right."[92]

Freund remained active in defending freedom of speech in the years after World War I, and his attention to the balancing of interests between the state and minority groups may account, in part, for his insistence that art be protected as free speech when First Amendment doctrine began to evolve in the years after World War I.[93] Responding to Harvard law professor Zechariah Chafee, Jr., whose advocacy for freedom of speech focused on political rather than artistic speech,

Freund insisted that "if you consider Freedom of Speech socially as well as politically," then Theodore Schroeder, founder of the Free Speech League and author of *"Obscene" Literature and Constitutional Law* (1911), "deserves a place in your bibliography."[94] That the august Freund recommended the work of Schroeder—the most vehement opponent of the Comstock laws in early 20th-century America and somewhat of an outsider—suggests the degree to which he prioritized a defense of literature and the arts.

While Freund had articulated a link between minority and individual rights and freedom of expression in the first decades of the 20th century, the major triumph for freedom of sexual expression in the interwar years, the famed *Ulysses* decision, proposed a different basis for allowing Joyce's book to circulate. Judge Woolsey asserted that the obscenity of a book must be judged on the basis of the book's effect on the *homme moyen sensuel*. At the time, this seemed like a sensible refutation of the Hicklin test—the principle, inherited from British case law, that one of the defining features of obscenity should be its tendency to deprave or corrupt the most vulnerable members of society—but in aligning freedom of expression with the perspective of the "average" person, that is, a member of the majority, this limited protection for the free speech of those who disagreed with the majority. Woolsey's celebrated decision was not as forward-thinking in this respect as Benjamin Greenspan's in *People v. Viking Press* (1933), which rejected John Sumner's argument that the "literati" who had submitted letters in support of Erskine Caldwell's novel *God's Little Acre* were "abnormal people" and that, following a statement in *People v. Pesky* (1930), "these matters must be judged by normal people and not by the abnormal."[95] It is perhaps not surprising that Greenspan, who had founded the Wall Street Synagogue in 1929 and served as its first president, would object to Sumner's characterization of such letter writers as the philosopher Horace Kallen and Solomon Lowenstein, the "executive and director of the Federation for the Support of Jewish Philanthropic Societies," as "abnormal," for much the same reason that any member of a minority group might feel excluded by a recourse to the "average."

While some American Jews had already embraced the discourse of "minority rights" while lobbying on behalf of the political protection of eastern European Jews in the wake of World War I,[96] the abrogation of

Jews' rights by the Third Reich was a further impetus for many Americans, Jewish and non-Jewish, to redouble their insistence on the U.S. Constitution's protection of minority rights. Nazism could also be understood as an impetus for broadening protections beyond already recognized groups. Jo Sinclair's prize-winning 1946 novel *Wasteland*, for example, envisions links between the protection of the rights of racial and sexual minorities. Sinclair's autobiographical character Deborah, a lesbian writer and a sister of the novel's protagonist, expresses her fellowship with other persecuted groups, with "Jews, Negroes, cripples of any sort."[97] When she remarks, a little earlier in the novel, that she has felt "isolated, part of a tiny minority of people who did not dare lift their eyes to the level of the rest of the world," Sinclair avoids specifying whether Deborah means that she felt marginalized as a lesbian or as a Jew or both: in any case, she was part of a "tiny minority."[98] The textual ambiguity works to emphasize the analogy, as if to say that since minority status functions analogically for people from these different groups, surely they deserve the same protection under the law. Another version of this analogy appears in the introduction that William Carlos Williams wrote to Allen Ginsberg's *Howl* (1955), which oddly proclaims that Ginsberg "has gone, in his own body, through the horrifying experiences described from life in these pages, . . . his Golgotha, his charnel house, similar in every way, to that of the Jews in the past war."[99] It is difficult to parse this comparison, except by considering the description of Ginsberg's struggles as "similar in every way" to the systematic murder of millions as deliberate hyperbole intended to align the abuse of a (Jewish) homosexual in the United States with the persecution of Jews (as well as homosexuals) by the Nazis in Europe.[100]

American obscenity law did briefly embrace the minority-rights argument for freedom of expression in the 1960s, and memories of World War II clearly influenced that development and thereby the overall liberalization of American obscenity law. One key event leading to that liberalization was a 1956 concurring opinion in the case of Samuel Roth written by Jerome Frank that prodded the Supreme Court to reopen the question of obscenity. Crucial elements of Frank's decision resonate with statements he made during World War II. In December 1941, he had contributed an article to the *Saturday Evening Post* explaining that Hitler's easy victory over France had dissuaded Frank from his former commitment to American isolationism. He mentions the anti-Semitism he personally encountered in the United States—being "barred from fraternities in college," finding he "was not wanted in a hotel or a club." He argues that "it is part of the great American tradition—a tradition which makes American Jews deeply grateful to America—that minority groups be respected."[101] This belief in the protection of the rights of minorities as an American tradition surfaces again in Frank's 1956 *Roth* opinion, in which he remarks that "some few men stubbornly fight for the right to write or publish or distribute books which the great majority at the time consider loathsome. If we jail those few, the community may appear to have suffered nothing. The appearance is deceptive."[102] Frank is concerned here with literature, not political speech, but he frames the issue in terms of a conflict between the "great majority" and the "few," which is exactly what previous generations of free-speech activists had been unwilling to do. It is noticeable, especially as he follows this passage with a quotation from Spinoza, that the principle of minority rights he emphasizes is a principle he had acknowledged as of special importance to American Jews, such as himself, during Hitler's reign.

The Supreme Court's decision in the *Roth* case did not embrace Frank's argument; Justice Brennan's decision asserted that "the standard for judging obscenity . . . is whether, to the average person, applying contemporary community standards, the dominant theme of the material, taken as a whole, appeals to prurient interest."[103] Again, the appeal to an "average person" and to "community standards" privileges the majority; as Justice Douglas objected in his dissent, "Under that test, juries can censor, suppress, and punish what they don't like. . . . This is community censorship in one of its worst forms."[104] The lawyer Charles Rembar, chief counsel for Grove Press, in his legal arguments in the wake of *Roth*, agreed with Douglas that giving the "average person" the power to determine whether a book is fit for suppression, or not, is a disastrous policy for minority groups. As Rembar phrases the matter, "the First Amendment is a cheap thing if all it provides is the assurance that one may say what a current majority is willing to hear."[105] Arguing cases on behalf of Grove Press in defense of books including *Lady Chatterley's Lover* and *Tropic of Cancer*, Rembar insisted that "the phrases 'average person' and 'contemporary community standards'" should not be interpreted so as to "limit writers and publishers to the average person's conception of the kind of writing that ought to be published, or to limit a minority of readers to the kind of reading that a majority might think good for them."[106]

As Justice Douglas had pointed out, it was generally accepted by this time that even if one person in a thousand in America supported a particular political program, it would be unconstitutional to restrict that person's speech on that subject because his or her ideas do not conform to the average person's thought. Rembar argued that the same should apply to sexual representations. Brennan's 1966 formulation, that "a book cannot be proscribed unless it is found to be utterly without redeeming social value,"[107] embraces the minority-rights argument: even if only the tiniest minority of Americans finds a book compelling and worthwhile, how could anyone claim it is "utterly without redeeming social value"? The result of this approach to obscenity was to grant virtually unlimited protection to speech precisely because it is the minority's right to speech that is being protected, even when the protected speech contradicts the beliefs of the majority. "It cannot be stressed too often," Rembar remarked, "that it was the United States Constitution that saved these books, and not the will of the people."[108]

Rembar was Jewish, a cousin of Norman Mailer's, but he does not seem to have made any claims about a link between his emphasis on minority rights and his background. Decades later, though, one of the most influential First Amendment lawyers of the following generation, Martin Garbus, made explicit the connection between the Holocaust and the minority-rights argument for a wide latitude in freedom of expression. In his memoir, *Traitors and Heroes* (1987), Garbus explains his commitment to First Amendment law in relation to his boyhood in the Bronx during World War II, when he was "terrified both by the people who ran this country and by the specters of Nazism and anti-Semitism." In an irony of which he is highly self-conscious, one of Garbus's professional accomplishments was to defend the National Socialist Party of America's right to march in Skokie, Illinois, in the late 1970s, suggesting just how far his commitment to freedom of speech went. He describes this commitment as seeming necessary to him as a member of a demographic minority. "The only alternative to freedom for any group is power," he explains. "But minority groups will rarely have the means sufficient to avoid injustice." In Garbus's view, free speech protects minorities from the kind of persecution that led to the Holocaust. "Does an absolute commitment to the protection of free speech ensure that there will not be another era of mass killings?" he goes on to ask. "Of course not. But on balance there is a better chance of its not happening again if the government is not given the power to decide what we can say."[109] Garbus makes explicit what by the 1960s had become an implicitly accepted idea, that self-consciousness of the danger of one's status as a member of a demographic minority—of being a part of one of the "minority groups" without "the means sufficient to avoid injustice"—is one key reason to argue for the defense of civil liberties generally and freedom of speech in particular.[110]

Anti-Anti-Semitic Pornotopia in the American 1960s

It is not difficult to locate examples in 1960s American culture in which frank discussions of sex of all kinds seemed like the solution to most problems, and particularly to the problem of anti-Semitism. As Allen Ginsberg explained to a courtroom in January 1965, in one of the cases about William Burroughs's *Naked Lunch*, Burroughs's novel contains the line "all a Jew wants to do is doodle a Christian girl" not to foment anti-Semitism but with the aim of "defending the Jews."[111] Another extraordinary example of this phenomenon constitutes an otherwise rather inexplicable aspect of a best-selling novel called *The Harrad Experiment*. Written by Robert Rimmer, it was first published in 1966 in a hardcover edition sold primarily by mail order. Then, as a seventy-five-cent Bantam paperback, marketed with the slogan "The Sex Manifesto of the Free Love Generation" on its cover, it sold a reported three million copies between 1967 and 1979 and was adapted into two feature films.[112] The novel describes the founding of a radical college campus with "a program designed to achieve sexual sanity." This fictional college, called Harrad and located in Cambridge, Massachusetts, innovates primarily in its rooming arrangements, in which "heterosexual couples would share . . . a study room, a bathroom, and a bedroom with twin beds." It also offers a thorough education in sexology.[113] The book consists of diary entries by four of the students who gradually manage to overcome their sexual fears and neuroses and to embrace Harrad's philosophy during their years at the school. By the end of the novel, they have sketched a political plan for the legalization of polygamy in one of the American states, and they have themselves committed to a six-person group marriage, with children, in a house in Philadelphia. The novel included a substantial bibliography of sexological sources and was not subtle about its goal of fomenting sexual radicalism. Indeed, it did inspire the formation of at least a few sexually radical communities, including Harrad West, in Berkeley, where members expressed the hope in 1969 "that perhaps six, eight or even a dozen or more adults can form 'marriage' relationships with each other as a means of attaining far more than monogamous marriages can offer."[114]

The book is awkwardly written and generally unsubtle. Rimmer regularly references books such as Betty Friedan's *The Feminine Mystique* or historical precedents for Harrad such as the Oneida community by simply having a character mention them. The main characters are cartoonish, and their psychological development takes place in convenient, implausible, spurts. The novel introduces Rimmer's ideas about sexuality without much indirection and with long expository speeches, in the fashion of Ayn Rand. It is not immediately clear, then, why the novel devotes so much energy to Jewish culture.

In an odd scene, one of the main characters, Beth Hillyer, the daughter of a Protestant doctor from Ohio, recounts a sexual experience with her Jewish roommate, Harry Schacht. "Last night, with Harry deep inside me . . . I was in a blissful, talkative mood," she begins and then presents a monologue in praise of Jewish cuisine: "Life would be very dull without potato latkes, bagels, lox, sweet and sour meatballs, stuffed cabbage, kishke, knishes, kreplach, chopped liver, gefilte fish, all the wonderfully crazy pareve food, all the enchanting desserts without leavening that have been invented for Passover." Harry interrupts this "breathless recital by kissing [her] breasts and gently probing them with his tongue," and he cautions her, "You may have a tendency to get too plump. I like skinny women." "Skinny women with big tits," Beth responds, "and a warm vagina." That settled, Beth returns to her praise of Jewish culture, which extends beyond food: she has also been pleased to discover "a whole new group of holidays. Rosh Hashonoh, Hanukkah, Passover to mention a few," as well as "a whole new Yiddish vocabulary. Hundreds and hundreds of useful onomatopoeic words, Shlecht, pisk, metziah, plotz, schlemiel, fresser, shicker, shmendrick, bobbe, kvetch": "In fact, I'm so entranced and there are such useful words for cursing, too, that I am compiling a dictionary of them" (227–28). While this material is introduced as clumsily as anything else in the book, the passage is remarkable both for the length of the list of foods and for the Yiddish words Beth introduces; she mentions not just bagels and lox but even "crazy pareve food," products that contain neither meat nor dairy and that, because of their flexibility, are staples in any traditionally kosher home. Why?

Why does this encomium to Jewish culture merit inclusion in a sexological *roman à thèse*, the self-described "sex manifesto of the free love generation"? The other three main characters' family backgrounds are briefly mentioned: Beth is an Ohio "WASP" from a "medical family" (132, 32); Stanley Cole's real name is Kolasukas, and his "family are poor Polish people" (21); Sheila Grove is the daughter of a hedonistic Texas oil baron. But the novel does not celebrate Polish, Texan, or midwestern Protestant culture or spend more than a page or two on any of them. The strangeness of the attention to Jewish culture in *The Harrad Experiment* is highlighted by the removal of that element of the novel when it was adapted to film: playing the part of Harry in the 1973 film, Bruno Kirby does not indicate in any way that his character is Jewish, and in the second film, which features scenes at Harry's parents' house, they appear to be wealthy suburbanites, not explicitly marked as Jewish, in stark contrast to the novel. Clearly Harry's Jewishness, and Beth's attraction to it, are not essential to *The Harrad Experiment*'s primary message about the pursuit and practice of radical sexual freedom.

Yet Jewishness figures intensely in Rimmer's novel, particularly in its second half. While at times Rimmer's characters mention Orthodox Judaism along with Catholicism as a traditional religion that constrains sexual behavior (e.g., 188), more frequently the novel concerns itself with Harry's family, who are "not really orthodox," though they do "respect [Jewish] customs" (132). Initially skeptical, Harry's family comes around to be remarkably accepting of the sexual radicalism practiced by the novel's young protagonists. When the group is "arrested for indecent exposure, and on a morals charge involving orgiastic behavior" on Cape Cod during their summer vacation, Harry, writing from prison, expects that his parents will disapprove: "they may be able to laugh at the subject of *yentizing* [*sic*] around when a Jewish comedian on the borscht circuit makes a 'funny' but as a practical family matter it quite obviously won't be admitted as a fit subject for laughter" (202–3). Even here, Harry makes clear that his parents are not puritanical toward discussions of sex, and as his journal entry continues, Harry recounts conversations he had with his father, Jake, earlier in the summer that suggest the older man's resistance to the Harrad students' sexual experimentation is rather superficial. Though Jake expresses concern for his son, he admits that his problem is not sex in itself but simply that Harry might be overdoing it: "Well, sex is all right," he says. "A growing boy has to learn, . . . but everyday you are living with that little blonde *meidele*. Day in, day out. You'll wear yourself out!" (203). Hardly operating on the assumption of sex as sinful—which the novel ascribes elsewhere to Catholicism and, inaccurately, to Orthodox Judaism—Jake simply fears that Harry will diminish his pleasure: "All this sex so young," he says. "You'll grow bored" (204). Jake's arguments are half-hearted, and Harry's rejoinders insist that his sexual practices do not contradict Jewish culture; when Jake suggests that Harry, who is studying to be a doctor, will lose his patients' trust if he is known to engage in polygamy, Harry responds with the example of his father's own doctor: "[He] has a girl friend. His wife knows it and couldn't care less. Old Jewish custom, really. Have you read the Old Testament lately?" (206).

Later scenes in the novel make even clearer Rimmer's idea that modern Jewish culture can accommodate free sexual expression. The novel recounts how the publisher of *Cool Boy* magazine—Rimmer's satire on *Playboy*—approaches Beth and asks her to pose nude. As a Harrad student, she understands what is at stake in this: her picture will be "hanging on college and barrack walls while sad little boys [play] with themselves" (236), but she finally agrees to pose in order to raise a thousand dollars for the group's plans. Along with giving Rimmer opportunities to lampoon *Playboy* and to explain that it succeeds only because of sexual repression—"magazines of the *Cool Boy* ilk would simply languish and die for lack of interest . . . once nudity was generally acceptable on the beaches, in public performances, and casually around the home" (282–83)—this plot point also gives the novel another opportunity to explore how Harry's Jewish family deals with sex. First, Harry's father, Jake, discovers the magazine and chides both Harry and Beth: "The girl you are going to marry . . . naked for everyone to see. Beth, tell me it's not you! . . . What would your father and mother think? Their daughter a sex-object!" (235). Again, while Rimmer presents Jake as expressing disapproval, his disapproval does not run very deep. Instead of articulating his own objection to Beth's posing nude, Jake evokes the potential reactions of Beth's Protestant parents. And, as Harry quickly points out, Jake could not have discovered the photos if he had not himself been a reader of the pornographic magazine. Jake's defensiveness, hearing this, is short-lived: "I look at it down at the drugstore. Since when should a father have to explain to his son? I look to see what a mess the younger generation is in. Maybe I like to look at pretty girls too" (235). Quickly the scene has turned from a father's disapproval of his daughter-in-law's posing for soft-core pornography to his rather unapologetic acknowledgment of his enjoyment of such material. Having heard the story of how Beth was approached to pose and why she agreed to participate, Jake accepts what she has done in terms that emphasize that his attitude is in some sense a Jewish one. "My lips are sealed," he says, "*Abi gezunt*" (243). The Yiddish phrase means "as long as you're healthy" and suggests that Jake acknowledges that there is nothing inherently unhealthy about what Beth has done.

In that scene, Jake suggests that Jewish women might not be as accepting as he is of such sexual expression: "Pray your mother and *bobbe* never hear about it," he tells Harry (243). Yet Rimmer represents Jewish women, in this family at least, as even more progressive than Jake. In the scene that immediately follows, Harry's grandmother ("*bobbe*") shows Beth a book of Eadweard Muybridge's photographs: "pictures of a young naked woman entitled 'Woman, walking and turning while pouring water from a watering can.'" She explains, with pride, that the woman is Harry's great-grandmother: "My mother was a pretty woman in her day." The scene suggests that any discomfort the family might have developed around photographing naked human bodies is a recent aberration; when Beth asks Harry's *bobbe* whether Harry's mother knows about the Muybridge photographs, she replies, "She should worry! A picture! The body is dust" (243): in other words, what harm did it do? Why get upset? In Rimmer's vision of this particular Jewish family, comfort with the graphic representation of the human body—indeed, with the very representations that Linda Williams understands as "the origin of porno"—evidently turns out to be, as Harry says of polygamy, an "Old Jewish custom."[115]

Rimmer insists that the sexually radical program he proposes should not threaten traditional Jewish culture but rather modernize it. Harry worries that "the basic idea of Harrad is ultimately against a world within a world like the Jews have made," but Beth explains that "the Harrad idea" is *not* "to obliterate cultural differences." She specifically cites the "strong sense of family unity" that Harry, "and many Jewish families, seem to have": "You are all . . . *landsmen* [*sic*]" (229–30).[116] Harry is quickly convinced, as Rimmer's characters tend to be, and he realizes that the experiment in group marriage he is participating in is precisely an extension of the Jewish family ideal that has begun to weaken under the pressure of sexual prudishness. "You and I, Jack and Val, Sheila and Stanley; we've replaced the vanishing family. We can give it an even larger existence and strength" (233). Part of Harrad's appeal to Harry, then, is its ability to preserve Jewish values.

If Rimmer's goal was a sexual utopia in which all humans could connect, why would he spend so much time in *The Harrad Experiment* insisting that his program is specifically congruent with modern Jewish culture? One way to answer this question is biographically: Rimmer explains, in an autobiographical essay appended to the twenty-fifth anniversary edition of *The Harrad Experiment*, that while his parents were nonpracticing Christians, as an adult, he found a place for himself in a Jewish community. In the late 1940s or early 1950s, Rimmer and his wife had joined in an informal group marriage with another couple, whom Rimmer calls David and Nancy; the two couples "were often casually naked together and slept with each other's spouses" but "never made love as a foursome." David and Nancy were Jewish, and as the two couples grew closer, Rimmer explains, "it was no longer a case of 'some of our best friends are Jews.' *All* of mine and Erma's friends were Jews." Rimmer became entranced by Jewish culture, and the speeches he puts in Beth's mouth, extolling it, are transparently his own expressions of enthusiasm. He notes, for example, "long before Leo Ros[t]en, and with no credentials, I was compiling a Yiddish dictionary," just like Beth.[117] Given that Rimmer began to write *Harrad* after more than a decade of a group marriage with a Jewish couple, it is not so mysterious that the novel associates sexual freedom and open-mindedness with Jews.

Yet Rimmer goes further than simply articulating affinities between the "Harrad idea" and Jewish culture. He also makes clear that his program for "sexual sanity" offers a solution to the problem of genteel anti-Semitism that persisted in postwar America. Rimmer had been concerned about anti-Semitism and understood it as an issue that could draw attention to his writing as early as 1959, when he was attempting to interest a publisher in his first novel, *The Rebellion of Yale Marratt*. In a pitch letter he sent to many of the publishers that rejected the novel, he explained that the first reason his book is "going to be a bestseller" is that "it has an idyllic love story which crosses religious lines and raises the deep undercurrent of anti-Semitism." Rimmer also understood that there would be particular interest in a novel on this topic being written by a non-Jew: "Since the author is Gentile, the Jewish community will be fascinated."[118] Rimmer's interest in anti-Semitism also has a clear biographical source: in his memoir, Rimmer notes that if he "hadn't met David and Nancy," he "never would have discovered just how anti-Semitic [his own] father and mother were."[119] His father, the wealthy owner of a printing company who seems to have bought and bullied his son's way into college and Harvard Business School, "belonged to a popular local club which excluded Jews" and "refused to come to [Rimmer's] house when David and Nancy (or any other Jews) were there" but "believed he wasn't prejudiced, because he did business with many Jews." Rimmer also reports that he was "shocked" that such prejudices were not uniquely his father's, upon traveling to Cape Cod with his friends and discovering "that there was no room at the inn when [the proprietors] saw David."[120] Such institutions, luxury hotels and country clubs, were among the few remaining places where Americans could find systematic anti-Semitism in the 1950s, and though they were hardly as threatening as the violent persecution of Jews in Europe or as widespread as the exclusionary practices in the early 20th-century United States, they remained troubling both to American Jews and to progressive non-Jews.

The novel registers these concerns directly. Beth's parents, described as "insulated Mid-Westerners" (90) and as WASPs, share the typical prejudices of the time. They "belong to a country club that seeks new memberships very carefully" to "avoid a 'Jewish takeover,'" for example (227). Some Harrad students also react with anti-Semitic stereotypes when Beth announces that she is dating Harry, impugning him as apelike with "an eagle proboscis" and accusing him of clannishness (77). As Beth and Harry grow closer, she reports of her parents, "[They] have been cordial with him but it is still a distant cordiality. Harry may be the finest boy in the world but, inescapably, to them, he is Jewish first and a man second. There is no overt anti-semitism in anything my family have said to me. It is indirect" (226). Rimmer is careful to show that these attitudes influence Beth and Harry, too, at least at the beginning of their relationship; Beth recalls, in retrospect, that when she first met him, she was "afraid": "He was Jewish, the way he thought, the expressions he used, they all seemed foreign and insular to me" (225). Meanwhile, Harry, early in their relationship, worries about what would have happened if Beth had been at his parents' home for Chanukah: "she would have felt foreign, . . . a *shicksa*, and while my mother and father would have tried to make her feel welcome, Beth would never feel a part of this life" (132). Beth's parents reject Harry as "Jewish first and a man second," but Harry knows that his own parents will at least try "to make [Beth] feel welcome." It is Beth whom he expects never to feel comfortable among Jews, and it is only thanks to Harrad College that she overcomes her prejudice.

The thesis of *The Harrad Experiment* is that this overcoming of anti-Semitism and other forms of retrograde superstition and irrationality and the resulting social problems will be inevitable if sexual puritanism is rejected and sexuality is taught, discussed, and studied openly and rationally. David Allyn notes in his history of the sexual revolution that no African American characters are included in Rimmer's utopian vision: Harry's Jewishness seems to be the outer limit of Harrad's possibility for overcoming difference; yet a few years later, Rimmer declared that "obviously, if a dormitory living program of the Harrad style was functioning, black students should be admitted."[121] The novel represents sex explicitly in modes ranging from the clinical—"the mucous will flow in my vagina and your penis will become erect" (41)—to the emotional language of Lawrence and Miller: "I could feel the soft undulating movement of her vagina keeping me happily within her" (73); "I never guessed that having you touch me and being so big inside me could be so warm . . . hungry . . . gentle . . . tender" (58); "Jack was gently kissing me between my legs and I was kissing his penis" (153); "I was taking a shower with Sheila, soaping her breasts and belly and pussy" (272).

There is no question that a paperback containing these passages—along with the words "prick" (19), "snatch" (19), "orgasms" (75), "ejaculations" (76), "seminal emissions" (78), "fuck" (107), and "tit-and-pussy chasers" (124)—would have been very difficult, if not impossible, to publish and distribute a decade earlier. Indeed, the book struck one reviewer, as late as 1969, as presenting "sly pornography" that Rimmer "offset" with his "stilted priggishness."[122] But a decade earlier, Rimmer had already come to the conclusion that if there was any hope of eliminating American anti-Semitism, it would be necessary to discuss sex more openly. As he wrote to a literary agent while attempting to market his first novel—and sounding a bit like Isaac Rosenfeld's channeling of Reich a decade earlier—Rimmer understood the "undercurrent hatred" of American anti-Semitism "as symptomatic of very much larger issues."[123]

The Harrad Experiment transparently draws its ideas from the sexological discourse that we have seen, throughout this chapter, to have been used by those who rejected sexual anti-Semitism since the early 20th century. It cites in its bibliography Wilhelm Reich's *Sexual Revolution* and Gershon Legman's *Love & Death*, as well as a book about the history of sexuality in religion by the Yiddish journalist Ben-Zion Goldberg and Victor Frankl's *Man's Search for Meaning*, a popular book by a survivor of concentration camps who asserts, as part of his program for finding meaning after the Holocaust, that "sex is a way of expressing the experience of that ultimate togetherness which is called love."[124] It is also noteworthy that Rimmer's bibliography emphasizes the work of two American Jewish psychologists, Abraham Maslow and Albert Ellis, citing three books by each and including brief, enthusiastic annotations. "Ellis will go down in the history of the sex revolution as the first man to dare to lift the curtain and reveal the smog behind it" (308), Rimmer notes, and "Abe Maslow will someday be widely recognized and perhaps be considered as influential as Freud on future developments in psychology" (310). While both of these psychologists were avowed atheists, like Reich, Legman, and other post-Freudian thinkers they developed their theories of human behavior and sexuality in part, at least, as a response to personal experiences of or intense concerns about anti-Semitism and particularly in response to the Nazi genocide of European Jews. Maslow's biographer notes that "he often referred both privately and publicly to the pervasive and intense anti-Semitism he experienced during his formative years and its profound effect upon his early outlook" and that it was "the spreading triumph of Hitler and fascism around the globe" that drove Maslow "to develop a comprehensive study of human motivation."[125] Ellis, for his part, notes in his autobiography that some of his relatives were among Hitler's victims, and he argues in his most widely read book that "sexual fascism"—for example, the "censoring and penalizing of harmless sex acts which run counter to some arbitrary authoritarian prejudice"—"stems from political fascism," specifically the sort embodied by the Nazis.[126] Whether or not Rimmer knew it, his idea that freedom of sexual expression would overcome the irrationality that drove genteel and "indirect" American anti-Semitism constituted a popularization for postwar America of a conventional sexological trope.

Rimmer's clearest dramatization of how the Harrad idea counteracts anti-Semitic tendencies appears in a scene in which one of the female Harrad students, Sheila, barely escapes being raped by knife-wielding gang members in a parking garage in New York City on New Year's Eve. When she returns to the hotel room where her friend Harry has been sleeping, she asks him how it is possible that the young men who assaulted her could want to inflict such sexual violence: "If they've loved someone in their lives, cared for someone once, how could they deliberately hurt a stranger?" "You haven't been reading your history lately," Harry replies. "Has man made any progress in the last twenty years? Really? The Nazi and Commissar mentality is still rampant." As if to demonstrate the sexual control that education and rationality confer on Harry, the scene continues, as Sheila narrates: "Harry held me close to him. We didn't talk. Though his penis felt big against my belly, he didn't try to make love" (130–31). As a contrast to the "Nazi and Commissar mentality"—in this case, the fascistic or totalitarian tendency, whether real or imagined, to inflict sexual violence on the vulnerable—the novel's representative Jew demonstrates both healthy sexual response and respectful self-control.

The Utopianism of Pornotopia

While sexual repression is often concomitant with other forms of social and political repression, sexual liberalism or radicalism are by no means always markers of progressive, pacifist, or healthy communities and cultures. Contrary to Isaac Rosenfeld's claim, anti-Semitism, in most of its manifestations, is not "a symptom of a . . . psycho-sexual disease" and cannot be said to coincide inevitably with any particular pattern of sexual behavior or even with any attitude toward or policy on the discussion and graphic representation of sex. Dreiser, Lewisohn, Rimmer, and the other cultural producers discussed in this chapter were not, in this sense, correct in the belief that the popularization of sexology would reduce the incidence of anti-Semitism. Their vision of a world liberated from sexual suppression and restriction and consequently freed of racism is a misguidedly utopian one, but that did not stop it from serving as inspiration for a great deal of American cultural production that links Jews and sexual expression or from providing motivation for individual Jewish and non-Jewish Americans to challenge, both in the courts and in the wider culture, the strictures of the law of obscenity.

2

The Prestige of Dirty Words and Pictures

Horace Liveright, Henry Roth, and the Graphic Novel

On September 14, 1933, Henry Roth wrote a note in his journal: "The novel is finished."[1] He had completed a draft of the manuscript that was to be published as *Call It Sleep*. Twelve weeks later, on December 6, federal judge John Woolsey announced his verdict in a case that must have interested Roth, *United States v. One Book Called "Ulysses."* Woolsey's decision would "determine whether" James Joyce's famous novel was "immoral and licentious," as the *New York Times* phrased it at the end of August, eagerly anticipating the ruling.[2] Roth read *Ulysses* in 1925, having borrowed a copy of Sylvia Beach's edition that his friend and patron, the NYU English professor Eda Lou Walton, had purchased in Paris and smuggled through U.S. customs. Joyce's novel fascinated Roth, and he and Walton and their friends would have known exactly what was at stake in the *Ulysses* trial, which received plenty of coverage in the press.[3] Would an internationally acknowledged literary masterpiece, a darling of the critics written by an artist of the first rank, continue to be suppressed by the U.S. government because it included a few graphic descriptions of sex and a smattering of taboo (so-called four-letter) words?[4]

We know, now, how Woolsey ruled; his celebrated decision freeing the novel from censorship, reprinted in the Random House edition of *Ulysses*, is among the most widely distributed U.S. legal decisions of all time. But consider Roth's perspective in the summer of 1933, when he was twenty-seven years old. He may have laughed at the boorishness and philistinism of the New York Society for the Suppression of Vice and its director, John Sumner, but he could not have been certain that Joyce's *Ulysses* would finally, after a decade, be freed by the courts. As far as Roth and his friends knew, it was possible—if somewhat unlikely, given Woolsey's liberal reputation—that *Ulysses* would be declared obscene again, meaning that no reputable American publisher would print it and that no American bookstore would display it and also that Joyce's work could still not be copyrighted in the United States or protected from literary pirates. Roth, it should be noted, had published virtually nothing at this point in his life. He had no contract for his novel, which he had dedicated the preceding four years, most of his adulthood, to drafting. Imagine, then, the courage or brazenness or foolhardiness required for Roth to include, in his manuscript, the same type of graphic representations of sex and the same four-letter words that had transformed Joyce's novel into contraband. If James Joyce was not permitted to use "dirty words," what made Roth dream that the authorities would allow the words "shit," "fuck," and "cunt" to stand in a first novel by an unknown writer such as him? Why would he take the colossal risk of attracting the attention of the censors and having his book suppressed?

The answer, of course, is that he had something to gain by doing so. This chapter explores how social and cultural marginalization provided one motivation for the use of obscenity by American Jews like, and very much unlike, Roth. Michel Foucault notes, in *The History of Sexuality*, that the public discussion of sex carries a "speaker's benefit,"[5] and scholars have since exhibited how directly Foucault's insight can be applied to literary history. Celia Marshik, for example, has shown that in the case of British modernism, while "censorship was repressive," it "also had productive effects," one of which was to enable "writers to construct public personae—such as that of martyr (in the case of Rossetti) or *enfant terrible* (as in the case of Joyce)—that exercise a strong hold on the imagination of readers even today."[6] It should be clear that obscenity differs from other practices, such as pimping and prostitution, engaged in by the desperately poor: to publish obscene novels, or even to write them, requires significant initial investments of capital. Engaging with literary obscenity is not, then, a means to stave off starvation. On the contrary, for some decades in the early 20th century, what obscenity offered was an effective way for writers and other cultural agents to transform their financial or social resources into cultural capital, or what we can more simply call literary prestige. This is one of the factors that drew so many American Jews, who had been denied more traditional routes to such cultural capital, to the use and defense of obscenity.[7] Yet engaging with obscenity also carried significant risks, especially for a marginalized and impoverished American. This chapter examines the "speaker's benefit" of obscenity—or its failure to materialize—in the careers of five literary figures: two publishers, Horace Liveright and Samuel Roth; one novelist, Henry Roth; and two pioneers of the graphic novel, Will Eisner and Jules Feiffer. In each case, a different constellation of marginalization, Jewishness, and obscenity emerged, and each suggests a different way that participating in the production of American literature could make someone's name—or ruin it.

The Rewards of Dirty Books in the 1920s: Horace Liveright

Some of the clearest examples of how literary obscenity could be used to transform one form of capital into another can be located in the history of a small group of Jewish men and women, children and grandchildren of immigrants, who revolutionized American literary and commercial publishing in the early 20th century. These men and women founded Random House, Knopf, the Modern Library, Simon & Schuster, Viking, and many other crucial publishing houses. Among them, perhaps the most fascinating and iconic was Horace Liveright. Having begun publishing only in 1917, Liveright's company was one of the key incubators of American literary modernism: he was the first American to publish books by Ernest Hemingway, William Faulkner, Jean Toomer, e.e. cummings, Djuna Barnes, Anzia Yezierska, and Nathanael West; he was, as mentioned in chapter 1, the stalwart publisher of Theodore Dreiser, as well as of Eugene O'Neill and Sherwood Anderson. Massively influential books that he published included John Reed's *Ten Days That Shook the World* (1919), Sigmund Freud's *A General Introduction to Psychoanalysis* (1920), and T. S. Eliot's *The Wasteland* (1922).[8] Part of Liveright's success can be attributed to his strategic engagements with obscenity, through which he was able to transform money—his wife's inheritance—into bankable literary prestige.

From childhood on, Liveright knew he wanted to be a player in literary and popular culture, but as a young man, his aspirations had been foiled on several occasions. Though his childhood home in Philadelphia contained a well-stocked library of English and American literature, his family did not have enough money to send him to a college-preparatory school; he considered his parents "poor relations" compared to his extended family, remembering later, "not dimly but clearly," how his family bought ice cream at a second-rate store, while his cousins, who attended expensive prep schools, ate the very best. At the age of eighteen, in 1902, Liveright interested a Broadway producer in staging an operetta he had written in the style of Gilbert and Sullivan, but the production fell through when he was not able to raise necessary funds. Eventually Liveright married the daughter of a wealthy paper manufacturer, and his father-in-law gifted him the money with which he founded his publishing house.[9]

Other Jews of his generation, with family fortunes behind them, had been doing the same. The question was how such fledgling publishers could attract authors to their lists. Alfred and Blanche Knopf began their publishing line in 1915, and they were at first unable to entice many American and British authors to publish with them; such authors preferred, sensibly enough, to work with established American houses such as Doubleday, Putnam, or Scribner. The Knopfs' first list included ten European translations and only five books composed in English. How could Liveright attract top talent a couple of years later, when he was a complete unknown on the publishing scene? Throwing money directly at the problem did not always work. As late as 1920, H. L. Mencken noted that Liveright had "offered" him and George Jean Nathan "a blank contract, including even 50% royalty," but, he said, "we are too comfortable with Knopf."[10] Along with Liveright's financial resources, to establish an attractive list he needed to find respected authors who were precisely not "too comfortable" with their current publishers. And one reason some authors were uncomfortable in those years was that publishers were unwilling to endure harassment and legal battles in order to publish unexpurgated literary works deemed worthy of suppression by Sumner and the NYSSV.

A remark by Adele Seltzer, who with her husband, Thomas, published and then defended in court D. H. Lawrence's *Women in Love*

(1922) after a couple of publishers had blanched at distributing the author's work unexpurgated,[11] makes clear how far a willingness to publish a controversial but critically acclaimed novelist could take a newly established firm: "Lawrence is a Titan," Seltzer wrote, "and I go about with an ever-present sense of wonder that we, Thomas and I, little, little Jews, should be the publishers of the great English giant of this age, publishers of him, not because with Jewish shrewdness we outwitted some other publishers & got Lawrence first, but because Lawrence's *Women in Love* went begging for a publisher."[12] Seltzer's "wonder" is understandable: publishing Lawrence in 1922 was a financial and even a legal risk for the Seltzers but not by any means a cultural one, given Lawrence's fame. Willingness to pay legal fees and even, perhaps, to go to jail was one of the qualities that could transform an unknown publisher into a cultural hero.

Liveright, for his part, promised in 1917—that is, at the very outset of his venture as a publisher—that he would distribute Dreiser's novel *The "Genius"* unexpurgated, despite the book's standing suppression by Sumner and the NYSSV.[13] This move made sense given the respect Dreiser commanded. The Authors League of America had stated, clearly and unequivocally, its opposition to the ban on the novel, so by financing a legal defense, and risking a jail term, Liveright had the opportunity of earning the regard of a vast number of American writers.[14] This was an example, then, of the powerful "speaker's benefit" that could be obtained by a publisher willing to defend the works of critically acclaimed authors accused of obscenity.

The 1923 "Clean Books crusade" in New York, and Liveright's response to it, furnishes an even clearer demonstration of how this worked. Toward the end of 1922, the outrage of a number of Christian religious groups at the "immorality" and "coarseness" of contemporary fiction began to swell, and Sumner, responding to the outcries, ramped up the NYSSV for a more aggressive than usual bout of book suppression directed against "a certain element in the publishing business."[15] Sumner's nascent coalition responded with alacrity when Judge John Ford of the New York State Supreme Court discovered, to his horror, that his own sixteen-year-old daughter had been given a copy of the Seltzers' edition of Lawrence's *Women in Love*. In February 1923, with Sumner's assistance, Ford gathered the support of more than a dozen religious and social groups to form the Clean Books League, which drew up a bill to revise the state's obscenity law so as to ease the conviction and punishment of book publishers.[16] Given how drastically the bill would have ceded editorial authority over the entire New York–based publishing industry to the self-appointed censors at the NYSSV, it received shockingly little opposition from established publishers and writers. The National Association of Book Publishers, for example, refused to oppose the bill (Sumner even claimed that several of the city's "reputable" publishers had helped to draft it), and fading literary eminences of the late 19th century celebrated the bill in the nativist spirit of the day. The critic Henry Walcott Boynton bemoaned the literary influence of "persons with alien names and frankly alien standards," while the novelist Mary Austin complained that "neither the Russian nor the Jew has ever been able to understand . . . that not to have had any seriously upsetting sex adventures may be the end of an intelligently achieved life standard."[17] Other nationally prominent authors and critics of the previous generation, including Hamlin Garland and Bliss Perry, came out explicitly for censorship and for the Clean Books League's bill.

Liveright opposed the Clean Books League bill almost single-handedly, with virtually no support from his fellow book publishers. This was an act of courage and conviction, perhaps, but it is also clear what he stood to gain from it. In an article published on March 17, 1923, Liveright contrasted would-be censors, such as Sumner, who have "little, if any, sense of value in literature, drama, and art generally," to publishers, who display "the highest quality of intellect and understanding" and who can be "severe and competent censors [who] judge by intelligent standards."[18] Opposing the Clean Books League was Liveright's opportunity to assert his position among the latter group, to establish himself as a publisher of "intellect" and "understanding." National opinion may not have supported him, but he rallied cultural authorities to his side: the bill was opposed by such literary eminences as Lawrence and Henry Seidel Canby, and the *New York Times* never vacillated in deploring it.[19]

Liveright, who unlike some of his fellow Jewish publishers never seems to have bothered to obscure his ethnic identity, could also count on support from the Jewish community. While Rabbi Stephen S. Wise, the country's most prominent Jewish leader, had been mentioned as one of the founders of the Clean Books League in March 1923, a month later Wise changed his mind and repudiated the bill in a sermon that was quoted at length in the *New York Times*.[20] Knowing that both cultural authorities and Jewish communal ones would sympathize with the campaign against the bill, Liveright could feel confident devoting time, energy, and money to it. When the bill was voted down in May 1923, his reward was a well-publicized dinner in his honor attended by literary eminences including Carl Van Vechten and Mencken (who just a few years earlier had said he would not publish with Liveright even for a 50% royalty). Senator James J. Walker, an opponent of the bill, credited Liveright in print as having been "solely responsible for defending the freedom of the press."[21]

In half a decade, Liveright transformed himself from an unknown parvenu to one of the most admired publishers in the country. While his defeat of the Clean Books League bill was hardly the singular stimulant to his growing reputation, it certainly helped the cause. In the wake of the victory, Waldo Frank featured Liveright in a celebratory profile in the pages of the *New Yorker*,[22] and soon the publisher added Sherwood Anderson to his stable of writers. In the years that followed, his firm managed to attract, at least briefly, such avant-garde talents as Hemingway and Faulkner.

Liveright's story is not at all unique. His commitment to freedom of expression parallels Ben Huebsch's publishing of Joyce's *Portrait of the Artist as a Young Man* a decade earlier, Seltzer's defense of Lawrence, Bennett Cerf's publication and defense of *Ulysses*, and perhaps even, to shuttle ahead to the late 1950s, Barney Rosset's defenses of *Lady Chatterley's Lover* and of Henry Miller's *Tropic of Cancer*. In several of these cases, the funds that covered the legal defenses of celebrated novels came not from within a publishing operation but from Jewish family fortunes earned in trades including tobacco, finance, real estate, and, in Liveright's case, paper products.[23] The publishing of obscenity was one means through which to convert such financial capital into a very precious form of cultural capital. It was, in other words, a way of purchasing literary prestige. And particularly in the years after World War I, this was something that some American Jews from wealthy families wanted and needed very much, as they were being denied access to prestige through more traditional channels.[24]

The Risks of Obscene Modernism in the 1920s: Samuel Roth

In the same period, American Jews from rather different personal backgrounds—specifically, poor eastern European immigrants—attempted to use obscenity to accrue cultural prestige, too, but the strategy tended not to succeed for them. Companies founded by the well-to-do Jewish publishers in the years after World War I remained blue-chip brands in the literary marketplace, but the "pariah capitalists" described in Jay Gertzman's excellent study *Bookleggers and Smuthounds: The Trade in Erotica, 1920–1940*, ended up running mail-order erotica-distribution operations that never rose to respectability and led their principals to be harassed, vilified, and jailed. Exemplary figures included Esar Levine and Benjamin Rebhuhn, friends who met at the City College of New York and spent most of the 1920s and 1930s defending themselves in courts, and Samuel Roth, who set out as a young man to craft a literary career for himself and wound up imprisoned for long stretches of his adulthood. Rehearsing some of the fascinating aspects of Roth's career helps to clarify the genuine risks of engagements with obscenity, especially for those gamblers who did not have family fortunes to fall back on.

Roth was born in a small town in the Austro-Hungarian Empire in 1896 and arrived in New York in 1903. He loved literature and claimed to have spent two years as a teenager reading all day at the public library while sleeping on the street at night.[25] He was committed to Jewish and Zionist literary culture in English: in 1914, he edited and published his first poetry anthology, *New Songs of Zion*, which reprinted verse from magazines including the *Maccabean*, the *Jewish Chronicle*, and the *Young Judean*. The collection included verses by internationally prominent Jewish writers such as Israel Zangwill and Emma Lazarus, as well as translations of Yiddish and Hebrew poetry by Morris Rosenfeld, Shimon Frug, and Chaim Nachman Bialik. Roth aimed to show, as he remarked in his editor's note, "that here in America, Zionism is a living movement the substance of which is of the very purest rock of human emotion."[26] Through all this activity, he earned himself a fellowship to Columbia University, but he soon dropped out to found a poetry bookshop in Greenwich Village. Roth's first collection of his own verse, *First Offering: A Book of Sonnets and Lyrics*, was published in 1917, and he reached a higher level of visibility and respectability when Liveright's firm released his next collection, *Europe: A Book for America*, in 1919. That book was reviewed sympathetically alongside Waldo Frank's *Our America* in the widely respected American Jewish monthly *Menorah Journal*.[27] Not all Roth's readers were impressed—Louis Untermeyer, writing in the *Dial*, remarked that his "chief impression" was "that of an honest, unflinching, and almost inspired triteness"[28]—but as Roth's work began to appear in *Harper's Weekly*, the *Nation*, and *Poetry*, he seemed poised for a role, if perhaps a minor one, in the embrace of literary modernism by American Jews in the 1920s, as a colleague of Waldo Frank, Ludwig Lewisohn, and Anzia Yezierska.[29]

In biographical sketches of Roth's career, this early phase, when he was a promising Zionist poet, tends to be overshadowed by the unfortunate path he trod in the following decades.[30] In the 1920s, Roth continued to pursue literary respectability: he founded a literary journal, *Two Worlds*, in which he included excerpts of James Joyce's "Work in Progress," which became *Finnegans Wake*, and later he printed expurgated chapters of *Ulysses*. Roth claimed that he had received permission from Joyce, through the intercession of Ezra Pound, to print the first of these excerpts, but the literary establishment condemned him for piracy.[31] In 1927, Lewisohn and Archibald MacLeish drafted a protest statement against Roth on Joyce's behalf, and a remarkable international coalition of 167 writers, critics, and philosophers signed on to it. At the same time, a few of Roth's countrymen in New York formed a group, the Clean Books Committee of the Federation of Hungarian Jews in America, to accuse him of obscenity, condemning his publication of Joyce's *Ulysses* in particular and harking back to the NYSSV effort that Liveright had helped to defeat.[32] The criticism of Roth rang out loud and clear, as if all the collective discomfort that many modernist writers had been feeling about the rise of Jewish publishers in New York—and the discomfort that some American Jewish literary types and businessmen felt about themselves as parvenus—were being projected onto "The King of the Jews," as the headline of a vituperative attack by the journalist Waverly Root in the journal *transition* characterized Roth.[33] In a letter to Joyce, the British poet Richard Aldington expressed his hope that the protest would succeed in "the confounding and suppression of Mr. Roth" but acknowledged that "the skin of the commercial person is hard, and he does not mind scorn if he can collect money." Aldington's language reflects Roth's transformation, in the eyes of the literary community, from a minor Zionist poet and aspiring literary editor into a "commercial person," a mean-spirited caricature of the stereotypical Jew who, like Shylock, lusts for money above all else.[34]

Sumner and the NYSSV recognized that once a minor, immigrant publisher such as Roth had been disavowed by the literary establishment, he was vulnerable to harassment and arrest as a scurrilous degrader of American culture. By 1928, Roth's offices were being raided on a regular basis by agents of the NYSSV. Probation followed and then arrests. After a raid on October 29, 1929, in which Sumner discovered copies of banned books including both *Lady Chatterley's Lover* and *Ulysses*, Roth was sentenced to serve four months in prison at Welfare Island; that stint was followed by two more months at Moyamensing Prison in Pennsylvania, as punishment for Roth's having sold a single copy of Joyce's *Ulysses* to a Philadelphia resident. If anything, Roth's sojourns in prison only increased his commitment to, and involvement in, the literary black market. By the early 1930s, while Henry Roth was scrawling his first novel in Eda Lou Walton's apartment, Sam Roth was off and running as a full-fledged publisher of banned books, erotica, and sensational political satires. He blamed his fellow Jews for his misfortunes, expressing bitterness and ire toward them in a passionately anti-Semitic screed, and he continued in the mail-order business for decades, enduring bankruptcies and long jail terms.[35] In a statement that echoed a resonant phrase from the Talmudic chapter *Pirke Avot*, the Ethics of the Fathers, Roth explained his commitment to the distribution of obscenity: "There must, under the circumstances, be someone courageous enough to publish such things. If not I, who?"[36] Despite his literary and cultural aspirations, Roth's legacy in American letters is as a criminal: the Supreme Court's decision against him, in 1957, which kept him in Lewisburg Penitentiary for the remainder of his five-year sentence, began the revision of the legal discourse of obscenity that allowed books such as *Lady Chatterley's Lover* and *Tropic of Cancer*, and *Portnoy's Complaint* after them, to be published.

Samuel Roth, like Liveright, had hoped to establish himself as a daring, progressive literary eminence. His failure to do so can be ascribed to any number of factors, but his lack of personal financial resources was certainly one of them. Whatever else his case reveals about the dynamics of American literary culture in the first half of the 20th century, it demonstrates that the transgression of legal and social standards of literary propriety was hardly a lark, especially for an impoverished immigrant without savings or a social or family support network to fall back on. As powerful as an engagement with obscenity could be for establishing a literary reputation and ensuring the legacy of a Liveright, so too were there powerful risks run by a Sam Roth who associated himself with obscene literature: particularly the risks of financial ruin, of prison sentences, and of public vilification.

Modernism and the Value of Perversity: Henry Roth

In the early 1930s, when Henry Roth was drafting his first novel and including taboo words in it, he occupied a social position closer to Sam Roth's than to Liveright's. Like the former, he was an immigrant, having been born in Tysmenitz, Galicia, in 1906. Though he had attended City College and befriended some wealthier New Yorkers, he had no savings to speak of and could not rely on his family to provide him with much in the way of financial or emotional support. He had been living in the Greenwich Village apartment of a New York University professor, Eda Lou Walton, who was romantically involved with one of Roth's childhood friends. Though like Sam Roth he had a group of literary acquaintances, he possessed little in the way of resources or skills to fall back on to support himself if his first effort as a novelist failed or if his patron lost her faith in his talent or her patience for his process. Yet he decided to include precisely the same obscenity in his novel that had rendered Joyce's *Ulysses* a financial disaster, subject to both suppression and piracy.

Obviously, Roth would only take the chance of winding up harassed by the police and the vice squads, jailed, impoverished, and vilified, like Samuel Roth, if he saw the potential of reaping a significant "speaker's benefit" from his engagement with obscenity. Unlike Liveright, though, Roth did not grow up in a middle-class American home well stocked with English and American literature, and he did not have the financial or social resources to fight court battles and wage publicity campaigns in defense of his writing. On the contrary, he was a self-loathing, immature, destitute immigrant. Yet Henry Roth complicates the pattern established by Sam Roth and other Jewish erotica dealers of the 1920s and 1930s, whose marginality jeopardized their publishing projects, because it was precisely in his painful personal situation, as an outsider's outsider, that he recognized potential for an extraordinarily valuable "speaker's benefit" that might accrue to him through his use of taboo language.

Literary historians have demonstrated that the pursuit of literary prestige has been especially appealing to members of disempowered groups—immigrants, the poor, colonial subjects, marginalized minorities—because it offers the possibility of social transformation and self-fashioning. Pascale Casanova singles out Henry Roth as exemplifying this phenomenon.[37] Yet Roth was not attracted to the socially transformative power of literature simply because he was a poor Jewish immigrant; in a passage from his late autobiographical fiction *Mercy of a Rude Stream*—in which Roth's young self is represented, in the third person, as a character named Ira Stigman—Roth makes clear that as a young man, he understood himself as even more desperate for what he calls literary "salvation" than other young Jews who grew up in similar circumstances. "It came back to the same thing," Roth's narrator remarks, "some kind of spasmodic, dumb determination he was going to find a way out of *himself*, out of what he had gotten himself into, cost what it might. Larry [a wealthy Jewish friend and NYU student] didn't have to pay that kind of price. He didn't need to. Neither did most everybody else, [City College] classmates Ira had begun to hobnob with: Aaron, Ivan, Iz, Sol. They didn't need to either. Ira did" (3:65–66). The main subject of Roth's late novels is, precisely, "what he had gotten himself into." The books track Ira's sexual development from the age of eight, when a stranger sexually abuses him in a public park, through his teenage years, when masturbation, which he associates with that early trauma, repulses him. As an alternative to masturbation, Ira discovers incest. He develops a method of mutual masturbation with his younger sister and soon moves on to intercourse with her and, later, with a cousin.

It is Ira's sexual behavior and resulting shame that make him feel he requires literary "salvation" more than any of his friends. Roth presents Ira as full of "shame and self-loathing" (3:15), both because of the abuse he has suffered and because of his incest. After that first experience of sexual abuse, Ira feels that "everything was steeped in something sinister, sinister, . . . ineradicable, an inescapable smut" (1:58). After practicing incest, which he refers to as "skulking, nasty lechery" (2:251), he regards himself as "perverted," as having "lusted for the prohibited" (3:120), as having "sinned" and having "been guilty of abomination" (3:116). His frequent characterization of incest as "sin" and "abomination" reveals that he understands it in the context of Leviticus and, to some degree, his Jewish identity, and the novels register the intensity of Ira's "guilt, guilt, guilt. . . . Guilt, guilt, and more guilt" (3:115).[38] For Ira, his being mired in "inescapable smut" is an intensification of another kind of social disability, "his inescapable East Side Jewishness" (3:157)—as if to say that while wealthy, native-born Jews were socially marginalized in the United States in the 1920s, and poor immigrant Jews even more so, none of them would be quite so contemptible as a Jewish immigrant who was both poor and sexually aberrant.[39] So, if literary prestige is especially attractive to socially marginalized people, Roth's autobiographical writing suggests, no one could be more desperate for literary prestige than his own young self.

For Roth and for Ira, literary modernism offers a "gateway to esteem, to prestige" (3:65–66). *Mercy* provides a vivid portrait of a young Jew's cathexis to high culture as a mechanism for self-transformation and for acquiring cultural capital. The particular attraction of literary modernism for Ira is that its alchemy has been demonstrated to be particularly effective in transforming into valued commodities precisely the elements of his own social marginalization: Jewishness, poverty, and sexual abnormality. One of his first glimpses of this power of literary modernism occurs when his friend Larry, a well-off German Jew (who, when they first meet, Ira imagines must be Protestant), reads him selections from Louis Untermeyer's anthology *Modern American Poetry* (1919) on the street in Manhattan. As Ira listens to a snippet of Vachel Lindsay's "The Congo," he feels "the familiar, the commonplace, become puzzling. . . . It was something like the way Larry transformed from gentile to Jew; only this went the other way" (2:200). Here, Ira listens to a wealthy and cultured Jewish young man (who can pass for a non-Jew) reading to him from a prestigious American literary anthology edited by a respected Jewish poet and, in particular, to an aristocratic non-Jewish poet's transformation of faux-African sounds into art. Through these intermediaries, Ira begins to understand the power of modernist art to defamiliarize its objects ("the commonplace, become puzzling") and, more importantly, to elevate the prestige of both its practitioners and subject matter. Just as the practice of modernism could transform nonsense faux-African sounds into art and ennoble Untermeyer (and, on a more personal level, Larry), Ira imagines that it might transform him, too.[40]

Joyce's *Ulysses* provides Ira with an even more relevant example of how literary modernism can transform sexually shameful experiences into prestige. Noting particularly the sexual and scatological elements of Joyce's novel, and comparing himself to Leopold Bloom, Ira comes to recognize the immanent value of his own distasteful childhood memories:

> If Bloom knew the hour when his wife cuckolded him, what did that compare to Ira's knowing the equatorial hour on Sunday morning when Mom and Pop were gone? And worse, worse than anything Bloom ever suffered: that agonizing afternoon when murder flapped bat wings over his plane geometry text, because Minnie hadn't menstruated. And talk about the nastiness of the diurnal—talk about the absolute vertigo of furore of a chance weekday break, what was looking up a statue's buttocks compared to that . . . or the colossal jape of compassionate Mamie's sentimentally "forcing" a greenback on him, a buck, right after he had hoisted her drippy kid daughter, Stella, on his petard. Hell, of nastiness, of sordidness, perversity, and squalor—compared to anyone in *Ulysses*, he had loads, he had droves, he had troves. But it was language, language, that could magically transmogrify the baseness of his days and ways into precious literature. (3:74)

As Ira understands it, his guilt-inducing sexual practices, "worse than anything Bloom ever suffered," constitute, in a literary context, a valuable resource.[41] Through Ira's introduction to Joyce, his most shameful moments—having sexual encounters with his sister "on Sunday morning"; contemplating her murder, when he fears he has impregnated her; accepting small gifts from his aunt after seducing her daughter—become resources for the creation of "precious literature." Not only can literary success transform him from a poor Jew into a respected American (as it seems, at least from Ira's perspective, to have done for

Untermeyer and for Larry), but it also has the power to make something attractive out of the sexual practices that burden him with guilt, shame, and self-loathing.

The quoted passage even models Joyce's formal influence, in the rhyming wordplay of "loads," "droves," and "troves" as descriptions of Ira's "nastiness," "sordidness," "perversity," and "squalor"—demonstrating *how* literature effects transformations by rendering shameful experiences into artistic forms. While "loads" and "droves" are ambivalent colloquialisms meaning "a large quantity," in neither a positive nor a negative sense, the final term, "troves," is "short for treasure-trove . . . in sense 'a valuable find.'"[42] As Roth proceeds through off-rhyme from word to word, then, Ira's potentially troublesome possessions transform into treasures, demonstrating on the level of diction how "language . . . could magically transmogrify" "baseness" into something "precious." In this passage's aping of the wordplay found in Joyce's work, then, it vivifies Roth's claim that "*Ulysses* demonstrated to [Ira] not only that it was possible to commute the dross of the mundane and the sordid into literary treasure, but *how* it was done. It showed him how to address whole slag heaps of squalor, and make them available for exploitation in art" (3:73).[43]

If Joycean wordplay is one of the crucial modernist techniques Ira discovers through which literature can mitigate his self-loathing by transforming its objects into prestigious and respected art, the mixing of registers typical of Joyce and T. S. Eliot is another. Ira first recognizes this artistic model early in *Mercy*, listening to a modern performance of Romantic music:

> When did [Ira] begin to recognize and enjoy that—that blend of pure and . . . and nasty? Yeah, yeah, instead of the one or maybe the other by itself. Like a dissonance in music maybe that repelled him at first, a perverse dissonance, like Wagner, like *The Meistersinger* when he first heard Mischa Elman play it in Izzy's house, and was so fond of it afterward. . . . But wasn't it something, Jesus, wild, when you joined the two together. (2:291–92)

As in Ira's exposure to Lindsay's "The Congo," this passage offers another richly overdetermined, multilayered occasion of culture as it is experienced in its contexts: Ira encounters Wagner, that paragon of high-art anti-Semitism and specifically an opera debuted in the midst of debates about Jewishness and German art, in which Jewish opera patrons embraced Wagner despite his anti-Semitic pronouncements—in a performance by a celebrated Russian Jewish musical prodigy, played on a phonograph at the house of one of his poor, music-loving Jewish friends.[44] What bears emphasizing is that Ira is thrilled here, as he is with Lindsay and Joyce, by the way that culture travels, by the way it transforms the lived experiences that serve as its subject matter and the people who produce and consume it. Here a musical composition that continues to be branded as anti-Semitic becomes an occasion for Jewish pride in a Jewish musical genius, as well as for an assertion of taste and cultural distinction by immigrants. Not only in the music but also in the dynamics of its circulation is there "perverse dissonance" and a "blend of pure and . . . nasty." Appropriately, Roth associates this quality of literary modernism with one of the signal aesthetic features of modernist texts: juxtaposition, the energetic mixing of registers of speech and literary discourse.

Of course, another signal feature of Anglo-American modernism—if not Eliot's, certainly Joyce's, Hemingway's, Lawrence's, and many others'—was authors' insistence that dirty words "were integral to their literary projects," as the literary scholar Loren Glass has argued.[45] Such authors, influenced by contemporary anthropology and psychoanalytic theory, understood obscenity not just as one more register of language but as a uniquely powerful one. In James Frazer's influential *The Golden Bough*, for example, taboo words are described as coursing with power: like people and objects, words may "be charged or electrified, either temporarily or permanently, with the mysterious virtue of taboo."[46] Sándor Ferenczi, a disciple of Freud, remarked in 1916 on the power of "obscene words" within the analytic setting; such words could, in some cases, overcome an analysand's "resistance." "The hearing of an obscene word in the treatment," Ferenczi wrote, "often results in unexpected disclosures and a gratifying progress in the mental dissection, which had perhaps been for some time at a standstill."[47] Whether in analysis or tribal life or in art, modernists understood dirty words as having the power to effect change, and this was the context in which Roth included dirty words in *Call It Sleep*.

In *Tropic of Cancer*, Henry Miller—Roth's contemporary and, like him, an artist committed to modernist aesthetics and to obscenity—offers perhaps the clearest statement of the aesthetic principles that Roth derived from his reading of modernism. Alluding to Walt Whitman, Miller expounds an artistic credo that serves equally well for Roth. "I love everything that flows," Miller writes,

> even the menstrual flow that carries away the seed unfecund. I love scripts that flow, be they hieratic, esoteric, perverse, polymorph, or unilateral. I love everything that flows, . . . the violence of the prophets, the obscenity that is ecstasy, the wisdom of the fanatic, the priest with his rubber litany, the foul words of the whore, the spittle that floats away in the gutter, the milk of the breast and the bitter honey that pours from the womb, all that is fluid, melting, dissolute and dissolvent, all the pus and dirt that in flowing is purified.[48]

Juxtaposing ancient and modern, sacred and profane—"hieratic" and "perverse" writing, "priest" and "whore"—Miller declares that it is precisely the convergence of these opposites, the recognition of their inseparability, that motivates his literary practice. In this sense, he shares in Eliot's and Joyce's poetics.[49] Moreover, in a gesture that exhibits continuities between his work and Roth's, Miller asserts that "in flowing," in this enthusiastic mixture of what Roth calls "pure" and "nasty," "pus and dirt [are] purified." Roth, like Miller and others, understood modernism as raising obscenity to the level of art.

Dirty Words in *Call It Sleep*

One might reasonably be suspicious that Roth's statements, in the 1990s, accurately reflect the thinking that drove his composition of *Call It Sleep* half a century earlier. Still, it is not implausible to read the novel as a brilliant rendering of the attractions of obscene modernism as an aesthetic technology for transforming Jewishness, poverty, and sexual shame into cultural prestige. In other words, we can understand the "speaker's benefit" that Roth sought to achieve through his use of taboo words in *Call It Sleep* as not only the opportunity to establish himself as a literary eminence the way that Liveright did but also, by transforming the sordidness of his childhood into the building blocks of literary art, the chance of assuaging his sexual guilt and reducing his self-loathing.

The novel dramatizes the risk and reward of obscenity in the modernist period in its scrupulous attention to the deployment of taboo words in David Schearl's consciousness. Given Roth's understanding of himself as marginalized because of his Jewishness, poverty, and sexual guilt, as explained earlier, it makes sense that the novel associates these qualities with taboo language. For example, the novel carefully tracks David's exposure to the word *shit*, which he learns from fellow immigrants, poor people, and Jews. He first hears it spoken in English by a neighboring kid and then by an adult carriage driver. He hears his aunt speak an equivalent word in Yiddish (which the novel represents, always, in English): the narrator reports her saying, "How long is it since you shit on the ocean?"; in Yiddish, she would have used the word קאַקן/*kakn*, in its past participle, געקאַקט/*gekakt*.[50] Not wanting readers to miss this bilingual point, Roth's narrator explains that "'kockin,' as David learned long ago, was a Yiddish word meaning to sit on the toilet" (160). This prepares the reader for a later moment when David is in *kheyder* (a traditional Jewish classroom for young children). One of his classmates speaks the word "shid" (229) just a moment after their teacher translates a line from Isaiah 6:1 (וָאֶרְאֶה אֶת אֲדֹנָי יֹשֵׁב עַל כִּסֵּא רָם וְנִשָּׂא) as "Isaiah saw God. And God was sitting on his throne, high in heaven" (226–27). As David ponders this image, his knowledge of the words *kockin* and *shit* lead his thoughts directly to blasphemous obscenity: "[God] was sitting on a chair," David thinks. "So he's got chairs, so he can sit. Gee! Sit Shit! Sh!" (230).

Consider these two words, "Sit Shit!" For one thing, they reveal that David's internal monologue, at least at this moment in the novel, occurs in English (contrary to Hana Wirth-Nesher's remark that David's thoughts "are experienced in Yiddish").[51] The transformation of "sit" to "shit" through their near homophony relies on the English words: the Yiddish equivalents, *zitsn/zetsn* (to sit) and *kakn* (to shit), lack any aural connection. More importantly, this specific slip is especially likely to have occurred to an Ashkenazic Jewish immigrant such as David. As Roth's biographer Steven Kellman explains (without noting the relevance of this history to this particular passage in *Call It Sleep*), the "post-alveolar pronunciation of 's'—almost as if it were 'sh'—was a shibboleth that stigmatized and handicapped Ashkenazic Jews" of Roth's generation, and "Roth's own sister, Rose, would be denied employment in the New York City public schools for this reason."[52] The intrusion of the taboo word into David's thoughts in this scene depends simultaneously on David's on-the-spot rendering of the teacher's Yiddish translation of Biblical Hebrew into his own English stream-of-consciousness and on the specific challenges of Americanizing Ashkenazic Jewish speech, which rendered the words *sit* and *shit* aurally indistinguishable for some speakers.

Obscene language is not only associated with Jewishness in *Call It Sleep*, but it is also a source of deep sexual shame. One of the novel's first reviewers, writing in the *New York Times* in February 1935, noted this, remarking that "though [David] learns to speak filth, it is always with a sense of sin, and this becomes in time an obsession."[53] The novel offers a clear sense of this the first time David himself thinks the word *shit*, while he is observing some birds in a park: "Funny, birds were. In the park on Avenue C. Eat brown. Shit green. On the benches is green. On the railings. So how? Don't you? Apples is red and white. Chicken is white. Bread, watermelon, gum-drops, all different colors. But—Don't say. Is bad. But everybody says. Is bad though" (174). In this brief dramatization of how unnatural language taboos can be, observation of nature leads David to contemplate biology, at which point he encounters the bizarre impermissibility of describing defecation. Birds eat brown-colored food, and their feces are green, he notices, while he, by contrast, eats multicolored foods, and his excrement turns out brown. This is a simple enough observation of nature, but by this point, David has internalized the language taboos that operate in the culture enough that he stops himself from articulating this simple observation, cutting himself off with the words "Don't say. Is bad." Unfamiliar with the acceptably Latinate synonyms that could be substituted as euphemisms for *shit* (such as the ones used earlier), David recognizes that "everybody says" *shit* (and *kakn*, too)—whether his aunt, his neighborhood, or non-Jewish adults on the street—but he still recognizes his responsibility not to utter, or even to cognitively countenance, what he refers to a few moments later as "bad words" (174). One critic, noticing moments such as these, has pointed out that for David, "excretion and sex are so evil that even thinking words that describe them is sinful," yet it is crucial to recall that David's feeling about these taboo words is not some sort of personal eccentricity.[54] Rather, he submits to a taboo imposed by his society on him and equally on Roth by American law. Even if David—or Jake Barnes or Lily Bart or any of the characters of early 20th-century American fiction—felt comfortable speaking or thinking the word *shit*, it would have meant taking a serious risk if the authors of the novels in which these characters appeared had represented that comfort.

For David, the uncontrollable nature of language—a universal feature of language especially obvious to immigrants—links it to sexual inappropriateness and shame. In an oft-quoted scene in which David learns a couple of slang terms for genitalia ("knish" and "petzel"), the boy discovers that his words have a mysterious power after he parrots his neighbor, Annie, thinking he is playing a game:

> "Yuh wanna?" [she says.]
> "Yea!" [he answers.]
> "Yuh wanna den?"
> "Yea, I wanna."

Annie leads David into a closet, and the conversation continues. She tells him,

> "Yuh must say, Yuh wanna play bad? Say it!"
> He trembled. "Yuh wanna play bad?"
> "Now, *you* said it," she whispered. "Don' forget, you said it."
> By the emphasis of her words, David knew he had crossed some awful threshold. (53)

Annie then informs David that anything that they do ("put yuh han' in my knish," she commands a moment later) has been summoned by David's speech act. Through this exchange, David discovers that even the most innocuous words can contain sexual meanings he does not want them to possess. Later, musing guiltily about his encounter with Annie, David thinks, "Everything shifted. Everything changed. Even words. Words, you said. Wanna, you said. I wanna. Yea. I wanna. What? You know what. They were something else, something horrible!" (102).

Simple words, "I wanna," can, David realizes, lead to "horrible" and frightening circumstances, if one is not careful with them. The closet scene is a masterful dramatization of a child's realization that language, in and of itself, tends to transgression if not carefully regulated—an insight, again, not incidentally related to the period in which Roth wrote, during which a lapse in authorial self-censorship could and did in some cases lead to prosecution, harassment, loss of copyright, and jail. As it did, repeatedly, for Samuel Roth.

The depth of David's shamefulness about taboo words arises in response to his *kheyder* instructor's gloss on Isaiah. Isaiah 6:5 reads as follows in the original and in the King James Version:

וָאֹמַר אוֹי לִי כִי נִדְמֵיתִי כִּי אִישׁ טְמֵא שְׂפָתַיִם אָנֹכִי וּבְתוֹךְ עַם טְמֵא שְׂפָתַיִם
אָנֹכִי יוֹשֵׁב כִּי אֶת הַמֶּלֶךְ יְהוָה צְבָאוֹת רָאוּ עֵינָי

> Then said I: Woe is me! for I am undone; because I am a man of unclean lips, and I dwell in the midst of a people of unclean lips; for mine eyes have seen the King, the Lord of hosts.

David's teacher, Reb Pankower, translates the passage with a few subtle changes: "Woe me! he cried, What shall I do! I am lost! . . . I, common man, have seen the Almighty, I, unclean one have seen him! Behold, my lips are unclean and I live in a land unclean" (227). Pankower's translation emphasizes Isaiah's description of himself as "unclean": while the Tanakh only has Isaiah call himself "a man of unclean lips," Pankower's version asserts that "unclean lips" metonymically represent Isaiah's entire person: the prophet, in Pankower's version, refers to himself as "I, unclean one." The difference between a tainted mouth and a whole tainted person surely matters, especially to a sensitive child such as David. In fact, David does not immediately accompany Pankower on the metonymic slide that equates "lips" with "I." At first, he focuses on the precise wording of the original text, wondering, "Why wasn't [Isaiah's mouth] clean, anyway?" David quickly answers his own question in the most literal, childish way: "He didn't wash it, I bet" (230).

Within a few paragraphs, though, which represent a few seconds of his stream-of-consciousness, David has moved on from that simple notion to the realization that Isaiah's problem was more than physical dirt. "He said dirty words, I bet," David realizes, and then he thinks of the dirty words he knows: "Shit, pee, fuckenbestit—Stop! You're sayin' it yourself. It's a sin again! That's why he—Gee! I didn't mean it" (231). In analyzing what he imagines to be Isaiah's grievous sin, David reproduces the proscribed behavior, transforming himself into one of the prophet's "people of unclean lips." As the passage continues, David conjectures that obscenity constitutes a special category of speech that defiles the person who uses it. "But your mouth don't get dirty," he muses. "I don't feel no dirt. (He rolled his tongue about) Maybe inside. Way, way in, where you can't taste it" (231). Bewildered by the abstraction of obscenity, the fact that saying the word "shit" or "fuckenbestit" does not produce physical harm, David, like generations of antismut crusaders, assumes that obscenity must then have the power to defile him in some vague but fundamental way, very much as Ira Stigman imagines his practice of incest to pervert and ruin him at his core. As Morris Dickstein has observed, "the self-loathing that bedeviled the young man in *Mercy*, especially his feelings of sexual guilt, carried over into his writing of *Call It Sleep*, where it was projected back onto his precocious childhood."[55] One major means of that projection is Roth's engagement with taboo words. In representing David's shame about "dirty words," Roth created a textual symbol for his self-loathing about his sexuality.

The project of the novel is to transform that shameful taboo language into the stuff of art, which it does through an embrace of modernist aesthetics. As the novel continues, David encounters more and more obscene speech as his shame and fear mounts until he reaches the point at which he can no longer stem the tide of obscene speech within himself. His crisis arrives when taboo language overtakes him: "A strange chaotic sensation was taking hold of him—a tumultuous, giddy freedom, a cruel caprice that made him want to caper, to skip, to claw at his hands, to pinch himself until he screamed. . . . 'Fugimbestit! Fugimbestit!' The pressure of his frenzy, too great to be contained seethed from his lips" (370–71). This tirade represents the failure of David's self-censorship; whereas he had succeeded, earlier, in stopping himself from saying "fuck," here he repeatedly unleashes the taboo phrase "fugimbestit!" That term resonates, of course, with David's imagined genealogy and guilt. Pankower refers to David as a "bastard" (presumably, he speaks the Hebrew and Yiddish *mamzer*, which Roth renders into its English equivalent in the text) just a few pages earlier (369). Fascinatingly, Roth's description of David's linguistic breakdown here evokes three parallel discourses: the disdainful language of the antiobscenity crusaders, who would not be surprised to hear of a child falling into a "frenzy" because of exposure to obscenity; the text of Isaiah, and its concern with unclean "lips"; and modernist literary cacophony, which promises both "strange chaotic sensation" and "tumultuous, giddy freedom."

David's fit continues, embracing the Joycean linguistic play that David self-censored, earlier, when he cut off the aural association of "Sit Shit" with the repressive "Sh." Now, David gleefully switches the vowel of "Fox" to form "fix" and then "fux" (that is: *fucks*). Similarly, he rhymes "Hee," the sound of his laughter, first with the Hebrew "V y'hee" (and will be), then with the innocuous "wee," and finally with "pee," one of those "dirty words" David conjectured Isaiah must have said along with "shit" and "fuckenbestit" to make his lips unclean. He imagines that he will expose his penis ("Take id oud! See! Look!") to "all de goils" and rejects his own silencing "Sh!" with a more aggressive rejoinder, "Shattop! Wot I care" (371). He then turns attention to non-Jews, whom he describes as "Goy sonn'vabitch!" (371) and of whose "goy-beads" (rosaries) he says "no good shitten them!" (378).[56] David's exuberant utterances of taboo words signal that the novel approaches its programmatically modernist climax, in which Roth presents a wide range of taboo words, equaling *Ulysses* and even *Tropic of Cancer* in their variety and vehemence and exceeding by far, in this regard, any other uncensored and unbowdlerized American novel until that time.[57]

In the novel's climactic chapter 21, as many critics have noted, *Call It Sleep* juxtaposes images and language sacred and profane, evoking Biblical prophecy but resonating even more forcefully with literary modernism and particularly with Miller's call for writing that is at once "hieratic, esoteric, perverse, polymorph, [and] unilateral." The crowd's taboo exclamations include "cunt" (410), "gash" (412), "fuck" (414), "fuckin'" (414), "balls" (412), "ass" (411), "pecker" (412), "putz" (413), "prick" (415), "shit" (411), and "jerkin' off" (418), as well as the culmination of the novel's treatment of the word *shit*, in an evocative and exuberant phrase, as "shit-hemorrage [*sic*]" (416). This taboo language appears in and around discussions of graphic sexuality and blasphemy, such as Mary the prostitute's anecdote about finding a used condom on a plate when she was a young waitress (411), and O'Toole's profanity, "Shit on de pope" (413). Self-consciously modeled on both Joyce and Eliot—the page layout suggests that Roth composed the section as an intersecting combination of blank verse and prose—this set piece incorporates taboo words as a crucial element in its modernist poetics, also including elaborate Joycean wordplay and a furious mixing of registers.

All this linguistic effusion results, appropriately, in a kind of purification for David, reported in oblique and lyrical language. After his electrocution, the boy experiences a version of Isaiah's initiation in which a coal ("one ember") is extended to him ("Nothingness beati- / fied reached out its hands" [430]). Afterward, not another taboo word appears in David's thoughts. This purification mirrors, or stands for, the purification that the author hoped to achieve for himself.[58] The promise Roth saw in modernism was that after having written and published a book like *Call It Sleep*, no longer would he be the type of poor Jew who "speak[s] like a Jew," in Miller's phrase. Having channeled his sexual guilt into David Schearl, and transformed it, in the process, into modernist literature, he would no longer suffer for it. Critics have debated whether the novel's ending implies a redemption or failure for David, whether his return to his parents' home represents newfound comfort in his environment or acceptance of his disillusionment, but such arguments miss the point.[59] A reading of the novel after *Mercy* and attending to its engagement with obscenity and modernism clarifies that the muted ambiguity of the novel's close is intrinsic to Roth's project, both because such ambiguity is a self-consciously modernist gesture and thus an end in itself and, more importantly, because David's redemption is not the primary project of *Call It Sleep*. The point of the book, as Kellman and Dickstein agree, was the redemption of Henry Roth. And among the means of effectuating that redemption was Roth's denuding taboo words—and the transgressive sexual acts, excretory functions, and genitalia that they signify—of their fearsome linguistic power, precisely by incorporating them into a modernist novel. If the novel's end tells us nothing else, it indicates what Henry Roth hoped modernism could accomplish.

Obscenity and the Reception of *Call It Sleep*

Roth did not turn out to be correct about modernism and what it would achieve for him. Writing *Call It Sleep* did not transform him into a literary celebrity (at least not for thirty years after the novel's publication), and it is unclear whether it did much to assuage his sexual guilt. Many critics have wondered why the novel did not reach a large audience until 1964 and why Roth did not publish another novel until 1994.[60] The book's engagement with obscenity suggests a partial explanation: when *Call It Sleep* appeared on February 15, 1935, it was an ironically inauspicious moment for that specific book, given its particular project and techniques. The *Ulysses* decision remained fresh in everyone's memories. Only six months earlier, on August 7, 1934, Woolsey's celebrated 1933 decision had been affirmed by the Second Circuit Court of Appeals, in an eloquent decision by Judge Augustus Hand.[61] Hand noted that *Ulysses* "has such portentous length, is written with such evident truthfulness in its depiction of certain types of humanity, and is so little erotic in its result, that it does not fall within the forbidden class"[62]—and he could have been describing Roth's novel with those exact words. Indeed, *Call It Sleep*'s first reviewers, as if writing directly in response to Woolsey's and Hand's decisions, frequently remarked on the book's use of taboo words but also on its length, its truthfulness, and its emetic, rather than erotic, effects. Some reviewers explicitly compared Roth's novel to *Ulysses*, too, emphasizing that *Call It Sleep* could only be understood in relation to, perhaps even as an imitation of, Joyce's celebrated and legally vindicated modernist novel.[63]

Writing in the *New York Times* in February 1935, H. W. Boynton dealt with the novel's obscenity directly, noting that Roth's readers "are spared nothing of what [David] hears and sees. In this and other connections the book lays all possible stress on the nastiness of the human animal. It is the fashion, and we must make the best of the spectacle of a fine book deliberately and as it were doggedly smeared with verbal filthiness."[64] Boynton's concession to "fashion" here—the fashion represented by the recently affirmed *Ulysses* decision, no doubt—suggests how difficult it would have been for the NYSSV or other book censors to mount a case against Roth's "verbal filthiness" in 1935. As Boynton wrote, "you find yourself conceding, against all qualms, the rightness as well as the (you would have said) unspeakable grossness of [the book's] human ingredients."[65]

Maxwell Perkins, the famed editor at Scribner who a few years earlier had infamously blanched at Hemingway's taboo language and bowdlerized *The Sun Also Rises* and *A Farewell to Arms*,[66] noted in a letter on July 29, 1935, with regard to publishing Henry Roth, "[It] would make no end of trouble for me on account of his contempt for conventional restraint—much worse than any one we have published." "Still," Perkins continued, "I wrote encouragingly and sent for [his next] book. We are publishers after all."[67] In one breath, Perkins affirms that *Call It Sleep* is "worse" in terms of its "contempt for conventional restraint" than Hemingway or any other writer he had edited, and he shrugs his famously prudish shoulders. The atmosphere of tolerance in which even Perkins could accept Roth's use of obscenity is the same one that prevented the NYSSV from mounting a campaign against the novel. Revealingly, the president of the NYSSV admitted in a 1935 report, "we cannot, in this age, when former notions of propriety and decency have so radically changed, attempt to take restraining steps which might not meet with broader views now taken by our courts. . . . Times have changed and we must change with them."[68]

Counterintuitively, this turns out to have been an unfortunate situation for Roth's book and for his career, as it left them both in a literary-historical limbo: not lionized like Liveright and *Ulysses*, if also not vilified like Sam Roth. An attack by the NYSSV could have spurred a community of authors, publishers, and critics to join together in defense of Roth's work, valorizing and publicizing it in the process, as had happened to *Ulysses*, Radclyffe Hall's *The Well of Loneliness*, and other novels. This would have constituted the speaker's benefit in action, but for Roth it did not happen. Publishers could not be certain that they would *not* be prosecuted for distributing a book like *Call It Sleep* in the 1940s and early 1950s, and apparently they could not afford the risk, even though many well-regarded critics praised the novel in print throughout those decades.[69] The decades-long uncertainty about the legal status of Lawrence's *Lady Chatterley's Lover* and the Supreme Court's upholding of a ban on Edmund Wilson's *Memoirs of Hecate County* in 1948 reminded American publishers that anything other than *Ulysses* itself could not be guaranteed legal freedom.[70]

The tenuous position occupied by *Call It Sleep* in the 1940s and 1950s is highlighted by a moment of testimony from one of the American trials of *Lady Chatterley's Lover* in 1959. The critic Alfred Kazin was on the stand, testifying in defense of Lawrence's novel. A defense attorney asked him whether there was any taboo language in Lawrence's book that he had "not seen in reputable and publicly accepted novels of the last several decades." Kazin answered, cryptically, "I know of a book which has not been banned and in which each one of these words occur." While it is possible Kazin was referring to some other book, it seems plausible that the book he had in mind was *Call It Sleep*—which he had praised enthusiastically a few years earlier in a symposium—but that he deliberately avoided mentioning its title so as to shield it from the attention of would-be censors.[71] It does not seem to be entirely a coincidence that only after *Lady Chatterley's Lover* and *Tropic of Cancer* had been vindicated by the courts, making clear to American publishers that no longer would books be suppressed because of these taboo words, was *Call It Sleep* republished as an inexpensive paperback, in which format it sold nearly a million copies. It did so not under the banner of daring obscene modernism triumphant over prudish Victorianism, though—which is how Joyce, Lawrence, and Miller are remembered—but rather as part of a postwar white-ethnic revival.[72] Thanks to unlucky timing and the contingency of the history of literary obscenity in the United States, the book was never officially suppressed, and so while Roth was never threatened with jail, neither did he receive the speaker's benefit that was due to him.

The Rewards of Graphic Sexuality in the 1970s: Will Eisner and Jules Feiffer

If the careers of Liveright and Samuel Roth suggest how necessary financial and social resources were for those who attempted to use obscenity to catapult themselves from social marginality into literary respectability, the history of *Call It Sleep* demonstrates how dynamic obscenity has been: taboo words that in the 1920s and 1930s could earn one a role among the cultural avant-garde had become safe and acceptable, even de rigueur, by the late 1960s. According to one count, seven of the ten best-selling U.S. novels of 1969 included the word *fuck*.[73]

Obscenity could, of course, still do cultural work in the 1970s and 1980s—indeed, we will see that it turned out still to be useful for Jews who hoped to accrue cultural prestige with their art—though most of the variables (obscenity, art, prestige) had by then been shifted places in the field of literary production. What had formerly been criminally obscene, for one thing, was now legal, and Jewishness, for another, was no longer marginal in American literary and popular culture. The graphic representations of sexuality by the Jewish pioneers of the so-called graphic novel (that is, literary comic book) in the late 1970s and early 1980s reflects these transformations.[74]

What remained marginalized in the 1970s was the comic book as a literary medium. Even though comics had been in more or less continuous, popular use since the rise of newspaper comic strips in the 1890s, they received precious little respect from institutions of cultural prestige.[75] How could this persistently disreputable form begin to attract the sort of critical attention and prestige typically reserved for literature? As this story is usually told, a handful of innovative comic books—Frank Miller's *The Dark Knight Returns*, Alan Moore's *Watchmen*, and Art Spiegelman's *Maus*—proved to critics and audiences in the mid-1980s that comic books could be every bit as skillful, as historically engaged, and as self-reflexive as the prose fiction that had by then already been widely canonized as American literary postmodernism.[76] Yet historical engagement and self-reflexivity were not the only, and perhaps not the key, factors in endowing comics with this new prestige.

The major impediment to the *littérisation*[77] of comic books, after all, had not been any sense that their creators were unskilled or simplistic but rather the very old idea that the form itself—in fact, any story told primarily as a combination of printed words and illustrations—was ideally suited to children, immature adolescents, and childlike, illiterate adults.[78] While copious evidence has always existed to counter this idea, the prejudice remained ubiquitous in the comics industry into the postwar period.[79] Will Eisner captures the spirit of the Golden and Silver Ages of comics in his remark that "between 1940 and the early sixties the industry commonly accepted the profile of the comic book reader as that of a '10-year-old from Iowa.'"[80] To transform the lowly comic book into the respected graphic novel, its creators needed to demonstrate that the proper reader for their work was not a semiliterate child but an intelligent adult. As Lawrence Levine's classic work on cultural hierarchy *Highbrow/Lowbrow* explains, "shared culture"—art that is "the property of many groups, the companion to a wide spectrum of other cultural genres"—is, precisely because of its accessibility, less powerful to "bestow distinction" on its audiences. Shakespeare and opera were so popular in 19th-century America, he explains, that they had to be "'rescued' from the marketplace" so as to become high culture.[81] In those examples, the audiences that needed to be excluded were immigrants and the poor; for comic books, the readers that needed excluding were children and immature adults.

In this sense, books such as *Maus* and *The Dark Knight Returns*, genuinely important and influential as they were, cannot be properly understood as the key texts in the rise of the graphic novel as a prestigious form. The intricacy and brilliance of their technical and narrative achievements did not limit their audiences to adult readers any more than Winsor McCay's or George Herriman's had half a century earlier. Children's librarians regularly recommend *Maus* and *The Dark Knight Returns* to other librarians and K–12 teachers; one professional educator, writing in *School Library Journal*, warns her colleagues that "there are several critically acclaimed graphic novels essential for building a core adult collection but inappropriate for your library's children or young adult section," and she then goes on to recommend Spiegelman's and Miller's books for young audiences, reporting with regard to Miller's, "I've never met a reader who didn't love this book, especially preteen and teenage boys."[82] *Maus* is often assigned in American public schools as required reading for children as young as eleven.[83]

Two graphic novels that appeared earlier did effectively exclude children and adolescents from their audiences.[84] These are among the works that, in the words of that school librarian, are "essential" for "adult" readers but "inappropriate for [a] library's children or young adult section": inappropriate because they were "graphic" in the sense, available to English speakers at least since 1856, of "explicit, esp. in the depiction of sex or violence." (Etymology is, in this instance, by no means a clear indicator of the word's meaning: even though *graphic* takes on this connotation along with the rise of the term *pornographic*, that term derives its suffix from the Greek *graphos*, that is, "writing," as in "writing about prostitutes," and this sense of graphic as "writing" has little to do with either of the particular senses of *graphic*—illustrated and explicit—that are relevant to the graphic novel.)[85] These books, by Will Eisner and Jules Feiffer, established an adult audience for comics and thus advanced the literary legitimacy of the graphic novel through graphic displays of sexuality.

This was an insightful response to the persistent association of comics with children, given the legal and social discourse about children and obscenity that developed in the United States in the 1970s. After broad latitude in the graphic representation of sexuality in fiction had been legalized by American courts in *Memoirs v. Massachusetts* (1966), ensuing judicial decisions insisted on a distinction between what can be shown to adult audiences and what can be shown to children.[86] As Justice Brennan wrote in *Ginsberg v. New York* (1968), even if some materials are "not obscene for adults, . . . the State has power to adjust the definition of obscenity as applied to minors."[87] This idea met widespread approval. In a 1978 editorial, the *Los Angeles Times* argued against enforcing obscenity laws in general but proclaimed that "common sense dictates that children should be protected from obscenity."[88] The Supreme Court ratified such "common sense" repeatedly in cases such as *FCC v. Pacifica* (1978) and *Pinkus v. United States* (1978), hammering home a message with which the majority of Americans seem to have agreed: there should be a differential standard of obscenity that protects children from graphic representations of sexuality that are legal for adults.[89] This helps to explain why Maurice Sendak's picture book *In the Night Kitchen* (1970) stirred up controversy as late as 1972 with its simple representation of a boy's penis.[90] As Perry Nodelman has noted, the question at issue in debates about Sendak's book was "whether penises should be on view at all in children's books, not the question about whether [Sendak's] particular depiction was meant to be sexually enticing."[91] If its images *had* been construed as "sexually enticing," there is no question, under *Ginsberg* and later decisions, that U.S. law would have deemed them unfit for children.

Creating comics in this context, Eisner and Feiffer displayed genitalia in unmistakably sexual contexts within their works, making clear that their books could not possibly be intended for children or young adults.[92] At the same time, these authors eschewed the pornotopic aesthetics of previous sexually explicit comic books, whether the ubiquitous

Tijuana Bibles or the underground comix that flourished in the 1960s, both of which genres frequently and characteristically included images of exaggerated, erect, ejaculating phalluses.[93] Instead, they presented standard tropes of graphic sexual realism: highly detailed representations of sexual failure, disappointment, and disillusionment.[94]

In Eisner's story "Cookalein," in *A Contract with God* (1978), for example, sexual escapades turn out to be, without exception, disillusioning experiences. A fifteen-year-old claiming to be nineteen is seduced by a married woman, but their coupling ends, miserably, in the boy's premature ejaculation and the appearance of the woman's husband. Meanwhile, a young couple court while pretending to be a wealthy entrepreneur and an heiress; it is when they are sexually intimate that they discover that neither of them is really rich, which leads the young man to attempt to rape the woman. Even that is a failure (we later learn he "didn't even penetrate").[95] Eisner's story "The Super" concerns a man who papers his walls with pornographic posters and pin-up calendars and succumbs to temptation when a ten-year-old girl offers him a glance at her genitals for a nickel. After briefly lifting her dress, the girl poisons the man's dog, steals his money, and exposes him as a pervert; rather than face arrest as a child molester, the super shoots himself. That story, then, far from evincing commitment to the presentations of sexually explicit images, seems to be a morality tale about how a pornography addiction can lead a man to pedophilia and then suicide. The narrative's concern about the danger of sexual spectacle is also mirrored in Eisner's management of sexual display: in *Contract*, he includes explicit renderings of a woman's pudendum and pubic hair and of naked, sexually engaged male and female bodies, but in several places he avoids explicit representation of sex. In "The Super," specifically, the key moment—the super's glance at the ten-year-old's genitals—is presented through a cropping of the frame and a quick shift of perspective that allow Eisner to represent the super's desire to look while keeping the object of his gaze invisible to the reader.[96] The text thus implies that an explicit illustration of a young woman's genitalia might pose a risk to the reader just as it does to the fictional super.

Feiffer's graphic novel *Tantrum* (1979) similarly presents nudity only at narrative moments of sexual frustration. Early on, Feiffer depicts the protagonist's wife naked in their bed, her nipple and the cleavage of her buttocks clearly delineated as she reaches out to her husband, who is cowering, turned away from her, eyes wild and unfocused. The illustration does not function as titillation—indeed, the woman's bare breast eerily echoes, in size and shape, her unmet eye—but rather signals the protagonist's isolation and inability to derive sexual satisfaction from his marriage.[97] The narrative climax of *Tantrum* is an even more dramatic scene of sexual failure: the protagonist, who at the outset of the story has magically transformed into an infant while maintaining his adult mind and desires, has insinuated himself with an exaggeratedly buxom secretary and joins her for a bath. She proceeds to wash his "face," "arms," and "chest," but as her hands descend lower on his body, her dialogue breaks off ("then we wash—"). At this moment, the narrative premise collapses, denying the character the sexual satisfaction he has longed for: he reverts to adult form and dashes naked away from the bathtub. As he does, his limp penis and his testicles dangle prominently at the center of a page.[98] As in Eisner's *Contract*, sexual explicitness here proffers an emphatic icon of sexual failure.

In *Highbow/Lowbrow*, Levine explains that "exoteric or popular art is transformed into esoteric or high art precisely at that time when it in fact *becomes* esoteric, that is, when it becomes or is rendered inaccessible to the types of people who appreciated it earlier."[99] By including these images, Eisner and Feiffer render these comics at least in principle inaccessible to children and, thus, as appropriate only for adult audiences. Their goal was unambiguously to transform comics into "high art." Eisner said that he seized on the words "graphic novel" in the hopes they would assist him "to develop . . . viable literature in this medium."[100] From the 1940s until his death, he consistently selected the words "novel" and "literature" to describe what he hoped to achieve in comics.[101] Feiffer's notes for a 1979 speech clarify this further: "All my life victim / Conflicting ambitions / 1. 2 b cartoonist / other, 2 b writer. / Cartooning was fun / Writing was prestigious. . . . I had the ambitions of a cartoonist & class pretensions of s.w. [a serious writer]. . . . 4 20 yrs or more I suspected I knew the answer 2 this dilemma Write a cartoon novel"—or, as he called it in a contemporaneous lecture, a "graphic novel."[102]

If an engagement with obscenity was one key technique through which lowbrow comic books were transformed into literary graphic novels in the late 1970s and early 1980s, is it meaningful that two Jews, Eisner and Feiffer, seized on this approach? The short answer is that it has nothing to do with any essential Jewish relationship with obscenity or visual representation and everything to do with the position of Jews in the U.S. culture industries. By the mid-1970s, Jewishness was just about coterminous with cultural and literary prestige in the United States. American Jewish writers won the top prize in the prestigious O. Henry Awards six times in the 1970s, as well as Nobel prizes in literature in 1976 and 1978. Key editors at many of the most venerated publishing firms were Jewish; the houses started by Jews in the interwar years had expanded, and Random House, in particular, had grown by 1975 into an industry-dominating company with revenues of almost $100 million annually.[103] Many influential participants in the system of literary production, from the book reviewers to the buyers and agents, were also Jewish. The proportion of Jews on the faculties of English literature departments did not rise as rapidly as it did on law faculties and in history departments, but Jews still accounted for 13% of English professors "in the better universities" by the mid-1970s.[104]

So when Feiffer kidded about sharing the pretensions of a serious writer, he knew whereof he spoke. He was friendly with Philip Roth, Bernard Malamud, and a number of the other Jewish authors who had been hailed throughout the 1970s as the leading American literary practitioners and who had received exactly the sort of adulation that Feiffer yearned for but never quite received. Eisner's comparison of his own output to that of the postwar American Jewish literati was, meanwhile, straightforward. "I've read *The Adventures of Augie March*," he once remarked. "I want to tell you that Bellow is doing nothing more than what I'm doing. . . . He got a Nobel Prize from that. I've been selling the same pretzel on the same street corner."[105] Any writer or artist, in any field, might have envied Bellow's massive international fame, but it is hardly surprising that an artist from a background as similar to Bellow's as Eisner was would have wanted a piece of the action.

Eisner and Feiffer had established themselves as comics creators in the 1940s, when doing so was a way to earn money for talented kids without tuition money for art school or college[106] and when Jewishness was—as Henry Roth knew well—something of a disadvantage in many areas of the U.S. culture industries. Eisner and Feiffer pioneered the graphic novel four decades later, when Jewishness was not only no longer an obstacle to accruing cultural prestige but a significant aid in obtaining it. As Pierre Bourdieu notes, "The propensity to move towards the economically most risky positions, and above all the capacity to persist in them (a condition for all avant-garde undertakings which precede the demands of the market), even when they secure no short-term economic profit, seem to depend to a large extent on possession of substantial economic and social capital."[107] Not only were Eisner and Feiffer both financially secure when they embarked on these projects, but they also possessed the cultural capital conferred on them by decades of work, as well as the advantages, in terms of what Richard Brodhead has called "literary access," conferred on them by their personal and professional connections with the American literary establishment.[108]

There was not any inevitability with which Jews supported their work; Eisner's *Contract with God* could just as easily be rejected by Oscar Dystel, the chairman and CEO of Bantam Books, as Feiffer's could be immediately accepted by his old friend Robert Gottlieb, who was then editor in chief and publisher of Knopf.[109] But the fact that Eisner could arrange a meeting with Dystel—who, as it happens, was born in the Bronx, a child of immigrant parents who met in a garment factory—distinguished him from the young underground comix artists of the 1960s who did not typically share such life experiences with leading publishing executives.[110] The publisher who did finally market *Contract*, Norman Goldfine, was an old friend of Eisner's who worked with him on commercial publishing projects and who identified with Eisner's stories of Jewish family life in the Bronx.[111] Upon the publication of *Contract* and *Tantrum*, they were unhesitatingly received as contributions to the field of American Jewish literature and immediately compared, deservedly or not, to works of such Jewish writers as Bernard Malamud, Philip Roth, Isaac Bashevis Singer, Franz Kafka, and Woody Allen.[112]

The value of Eisner's and Feiffer's accumulated cultural capital can be highlighted through a comparison to the early career of Harvey Pekar. Jewish like them, he also aspired to produce comics for serious adult readers (in 1979, he expressed in print his hope of going beyond "the guys who do that animal comic an' super-hero stuff" as well as the "underground comics": "You c'n do as much with comics," he wrote, "as the novel or movies or plays or anything").[113] But Pekar, who was a decade younger than Feiffer and twenty years younger than Eisner, could not himself draw and had had relatively little experience in any creative field. He lived far from the seats of literary and cultural power, in Cleveland, and he had few connections to American literary institutions, unless one counts his friendship with the celebrated underground comix artist R. Crumb. So despite having begun to self-publish gritty, realistic comics stories in the mid-1970s, it took a decade of commitment to a virtually nonexistent readership before Pekar finally achieved what Eisner and Feiffer had done half a decade earlier with considerably less struggle. In the mid-1980s, that is, he gathered a selection of his comics stories into a trade book that was taken seriously as literature.[114] Notably, while some of Pekar's earliest stories had contained almost Tijuana Bible–like graphic sexual images that were consistent with the aesthetics of the underground comix, his first book, published as a Doubleday paperback, excluded those particular stories in favor of less sexually explicit ones about art and politics.

That book of Pekar's stories appeared in 1986, the same year that Spiegelman's *Maus* was transformed from an insert in an avant-garde comix magazine to a widely accessible book and while Frank Miller's *The Dark Knight Returns* and Alan Moore's *Watchmen* were busily deconstructing the superhero genre. Each of those projects, in its own way—through postmodern self-reflexivity, historical and generic engagements, and aesthetic innovation—advanced the case for the legitimacy of the graphic novel. But half a decade earlier, two established comics creators had gotten there first, inaugurating the American tradition of the graphic novel with explicit displays of sexuality, motivated by their yearning for the respect that they deserved as American Jewish storytellers and artists.

The Speaker's Benefit Changes

The case of the graphic novel demonstrates that a "speaker's benefit" for the explicit representation of sexuality persisted in the United States even beyond the period that stretches from the establishment of obscenity law in the late 19th century to the liberalization of that discourse in the 1960s. It also makes clear, however, that the particulars of the speaker's benefit changed along with the social and legal discourses around obscenity and other shifts in American culture. Whereas in the interwar period an embrace of obscenity could be incorporated into an avant-garde pose, by the last few decades of the 20th century obscenity was transformed into a marker of artistic legitimacy in the face of an increasingly hegemonic commercial market that demands that culture be "family friendly." The artists deploying obscenity by then were just as likely to be of retirement age as young turks. And, just as importantly, in the four short decades of Eisner's and Feiffer's careers, Jews transitioned from occupying relatively marginal positions in American culture to comparatively dominant ones.

The utility of obscenity as a medium of exchange that can transform financial or social capital into cultural capital cannot be assumed to operate except in relation to a complementary set of historical circumstances, such as those at work in the 1920s. It was the social and cultural marginalization of Jews in the first half of the 20th century in the United States, and the concurrent stasis in the legal discourse of obscenity, that created opportunities for insightful participants in the culture, such as Horace Liveright, to benefit from the situation. Understanding this helps both to explain why Jews, from Liveright to Eisner, engaged in the defense and circulation of obscenity and to appreciate the consequences of their interventions for the development of contemporary American culture.

3

Otherfuckers and Motherfuckers

Reproduction and Allegory in Philip Roth and Adele Wiseman

Another way that the debates about the law of obscenity resonated with particular intensity for some American Jews is in relation to their shifting anxieties about reproduction, both biological and cultural. The emphasis on reproduction in rabbinic Judaism would be hard to overstate: it is frequently noted that the first *mitzvah* (commandment) that appears in the Torah is פְּרוּ וּרְבוּ (*pru urvu*), in Genesis 1:28. Typically translated as "Be fruitful and multiply," this conveys the divine imperative to reproduce. As basic a command as this may seem, rabbinical tradition anticipated contemporary theorists such as Pierre Bourdieu in acknowledging the complex interweaving of the biological and the cultural in processes of reproduction, and individual Jews and Jewish communities have often understood reproduction and its challenges in vastly divergent ways.[1]

To be specific, American Jews' attitudes toward reproduction have shifted dramatically in the period between the establishment of modern obscenity laws in the 1870s and the present. In the late 19th and early 20th centuries, many American Jews resisted the Comstock laws (which criminalized both sexual representation and the circulation of information about birth control) because their anxieties about Jewish overpopulation made individual control of biological reproduction seem necessary, especially as it pertained to the marketing of contraception and making abortion accessible to poor, urban immigrants. Between the 1920s and 1960s, the symbolic subject of contraception activism was extended beyond the crushingly poor (prototypically Jewish) "factory girl" to the middle-class (often Jewish) working woman. This transformation of reproductive rights from an issue understood to affect the urban poor to one meaningful as a broader cause can be traced in nationally celebrated literary texts, too; in the postwar period, such texts went so far as to count even male, Jewish intellectuals among the potential victims of anticontraception Comstockery. That historical trajectory, in which American Jews contributed to the legitimation and normalization of birth control and abortion from the beginning of the Comstock laws to their overturning, met its countertendency in the postwar decades, when, in the wake of the Holocaust, American Jewish leaders began to see contraception and abortion as threats to the waning Jewish population.

Surveying these legal and cultural engagements, this chapter turns to focus on the literature of the 1960s and 1970s, examining how novels of that period use explicit representations of sexuality, formerly prohibited as obscene, to allegorize the particular Jewish reproductive anxieties of that moment—specifically, fears about the failures of Jewish *cultural* reproduction, that is, of American Jews' inability to produce identifiably Jewish offspring—in ways that revisited traditional Jewish literary tropes, revivifying them to reflect on and to resonate in the postwar period. This chapter demonstrates how, for American Jews, the stakes of the law of obscenity, and of the constraints it placed on reproductive freedom and literary expression, changed with Jewish demographics—and that obscenity, in the age of its liberalization, made possible the reinvigoration of a set of classic Jewish narrative tropes.

Comstock and Sadie Sachs

The 1873 federal statute that has been called the Comstock Act, in tribute to its most ardent proponent, forthrightly criminalized the mailing of any "obscene, lewd, or lascivious book, pamphlet, picture, paper, print, or other publication of an indecent character" but also "any article or thing designed or intended for the prevention of conception or producing an abortion . . . [and] any written or printed card, circular, book, pamphlet, advertisement or notice of any kind giving information, directly or indirectly, where, or how, or of whom, or by what means either of the things mentioned may be obtained or made."[2] The Comstock Act, in other words, yoked together textual explicitness about sex, birth control devices, and information about abortion into one conceptual category, presenting itself as a means through which the Christian establishment could rein in the excesses of what it understood as sinful, un-Christian sexuality.[3]

Notwithstanding the religious imperative commanding Jews to reproduce, there was little support among American Jews for the Comstock Act. Indeed, as mentioned in the introduction, those laws were passed in part so as to give Comstock an edge over abortionists as well as manufacturers and distributors of birth control devices, a number of whom were deliberately identified in Comstock's papers and in the press as Jewish.[4] That generation of abortionists and entrepreneurs of the 1870s left little testimony as to why they took up this particular line of work, but it is clear that Jews who engaged in such activities in the following decades, particularly after eastern European refugees began flooding into New York City in the 1880s, recognized the burden the Comstock Act placed on immigrant women who could not afford to cede control over their sexual reproduction to the government or to self-appointed moral authorities.

By the mid-1880s, hundreds of thousands of impoverished Jewish immigrants lived in desperate conditions in urban ghettos, and for these Jews even one additional unplanned pregnancy could be a grievous financial burden.[5] Other immigrants to the United States, including plenty of Irish, Italians, and Poles, lived in relatively similar straits, but Jews were generally more open to birth control and abortion because no absolute opposition to such practices inhered in rabbinic discourse, and, in any case, Jewish religious leaders exercised less influence over American Jews than Catholic leaders did over American Catholics.[6] Poor Jews felt the need for birth control themselves, and many wealthy or socially established Jews felt responsible for disseminating birth control information to alleviate the suffering of their coreligionists and particularly of poor Jewish women. The anarchist Emma Goldman, for one, felt that information about birth control was especially relevant to Jewish immigrants. In her autobiography, she recalls, "[I decided] to make public the knowledge of contraceptives, particularly at my Yiddish meetings, because the women on the East Side needed that information most."[7] Goldman's many clashes with the Comstock Act were not limited to her dissemination of birth control information (as the act had been tailored in 1908 also to target anarchist publications), but the criminalization of birth control by Comstockery offered her one compelling reason to oppose it.[8] Goldman's associate Margaret Sanger, the celebrated Catholic-born crusader credited with the popularization of contraception in America, often explained that her inspiration to devote her life to disseminating birth control information was "a small, slight Russian Jewess, about twenty-eight years old," named Sadie Sachs, who died from complications related to pregnancy after being refused information about contraception by a doctor.[9] While scholars have raised doubts about the veracity of Sanger's anecdote, that she chose repeatedly to tell her own narrative of vocation in this way, with a Jewish (rather than an Italian or Irish or Polish) immigrant woman as her representative martyr to Comstockery, reflects the positioning of the poor Jewish immigrant woman as the paradigmatic beneficiary of this phase of U.S. reproductive-rights activism.[10]

Part of the reason a Jewish woman could serve in this symbolic role was that, as noted earlier, the American Jewish community mounted less resistance to birth control activism than other immigrant communities. Sanger founded the first U.S. birth control clinic in Brownsville, Brooklyn, on October 16, 1916, and later noted why she had selected that neighborhood: "here in this Jewish community I need have no misgivings over breaking of windows or hurling of insults."[11] The receptivity of the American Jews of this period to birth control and abortion activism can also be observed in the range of Yiddish-language texts and plays that treated the subject. Ben-Zion Liber's oft-reprinted and revised 1915 pamphlet *Dos geshlekhts lebn fun man un froy* (The sexual life of man and woman), for example, devotes attention to birth control among other aspects of sexual hygiene.[12] In a preface, Liber notes that he could have simply translated another book on the subject—indeed, Sanger's *What Every Girl Should Know* and Auguste Forel's *The Sexual Question* were soon thereafter translated into Yiddish, likewise discussing abortion and birth control[13]—but he explains why he had written his own book: "to speak from the perspective of the Yiddish reader, and for the Yiddish reader, whose needs I know so well."[14] The Yiddish theater foregrounded birth control in productions such as *Birth*

Control or Race Suicide, which premiered in New York in July 1916, and *A Woman's Duty in Birth Control*, which played in Chicago.[15] As will be discussed in chapter 4, because such texts and performances circulated in Yiddish, they almost never encountered government suppression, unlike Sanger's pamphlets in English. In the years that followed, Jewish women and men played key roles in the contraception movement. The medical director of Sanger's Birth Control Clinical Research Bureau of New York beginning in 1923 was a pioneering female Jewish doctor, Hannah Mayer Stone, who was also the physician Sanger chose to represent the movement in an orchestrated test of obscenity law, the key case that became known as *United States v. One Package of Japanese Pessaries* (1936).[16] The historian Hasia Diner identifies half a dozen other Jewish women who ran birth control clinics in the interwar years and notes that as late as 1939, the biologist Raymond Pearl remarked in *The Natural History of Population* that "urban American Jews constitute the most ardent birth-controlling group in the population. Regardless of economic or educational status the Jews seem overwhelmingly to be of the opinion that contraception is the thing."[17]

The acceptance of birth control by the American Jewish community may have contributed to the motivation for individual Jewish entrepreneurs and doctors to produce and distribute contraceptives, even when they were not themselves part of the vast multitude of eastern European Jewish immigrants. The leading American producer of condoms in the first half of the 20th century, and the creator of the iconic Ramses brand, was a German Jewish immigrant, Julius Schmid, who began to manufacture condoms in 1883 as a black-market sideline while earning seven dollars a month cleaning animal intestines at a sausage-casing factory. Schmid's workshop was raided by Comstock in 1890, and he was arrested, convicted, and fined for those activities; but he persevered and by World War I had become the official vendor of prophylactics to the U.S. military.[18] On the other end of the spectrum of respectability was Dr. Abraham Jacobi, likewise a German Jewish immigrant. Rather than an entrepreneur, though, Jacobi was, as one medical historian has phrased it, "the founder of American pediatrics, and one of the most influential American physicians of the late nineteenth and early twentieth centuries." He had arrived in New York in 1853 and committed himself to serving poor immigrants in the Kleindeutschland neighborhood.

Though he was at first excluded from the German medical community in New York, both as a former radical and as a Jew, he persevered and rose to national prominence in his profession.[19] As president of the American Medical Association in 1912–1913, Jacobi became one of the first nationally prominent doctors to speak out in favor of birth control, and, introducing a book on the subject of contraception, he derided the Comstock Act, noting that "our Federal and state laws on the subject of prevention are grievously wrong and unjust. It is important that these laws be repealed at the earliest possible moment."[20]

Of course, Jewish medical professionals and entrepreneurs must have been motivated in their support of reproductive rights by many considerations irrespective of their ethnicity or religion. By the time Jacobi announced his support of birth control, he had been an attending physician on the staff of Mount Sinai Hospital in New York City for half a century, and in that role he had certainly witnessed the suffering of innumerable Jewish immigrants who had a desperate need for birth control information. But he had also worked at other local hospitals and would likely have understood himself as aiming to improve the health not just of Jewish children but of all American children and of poor ones especially.[21] Still, the Jewish community's relative acceptance of contraception and abortion may have at least removed one significant obstacle toward such work that would have been present for some non-Jews in these professions.[22]

Defending Contraception and Obscenity Together: Harriet Pilpel

In the 1920s and 1930s, birth control began to be represented in American literature as the prerogative of middle-class women (and sometimes men), rather than simply as a necessity for Sadie Sachs and her fellow tenement-dwelling immigrant factory girls.[23] If birth control and abortion remained illegal in many places and situations, such services were nonetheless by then widely available, and novelists and memoirists could treat the question of birth control and abortion not only from the perspective of the desperate poor but more frequently as a means through which working women made choices, for better and worse, about their personal and professional lives. By the mid-1930s, obscenity laws no longer officially yoked together literary representations of sex with information about birth control under the category of obscenity, but talking about these two behaviors together began to make sense for a different reason—because, as the literary scholar Alan Ackerman has pointed out, increasingly women's choices about birth control and abortion were choices about their careers, literary and otherwise.[24]

Lillian Hellman, who attended Columbia and New York Universities before taking a job reading manuscripts at Boni & Liveright (the publisher of American modernism discussed in chapter 2), describes how on the morning after her first abortion, in 1925, she returned to the office, where Horace Liveright himself offered her "a glass of mid-morning champagne."[25] The recollection emphasizes that abortion was what allowed Hellman to continue participating in Liveright's raucous, hard-drinking literary organization. Tess Slesinger's 1934 novel *The Unpossessed* dramatizes the link between a woman's reproductive and professional decisions in its final chapter, in which Maggie Flinders reflects that she and her husband, self-conscious "intellectuals," have aborted "a baby for economic freedom which meant that two of them would work in offices instead of one of them only . . . [and] for intellectual freedom which meant that they smoked their cigarettes bitterly and looked out of the windows of a taxi onto streets and people and stores and hated them all."[26] Maggie resents her husband's having compelled her to abort a pregnancy because she understands that he has done so not out of financial desperation but rather as a choice about the professional and "intellectual" lives he wants them to lead.

While the courts separated birth control and abortion from the legal category of obscenity in *United States v. One Package* in 1936, the Comstockian association of the two issues continued to exert influence on the imagination of activists and artists.[27] The enduring consequences of the original linkage between these issues is apparent in the career of Harriet F. Pilpel (1911–1991), a pioneering lawyer and stalwart opponent of both prongs of the Comstock Act.[28] Pilpel graduated Vassar in 1932, having written her senior thesis on censorship, and went on to Columbia Law School, where she stood second in her class and served as the articles editor of the *Columbia Law Review*. The New York judge who regularly hired Columbia's second-best student told her flatly that he refused to employ a female clerk, and most New York law firms discriminated openly against both women and Jews at the time. Pilpel set her sights on joining the firm of Greenbaum, Wolff, and Ernst. Morris Ernst had made a name for himself through his successful defenses against obscenity charges as counsel both for authors and publishers, most famously in the *Ulysses* case, and for birth control advocates such as Mary Ware Dennett. Pilpel devoted herself to defending obscenity, in both of these senses, throughout her career.

Pilpel is mostly remembered now for serving as general counsel to Planned Parenthood during the decades in which abortion was legalized by the Supreme Court, as well as for her leadership role at the ACLU. She insisted, in a crucial 1964 address, that the latter organization dedicate itself to the defense of women's reproductive rights and of civil liberties for gay men and lesbians, which it had refused to do up to that point.[29] Less frequently recalled are Pilpel's contributions as a tireless anticensorship advocate in both professional and popular forums. She argued against movie censorship in the *New York Times* in 1946, anticipating that the Supreme Court would reverse its 1915 decision and offer First Amendment protection to film, as it did a few years after her article.[30] In 1957, she won the Kinsey Institute the right to import sexually explicit materials for scholarly study.[31] As a monthly columnist for *Publisher's Weekly* for decades, she kept authors and editors informed about relevant developments in law, including the changes in the enforcement and legal meaning of obscenity.[32] One indicator of Pilpel's prominence within the cultural as well as legal sphere was an article, "Lady Chatterley and the Courts," which appeared in the 1960 issue of *New World Writing*, alongside an early story by Thomas Pynchon and the first publication of Tillie Olsen's "Tell Me a Riddle."[33]

Approaching the Comstock Act from the perspective of a female professional, Pilpel understood the threats of obscenity laws better than many male First Amendment lawyers. It was typical of them to quail or prevaricate when they considered the consequences of their legal victories. Pilpel's mentor, Ernst, in 1970 decried the use of "the four-letter word, out of context," as well as "sodomy on the stage and masturbation in the public arena," and Grove Press's lawyer Charles Rembar was, in the words of his cousin and client Norman Mailer, "troubled just a hint by the liberties [he] won."[34] Pilpel, by contrast, remained steadfast in opposition to the law of obscenity, without cavil. In *Obscenity and the Constitution*, a lecture she gave to publishing executives in 1973, Pilpel outlined the challenges to free expression imposed by recent decisions, particularly *Miller v. California*, and argued for a redoubled commitment to First Amendment protections, broadly interpreted. "There should be as free a marketplace for sexual ideas and descriptions," she thundered, "as we have now with reference to other kinds of ideas and descriptions."[35] Speculating on why the court had recently retreated from its more liberal positions of the 1960s, Pilpel suggested that this may have come about because "the Court majority consists of middle-aged or elderly gentlemen of the upper middle class . . . [who] are not completely comfortable about sex and therefore objectify their subjective concerns" and who display "conventional middle class distaste for the vulgar and profane." In contrast, she remarked, "I'm all in favor of good taste, but I don't think it should be enshrined as a matter of constitutional law"[36]—precisely, her remarks suggest, because she perceived the Bourdieuian insight that "taste" so often works to reproduce the privilege of "gentlemen of the upper middle class."

Raised as a Reform Jew, active as an adult in the Ethical Culture Society, and married to a man who worked for a major nonprofit Jewish community agency, the Joint Distribution Committee, Pilpel, like most lawyers, never seems to have attributed her commitments in the field of obscenity law to her Jewishness. But her remarks on the subject emphasize the way that prosecutors use "obscenity charges as a means of suppressing views which are dissident, satirical, irreverent, or merely unpopular"[37] and that "censorship of obscenity . . . sets the stage for a censorship or censorious mentality which can pour over from obscenity to other things we may not like"[38]—arguments, as noted in chapter 1, that had particular resonance for American Jews who were self-conscious about their vulnerability as members of a demographic minority. Linking herself to other women who came of age in the 1920s and 1930s, like Hellman and the fictional Maggie Flinders, Pilpel remarked that birth control was necessary, given her commitments to her career and family. "Birth control and the freedom of women to choose whether or not to have children was of burning interest to me," she noted, "partly because I always wanted to have a career and children, but if I had no control over when I had the children it wouldn't have been possible for me to plan my career."[39] It is perhaps just a historical accident that the battles begun by Goldman and Sanger to deliver contraception to

Jewish immigrants at the turn of the century were fought and largely won, decades later, by a professionally empowered Jewish woman, but Pilpel's career exemplifies the transformation of birth control from an issue affecting primarily impoverished immigrants to one affecting the middle class and suggests why many professional women, like her, rejected the Comstockian law of obscenity.

Jewish Intellectuals and Contraception at Midcentury: Saul Bellow and Philip Roth

Pilpel's career reflects the evolution of the symbolic beneficiary of the birth control movement in pace with the socioeconomic changes that confronted American women, Jews no less than anyone else, with choices to be made about motherhood and career. The shift of the imagined beneficiary of the movement is also registered in literary texts and not coincidentally in the handful of prominent fictions that marked the arrival of American Jewish men as dominant presences on the postwar literary scene. By the mid-1950s, these texts had the temerity not only to figure the male Jewish intellectual as a preeminent American type, as critics have regularly remarked, but also, more oddly, to represent him as the symbolic subject of U.S. contraception activism.[40] In doing so, these novels about young Jewish men present abortion and contraception not primarily as technologies for the control of biological reproduction but as reflecting the complexities of social and cultural reproduction.

One significant episode in Saul Bellow's *The Adventures of Augie March* (1953) follows the titular protagonist as he supports a friend and housemate, Mimi Villars, who is seeking an illegal abortion. Mimi is not, as Augie puts it, "a timid little knocked-up factory girl."[41] While she works as a waitress "in a student hashhouse on Ellis Avenue," Mimi is the daughter of a Hollywood actor and "came to Chicago to study"; she was "expelled from the university for going past the bounds of necking at Greene Hall, in the lounge" (234–35) but remains within the orbit of the university. Her lover is "a graduate assistant in Political Science" (235), so while the couple with the unexpected pregnancy is poor, they are a far cry from the blue-collar laborers who served, in the first decades of the century, as the symbolic subjects of contraception activism. Mimi is no Sadie Sachs (that mythic "Jewess" who inspired Sanger), nor is she Roberta Alden, the "poor factory girl" of Theodore Dreiser's *An American Tragedy* (1925) who, ignorant about birth control and unsuccessful in finding an abortionist, is murdered by the man who has impregnated her and who would rather kill her than marry her.[42]

Bellow emphasizes the difference between Mimi and a factory girl again when, after the procedure, her heavy bleeding and fever impel Augie and another friend of his to take her to a hospital. They lie, telling the hospital staff that "she's a working girl and couldn't have a kid" (318). This is what they think the doctors need to hear, but in fact, Mimi is an assertive, powerful woman who has indicated that she does not see the value in bringing another life into a world of pain and difficulty. Augie has suggested that she keep the baby, noting that he "can't complain about having been born," but she disagrees. "Maybe you like the way you are," she tells Augie, "but most people suffer from it" (291–92). Even if one does not entirely credit Mimi's bravado in that conversation as genuine, her remarks to Augie about abortion insistently shift the discussion from one of economic necessity to the more philosophical issues of when life begins and what responsibilities the living have to the not-yet-conceived and not-yet-born. And while the novel acknowledges that the problem of contraception is much more tangible for women than for men (Mimi makes clear to Augie, "you, a man, could talk, but she was the one for whom it was the flesh and blood trouble" [292]), because the chapter is narrated by Augie and presents *his* experiences of the events around the abortion, rather than Mimi's, emphasis is placed on the consequences of a failure of contraception not for her but for him. In the midst of this episode, Augie meets up with an old friend, Jimmy Klein, who explains how he has wound up "married" with "a kid": "It's all that you want from life comes to you as one single thing—fucking; so you and some nice kid get together, and after a while you have more misery than before, only now it's more permanent. . . . I fooled around with her, I got her in the family way, and I married her" (306–7). To describe the desire that began his troubles, Jimmy uses the still somewhat taboo word "fucking," which, like the birth control of which he seems not to have been aware and the abortion that he does not seem to have considered, was criminalized by the Comstock Act.

From Jimmy's adult perspective, sexual desire must be understood as a biological trap for men. He describes sex with the same analogy of fireworks for the action of erection and ejaculation that Joyce does in the "Nausicaa" chapter of *Ulysses*, though what Jimmy experiences in the aftermath of his own ejaculation is not the mawkish gloom and depression that Bloom feels but rather the serious consequences of sexual intercourse without contraception: "You're set up like the July fourth rocket. . . . Just charge enough to explode you. Up. Then the stick falls down after the flash. You live to bring up the kid and oblige your wife" (306–7).

Jimmy illustrates the potential consequences of the illegality and unavailability of contraception and abortion for a young intellectual like Augie. What happens to Augie, more specifically, as a result of his helping Mamie abort her pregnancy is that he loses his chance to vault into bourgeois respectability by marrying the wealthy girl to whom he is engaged. Augie and Mamie are seen outside the abortionist's office, and word gets back to Augie's brother Simon and to the Magnuses, the parvenu family into which Augie had been angling to marry. His prospective father-in-law tells him, in no uncertain terms ("No dough if she marries you!" [320]), that because word has gotten out about his involvement in Mimi's abortion, Augie will not be invited to join the moneyed classes. Even if the girl still agrees to marry him, she will be cut off by her family, and Lucy chooses to side with her family, not Augie. In this case, the stakes of reproductive rights are the line they draw between the morality of an up-and-comer like Augie and the bourgeois morality of a parvenu family: it is precisely his support of a woman's right to control her biological reproduction that ends up enforcing a kind of *class* reproduction. The way Augie has put it is that in his pursuit of this girl, "what had to be established was whether [he] was qualified in pocket to mix with the sons of established fathers" (281), and it turns out to be his complicity in Mimi's abortion that renders him *disqualified* to mix with such sons.

These turn out to be precisely the same stakes of a conflict over contraception in another of the classic works that marked the emergence of the postwar generation of American Jewish writers, Philip Roth's novella *Goodbye, Columbus* (1959), which Bellow enthusiastically praised. As Beth Widmaier Capo and others have noticed, the series of events with which that novella reaches its conclusion turns on birth control: Neil Klugman's summer girlfriend, Brenda, agrees to acquire a diaphragm, and her mother is outraged upon discovering it, hidden in a drawer, after Brenda has returned to college.[43] Just as the discovery of Augie's involvement in an abortion leads Lucy Magnus's parents to forbid that she continue to see him, here again the discovery of Brenda's diaphragm causes her *alrightnik* parents to forbid her to associate with her boyfriend. As in *Augie March*, here too the young man makes clear that the young woman faces a choice between her wealthy parents and himself, and here again the woman chooses her parents on the basis of the financial support that the young intellectual cannot offer.

"You can go home or not go home," Neil tells Brenda, ostensibly discussing her plans for the Thanksgiving holiday but obviously referring to the possibility that she reject her parents' demands and begin a new life with him. Her answer echoes her father's recent demanding letter: "They did send me to the best schools, didn't they? They have given me everything I've wanted, haven't they? . . . Then how can I not go home?"[44] Like Augie's relationship with Lucy Magnus, Neil's with Brenda promises him entry into a newly wealthy family and all that that entails (of which he offers an inventory: "gold dinnerware, sporting-goods trees, nectarines, garbage disposals, bumpless noses, Patimkin Sink, Bonwit Teller" [71]), and Neil's insistence on Brenda's use of contraception scuppers all that, impeding his upward mobility—the irony, of course, being that if Neil had not used contraception in his sexual relationship with Brenda, the Patimkins would in all likelihood not so easily have been able to dispense of him.

These texts by Bellow and Roth shift the emphasis of literary representations of contraception and abortion away from a focus on the bodily and social issues these technologies raise for women and onto the ramifications of reproductive rights, in terms of social and class reproduction, for young intellectual men in particular. Accepting abortion and contraception, Augie and Neil show themselves to differ from their prospective well-to-do in-laws and from the young women who choose their parents over their boyfriends (or, in Werner Sollors's still useful terms, who privilege descent over consent),[45] and the texts in which they appear suggest just how deeply entwined the issues of contraception and abortion can be with larger social relationships—in these cases, between the newly wealthy and the upwardly aspirational middle class.

From Biological to Cultural Reproduction: *Letting Go*

In the novel that Roth published after *Goodbye, Columbus*, he addresses at much greater length the relationship between biological contraception and reproduction and their ethnic, religious, and social analogues, especially as they impinge on the fortunes of young Jewish men. That novel, *Letting Go* (1961), can be described as a six-hundred-page meditation on the problems of reproduction, in many of its most recognizable literal and metaphorical forms, including pregnancy, birth control, abortion, the births and deaths of children, and the relationships between parents and their children—but also, specifically, adoption and religious conversion, two processes that attempt to reproduce socially what can otherwise be reproduced biologically. The novel extends the metaphorization of contraception at work in Bellow's and Roth's earlier texts and renders explicit the link between American debates about reproduction and the laws governing it, on the one hand, and the complexities of making new Jews, on the other.[46]

Letting Go piles up plot points that allow Roth to describe the challenges of biological reproduction and their consequences for young intellectuals. As in *Augie March* and *Goodbye, Columbus*, in *Letting Go* the character who is represented as using a diaphragm, and then having an abortion, is no poor factory girl. She is a middle-class college dropout, Libby, and the father of her child is a young Brooklyn-born Jew, working on his doctorate. Much of the novel's plot concerns Libby, though it is less often focused directly on her than on the men in her life, particularly her husband, Paul Herz, and his fellow graduate student Gabe Wallach. After Libby and Paul marry, her birth control fails, and Paul convinces her to have an abortion. Later, Libby wants to have a child but is told she is now too frail to endure pregnancy and childbirth. By the end of the novel, she and Paul have adopted a newborn, with considerable help from Gabe. In the novel's other main plot, Gabe dates and moves in with Martha Reaganhart, another college dropout and a single mother of two children. Most of the meager criticism that has addressed *Letting Go* barely mentions any of these events,[47] but one of the main achievements of the novel is to illustrate, through Libby and Martha, the double bind of pregnancy for a middle-class woman with intellectual inclinations in the 1950s, when abortions were widely available though still mostly illegal. In Libby, Roth depicts the dissatisfaction of such a young woman who has chosen to abort a fetus, while Martha represents both the joys and hardships associated with a young woman's deliberate decision *not* to abort unplanned pregnancies.[48]

What has been even less noted by critics of the novel is the perceptiveness of Roth's treatment of the questions of Jewish conversion and adoption, which have since become key issues in discussions of Jewish identity. This makes *Letting Go* a prescient exploration of crucial problems of Jewish reproduction that would be more widely discussed in the following decades. In the novel, these phenomena reveal confusion and incoherence in American Jewish identity.

Libby was raised as a Catholic, and Paul as a Jew. Their families view the marriage as a rejection of religious and cultural responsibilities, and so they unilaterally sever connections to the young couple. Libby, in an attempt to reestablish a relationship between Paul and his parents, converts to Judaism. She describes the process of conversion in terms that locate it theologically with some specificity: "I read six thick books on the plights and flights of the Jews," she says. "I met with this cerebral rabbi in Ann Arbor once a week, and finally there was a laying on of hands" (22). Later, Libby is clearer about what she means by "a laying on of the hands": "The rabbi in Ann Arbor took me to the swimming pool at the Y, and in my old blue Jantzen I had this *mikvah* [ritual immersion]" (53). This makes clear that Libby's was almost certainly not an Orthodox conversion: both the "old blue Jantzen" bathing suit and "the swimming pool at the Y" would be questionable according to traditional Orthodox and Conservative practices. Paul's parents are not themselves Orthodox—at least not punctiliously so with regard to *kashrut*, given that Paul's mother joyfully recalls how, as a child, Paul "ate shrimps till they came out of [his] ears" (413)—but the Herzes view Libby's conversion just as dismissively as an ultra-Orthodox rabbi would. "I was a daughter of Ruth, the rabbi told me," Libby remembers, but "in Brooklyn . . . no one was much moved by the news. . . . I might be Ruth's daughter—that didn't make me theirs. A shikse once, . . . a shikse for all time" (22).

The novel's language here evokes the reproductive paradox of Jewish conversion practices, which allow for individuals with no biological connection to Jewish culture to assert a Jewish identity through their voluntary actions but which do so in part by positing an imagined biological link between the new converts and Jewish heredity, renaming them in Hebrew as "sons of Adam" and "daughters of Ruth." Thus, a practice that directly counters racial visions of Jewishness by providing a mechanism through which anyone, regardless of biology, can become Jewish also reinforces the idea of Jewishness as an inherited trait. Libby's gender matters here; if she were a non-Jewish male, married to a Jewish woman, their children would be considered Jewish by traditional rabbinic authorities according to the matrilineal principle.[49] Whatever other complications there are in conversion to Judaism—and in the United States, where Reform and Conservative Jews have composed the majority of the Jewish population but where Orthodox Jewish leaders, based in the United States and Israel, have retained a surprising amount of authority over many areas of Jewish religious practice, including conversion, disagreements have proliferated about the nature of Jewish inheritance and standards for conversion—the pressure point for any discussion of a woman's conversion to Judaism tends to be the question of reproduction, which is to say, the issue of whether her children will be accepted as Jewish.[50]

It is not clear whether the Herzes would have been so quick to reject Libby's conversion as meaningless if it had been carried out by an Orthodox rabbi, but, in a further irony, to engage in such a conversion, Libby would have had to become much more zealous about Jewish religious practice than the Herzes themselves. Yet another irony is that Libby actually *looks* Jewish. She passes for "a *yiddishe maydele* [a little Jewish girl]" (128): "Jewish store owners were always taking her for a nice Jewish girl" (119). Still, the Herzes are not the only ones who reject Libby's conversion. Paul reflects, at one point, that he is "almost glad that his parents had not been fooled by it. Nobody else had, not even (most wretched of all) the convert herself" (142). Later in the novel, one of Paul's childhood friends, a former girlfriend, suggests that he was never attracted to "Jewish girls," and when he reminds her that his current "wife is Jewish," she clarifies, "not flinching," that she meant Jewish "by birth" (422). This prejudice—an instinctual unwillingness to accept converts as fully or authentically Jewish—is by no means unique to an unsympathetic character within Roth's novel; indeed, one of the most revealing aspects of the reception of *Letting Go* is that many of its reviewers, including Irving Feldman and James Atlas, neglect to mention Libby's conversion at all and refer to the character, without qualification, as a Catholic young woman.[51] They do so, presumably, not because they uphold Orthodox standards of conversion but because they take for granted a racial concept of Jewish identity that remained remarkably tenacious in the postwar United States. Such racialism requires them to ignore the ability of conversion to effectuate Jewish reproduction in the absence of biological reproduction—that is, to make a new Jew through a process other than pregnancy.

Paul himself recognizes that the reason Libby's conversion has failed to win over his parents is that the elder Herzes rely on a biological sense of Jewish heredity. Before Libby's abortion, he considers the potential benefit of having a baby in repairing his relationship to his family: "Would not a baby's coo soften their hearts? How could they resist a little dark-eyed child? This would be different from Libby's conversion; this was nature, not design" (142). In other words, Paul knows that establishing a racial/biological ("nature") connection between Libby and his Jewish family (through the intermingling of their genetic material in a hypothetical "dark-eyed" child) would be more meaningful to his parents than the social ritual ("design") of conversion. It is perhaps this sense of racial Jewish identity that Paul defies in the moment when he commits to aborting the fetus inside Libby: ambiguously, at that moment, instead of consulting with Libby herself, Paul thinks of the New York rabbi who refused to marry them and then thinks of his family and *then* shakes the abortionist's hand (127). Having a baby would be a solution to his problems, but he refuses to do it since that would accede to the racialization of Jewishness.

The novel's adoption plot points up another instance of the persistence of a racialized understanding of Jewish identity in the postwar United States, but in this case it allows some room for progress. Paul and Libby, having decided to adopt, face a problem: "there's over a three-year waiting list" for those who wish "to adopt a Jewish baby" (313). To contemporary readers, this may sound bizarre—why not just adopt any baby?—but Paul and Libby do not have a choice. The laws governing adoption in the United States from the 1930s to the 1960s "mandated that adoptive parents and child 'are suited to one another by religious affiliation.'" In other words, Jewish couples could only adopt Jewish babies; Catholic couples, Catholic babies; and Protestants, Protestant babies. Such policies, and the religiously specific orphanages and adoption agencies that enacted them, arose largely in order to protect orphaned Jewish and Catholic children from Protestant evangelism. Religious identities were assigned even to newborns, who would be identified as sharing the religion of their birth mother, and, astonishingly, religions were assigned even to babies anonymously abandoned at hospitals and orphanages.[52] This is why, when Gabe finds a young nominally Catholic woman with an unwanted pregnancy who is willing to give up her child for adoption by the Herzes, "it was best for the hospital to know nothing of the adoption; should they find out the exact circumstances, they would most certainly bring pressure upon Theresa to give up the child to a Catholic family, or even to an orphanage" (475). As far as the state and adoption agencies are concerned, a Catholic mother's child is Catholic, however theologically and practically meaningless it might be to assign religion to a newborn—a fictional development that had a legal precedent in a 1954 decision by the Massachusetts State Supreme Court to deny "a Jewish couple's petition to adopt twin boys born to a Catholic mother, even though the mother herself had consented to the placement."[53]

In the novel, a comment by Martha Reaganhart points up the strangeness of the notion that children could be religious at birth: speaking of her seven-year-old daughter and four-year-old son, she says, "my kids, you know, are little Protestant kids," but in the next breath she notes that Markie, her son, is "a slow learner, . . . and it may take him fifteen years to figure out what a Jew *is*" (212). The sort of identity that one can possess without any understanding of it is, of necessity, biological. In postwar America, religious identity was gradually coming to be seen as voluntary and based on personal declarations of faith rather than imposed by heredity, but Roth's novel provides a reminder that adoption laws meanwhile reflected the tenacity of racialized visions of religious identity.[54]

Miraculously, though, in the novel's conclusion, it holds out hope of a departure from such conservative, biologically determined visions of Jewish identity. Despite the rejection of Libby's conversion and the obstacles to adoption, she manages to transform herself into a Jew by the end of the novel. Gabe tells her, "You have certainly become a very Jewish girl" (536), and even if he is being sarcastic, Libby takes him quite seriously. Moreover, Paul's mother reestablishes contact with Paul and Libby, reconnecting them to his Jewish family. What is even more impressive about this is that Libby transforms herself not into a religious Jew but into an *ethnic* one—precisely the kind of Jew for which there is no acknowledged conversion process. "I don't know whether I believe in God," she tells Gabe, but that does not trouble her. "What's important is being something": that is, having an identity.[55] She makes the case for this sort of Jewishness through a radical interpretation of a Jewish ritual: "Chanukah . . . doesn't even require that you believe in God," she says. "It's the people it commemorates" (536–37). Others might argue that the modern Chanukah story offers *both* a historical triumph (the military victory of the Maccabees) and a theological miracle (the miracle of the lamp that burned for eight days), but for Libby, who uses a guidebook of "suggestions for the Jewish homemaker" (353) and has a child of her own to raise as a Jew, Jewishness can be asserted simply by acting Jewishly—and by reproducing Jewishness, even if there is no biological content whatsoever to that reproduction. Libby fulfills the first commandment, *pru urvu*, in that she will raise a Jewish child and in doing so legitimates herself as a Jewish woman—an identity to some degree defined, in the rabbinic tradition that established matrilineal descent, by a woman's ability to bear Jewish children.[56] In giving her this opportunity, Roth's novel holds out hope for an understanding of Jewish reproduction in the postwar United States that need not be strictly biological. Libby is a Jewish woman with no biological connection to Jewish people, raising a Jewish child with no biological connection to Jews, including herself. It seems, then, that the function of abortion in the novel has been specifically to foreclose the possibility of biological reproduction so as to carve out a space in which to demonstrate what purely cultural reproduction would look like.

Allegories of Assimilation

The treatment of reproduction in *Letting Go* was wildly ahead of its time. Just after the novel was published, and in the same years that contraception and abortion were finally being legalized by the U.S. legal system, a different reproductive anxiety began to dominate discussions about the American Jewish population that once again, and with increased rhetorical brashness, conflated biological and cultural reproduction. Responding to two phenomena discovered by demographic studies of American Jews in the 1960s—a decline in Jews' birthrates and a rise in the rate of Jews marrying non-Jews—observers began to make broad, apocalyptic claims about the future of the Jewish population in the United States, and these often invoked the Jewish embrace of contraception as one contributor to the problem. In 1963, suggesting to fellow Jews, "we are failing to reproduce ourselves," and lamenting the support of contemporary rabbis for contraception and abortion, Milton Himmelfarb invoked both "loss by infertility" and "loss by intermarriage" as threats to Jewish "survival."[57] Michael Staub has shown that such claims were repeated incessantly in the Jewish press in the decade that followed, even while most Jews continued to support contraceptive freedom.[58]

Such formulations conflated biological reproduction and cultural reproduction into a single phenomenon: low birthrates represent a failure of the former, while intermarriage putatively represents a failure of the latter—not that anyone believed that intermarried couples would fail to bear children; rather, such couples allegedly failed to produce children who turned out to be Jews. Himmelfarb remarked that "only about 30 per cent of the children in Jewish intermarriages are raised as Jews or are considered to be Jews by their parents."[59] Like the resistance to conversion and adoption dramatized in *Letting Go*, this declaration assumes that biological reproduction is the only truly effective form of Jewish reproduction and that it is a prerequisite for cultural reproduction. In other words, Himmelfarb—like so many other conservative commentators who followed him in decrying intermarriage—hones in on the biological non-Jewishness of a Jew's spouse as the bugbear of American Jewish reproduction. This was, by then, already a very well-worn idea. For whether or not intermarriage is now, or ever has been, necessarily predictive of the attrition of Jewish identity in the children of the couple—and sociologists and demographers will debate that question ad infinitum[60]—there is no doubt that intermarriage, figured narratively as the sexual attraction of the non-Jewish woman, has always been textually useful to metaphorize the threat of what has been called "assimilation" or, in other words, as a literary shorthand for failures of Jewish cultural reproduction.

The Biblical scholar Tikva Frymer-Kensky has remarked that in the Tanakh, "stories about marriages to outside women . . . were the natural vehicle with which Israel expressed and explored . . . crucial national issues of survival and self-definition."[61] The threat posed by the non-Jewish woman is etymologically clear in the epithet *shiksa* or *shikse*, employed widely in modern Yiddish and English to refer to non-Jewish women and, as we have seen, in Roth's *Letting Go*, where, from the perspective of Paul's parents, "a shikse once . . . [is] a shikse for all time." The Biblical Hebrew שקץ (*sheketz*) is translated into English as "'unclean creature,' reptile; abomination, detestation, uncleanliness," and in the Biblical dietary laws, this word denotes dirty, unpleasant creatures unfit for consumption, such as shellfish and insects.[62] Leviticus 7:21 describes the consequences of consorting with such objects for the Israelites involved with Temple sacrifice: "Should a person touch . . . any unclean abominable creature [בְּכָל שֶׁקֶץ טָמֵא] . . . that person shall be cut off from his kin."[63] The perspective always implicit in the modern term *shikse*, then, is that just as detestations taint the ritual purity of a Jew, requiring that he be "cut off from his kin," so too does a non-Jewish spouse, sexual partner, and mother for his children irreversibly detach him from the Jewish community—again, recall how in *Letting Go* marriage to Libby severs Paul's connection to his Jewish family. One anecdote in the Talmud goes so far as to imagine that sexual intercourse with non-Jewish women, in and of itself, threatens Jewish cultural reproduction even in its most concretely embodied manifestation: in *B. Eruvin* 19a, we learn that "our father Abraham" will prevent Jewish sinners from ending up in *gehenna* (hell) "except such an Israelite as had immoral intercourse with the daughter of an idolator, since his foreskin is drawn and so he cannot be discovered."[64] According to this text, if perhaps only this text, a Jewish man who has had sex with a non-Jewish woman can no longer be identified as Jewish, even by a prophet with superhuman faculties of perception. This exemplifies the extent to which sex with a non-Jewish woman could be used to symbolize a failure of Jewish cultural reproduction.

Allegorical representations of attractive non-Jewish women as embodying the threatening allure of non-Jewish culture, consonant with this etymological and textual history, recur in a variety of modern Jewish narratives. I. L. Peretz's Yiddish ballad "Monish" (1888), with what the critic S. Niger called its "direct and indirect allegorism," provides one excellent example: Peretz's poem relates the tale of a prodigy, the pride of his pious generation, who is lured away from Jewish tradition by a golden-haired temptress named Marie who represents the appeal of Western culture.[65] S. Y. Agnon's Hebrew fable "The Lady and the Peddler," published in Hebrew in 1943, provides an even more powerful example of the continuity between ancient and modern Jewish narrative traditions in their use of this allegorical trope. Agnon's story centers on Joseph, who while peddling in an unidentified wooded region arrives at a lady's manor and strikes up an intimate relationship with her. They cohabit comfortably until Joseph discovers that she is a flesh-eating, blood-drinking monster bent on devouring him.[66] As Baruch Kurzweil observes, the story is an allegory for "the relations between the people of Israel and the nations of the world, the problem of assimilation"[67]—and particularly for how German culture, in which Agnon was raised, first seduced and then attempted to destroy Europe's Jews. The lady's name, Helen, evokes the classic example of a society that threatened Jewish identity because of its allure, and Agnon alludes explicitly to the stories of Joseph and Potiphar's wife and to Samson and Delilah, two Biblical narratives about the dangerous attractions of non-Jewish women.[68]

Dozens of narratives about intermarriage were also written by American Jews, long before intermarriage was a significant social phenomenon in the United States.[69] Working separately, the literary scholars Frederic Cople Jaher and Adam Sol have cataloged nearly three dozen examples of novels or short stories by American Jews that concern themselves primarily or substantially with interfaith relationships, many of them published in the first half of the 20th century, when intermarriage was exceedingly rare. These lists are not exhaustive, either.[70] Many texts also describe Jewish women attracted to non-Jewish men, but it is crucial to recall that the nearly universal acceptance of the matrilineal principle among Jewish religious authorities until the 1980s meant that the so-called *shaygets*—the male equivalent of the *shikse*—could not help but father Jewish children, if he married a Jewish woman, whereas a *shikse* was understood as posing a direct and dire threat to Jewish reproduction.[71] As in Agnon's fable and in rabbinic literature, American Jewish writing employs narratives of romance between Jews and non-Jews as a means of addressing perennial questions about identity, continuity, and cultural reproduction that have been posed simultaneously by Jewish sociologists, theologians, and other communal leaders. In some cases, of course, authors may have simply been reflecting on their own personal romantic experiences. But in many other cases, the aim of such narratives was not autobiographical but patently allegorical; the novelist Myron S. Kaufmann, for one, "never dated a girl who was not Jewish" and yet devoted more than six hundred pages of his 1958 best-seller *Remember Me to God* to dissecting the affair between a Jewish Harvard undergraduate and a Radcliffe blue blood.[72] For Kaufmann, as for a host of other American Jewish writers, narratives of interfaith relationships have provided unparalleled opportunities for exploring identity conflicts in fiction.[73] This was clear as far back in American Jewish literary history as Ezra Brudno's *The Tether* (1908), in which the Jewish protagonist, David, falls in love with a Baptist, Mildred. Though the novel details the couple's courtship expansively, the narrator explains that "instead of a personal matter, [David's] love for Mildred presented itself to him in the form of a general question, a problem to be solved—the problem that had faced his race in all lands and at all times."[74] Rather than an individual dilemma, in other words, David and Mildred's affair is understood, even by David himself, as an allegory for community interactions. The influential critic Leslie Fiedler noted this, too, in his foundational essay on American Jewish fiction. In the first half century of novels about Jews in America, he wrote, problems of "identity and assimilation" are "posed in terms of sexual symbols": "it is in the role of passionate lover that the American-Jewish novelist sees himself, . . . and the community with which he seeks to unite himself he sees as the *shikse*."[75]

Passionate as Jewish writers may have imagined themselves to be, until the 1960s they were constrained both by obscenity law and by their own notions of literary propriety from representing lust for America graphically. Euphemisms abound in these texts. In Mary Antin's famous memoir *The Promised Land* (1912), the author's sexual relationship with a non-Jewish man is skillfully elided; in its place, Antin relates in substantial physical detail her first experience chewing and swallowing "a pink piece of pig's flesh."[76] Anzia Yezierska seizes on less concrete metaphors to describe the sexual intimacy of interracial lovers at the center of her novel *Salome of the Tenements* (1923): "It was as if their spirit had found expression at last," she writes, "through the flesh merging their hearts into one consuming flame of love."[77] This typical mess of mixed metaphor and banality conveys the vaguest reference to the mechanics of sex with only a slight hint of concreteness in the sometimes controversial word "flesh."

Even Ludwig Lewisohn, committed as he was to sexual frankness, as discussed in chapter 1, would not or could not be any more explicit than Antin or Yezierska in representing the physical intimacy of Arthur Levy and his non-Jewish virgin lover, Elizabeth, in *The Island Within* (1928).[78] The narrator describes their first experience of sexual intercourse as follows:

> The world of reality was drowned for the hour in another world that was magical and mad and overwhelmingly tangible, too. . . . He was not surprised that she went back to his apartment with him, nor that she entered, nor at her white, scared face, nor at her utter yielding, nor at her straining to him, nor at her sweet ways or beauty of body. . . . Then the magic snapped. . . . She sat on the edge of the bed, wrapping a silk coverlet about her, her face haggard with pain and a touch of brooding horror. "Is that all?"[79]

The ellipses in this quotation, it should be noted, all belong to Lewisohn, as do the oblique and euphemistic phrases. They demonstrate Lewisohn's refusal to describe a sexual experience concretely. Elizabeth's "utter yielding," "straining," and "sweet ways" all refer indirectly to sexual actions; and her "beauty of body" is, of course, an allusion to the arousal Levy experiences in seeing her naked. But nothing here conveys the "overwhelmingly tangible" nature of sexual contact, while the narrator refers repeatedly instead to the opposite of concrete experience, "magic." Later Lewisohn's reader learns that Elizabeth is pregnant with Arthur's child, and the conversation touches on whether Arthur "had taken proper precautions" (without, of course, clarifying what constituted such precautions for the daring intermarried couples of the World War I era).[80] The recourse to innuendo, florid language, asterisks, ellipses, and well-placed paragraph breaks to euphemize intercourse in fiction was hardly unique to American Jewish writers; on the contrary, it was what American law demanded of them and of everyone else. Ellipses serving this purpose were so widely recognizable that Philip Wylie's 1928 novel *Heavy Laden* could jokingly interrupt a scene headed toward the bedroom with the exclamation, "Now, damn you, take your row of dots!"[81] Along with all the Comstock Act's other effects, it barred American writers from representing the attraction of the *shikse*, as symbol of the appeal of America, in its sexual dimensions.[82]

Graphic Sexual Allegory: *Portnoy's Complaint*

Thanks to changes in obscenity law, the trope of the attraction of the *shikse* could be rendered with considerably more explicit detail in the 1960s and could reflect the growing anxiety about Jewish cultural reproduction through a more powerful set of sexual metaphors just as intermarriage, which had not previously been a serious demographic phenomenon, increased in popularity. In other words, what had previously been just a literary metaphor became enlivened with bodily possibility, which could now, rather conveniently, be rendered explicitly in literary prose. In Philip Roth's *Portnoy's Complaint*, the allegorical tradition adumbrated earlier in this chapter collides with the representational latitude of the late 1960s. Alexander Portnoy's infamous obsession with *shikses*, that is, allows Roth to rewrite the allegory of exogamic desire as representing communal affiliation in graphic sexual terms. One need not scour Roth's archives for proof of this, either, as Portnoy all but shouts it from the rooftops: "O America! America! it may have been gold in the streets to my grandparents, it may have been a chicken in every pot to my father and mother, but to me, a child whose earliest movie memories are of Ann Rutherford and Alice Faye, America is a *shikse* nestling under your arm whispering love love love love love!"[83] In a sharp reading of this passage and related moments in the novel, the literary scholar Sam Girgus contextualizes *Portnoy* within an allegorical tradition in which America has been represented as a "feminine pastoral image" and asserts that the novel's "Gentile women . . . are not merely Americans; they embody America."[84] As if stating outright that "America is a *shikse*" did not render this quite clear enough, it seems worthwhile to remark that Portnoy's opening apostrophic exclamation here is a sly evocation of John Donne's "Elegy 19: To His Mistress Going to Bed," in which the poet compares his lover to the newly discovered continent:

> License my roving hands, and let them go
> Before, behind, between, above, below.
> O my America! my new-found-land,
> My kingdom, safeliest when with one man manned,
> My Mine of precious stones, my empery,
> How blest am I in this discovering thee![85]

Whereas for Donne's speaker the analogy of woman-as-country serves to concretize sensual desire (that is, "before, behind, between" is a fairly precise description of where a lover might want to place his "roving hands"), Roth works the allegory forcefully in the other direction, intensifying the political meaning with the obscenity available to him.[86] In one of the book's most frequently cited passages, Portnoy remarks, "I don't seem to stick my dick up these girls, as much as I stick it up their backgrounds—as though through fucking I will discover America. *Conquer* America—maybe that's more like it" (235). Here, it is literally "fucking" that is the means of discovery and conquering and that has consequences for Portnoy's communal affiliations; Portnoy's "dick" is the medium through which he embarks on his adventures of identity and alienation. With the obscene language made available in the 1960s, then—and it is noteworthy, in this regard, that in Roth's papers one finds an earlier typescript of this passage that reads, instead, "As though sex is my way of discovering America"—*Portnoy's Complaint* extends an allegorical tradition of Jewish narrative to the American Jewish situation.[87]

Many readers of *Portnoy's Complaint* have recognized what Roth is up to when it comes to the allegorical resonances of Portnoy's *shikses*. Portnoy's "relations with women approximate those with society," one critic notes; another explains that "'The Pumpkin,' 'The Pilgrim,' and 'The Monkey' [are] all the forbidden *shiksa* in her respective guises as Middle-American wholesome, old New England establishment, and blue-collar ex-hillbilly."[88] Roth himself acknowledged his allegorical intentions for the novel, noting that his method in *Portnoy* was "to ground the mythological in the recognizable"; the Portnoys were meant to serve, he explained, as the "legendary Jewish family dwelling on high, whose squabbles over French-fried potatoes, synagogue attendance, and shiksas were, admittedly, of an Olympian magnitude and splendor, but by whose terrifying kitchen lightning storms were illuminated the values, dreams, fears, and aspirations by which we mortal Jews lived somewhat less vividly down below."[89]

It is by no means unfaithful to the text's spirit, then, to note how sharply a received idea about American social life could be rewritten and reanimated through the use of obscenity. It was no news to American Jews by 1969, for example, that the entrenched Protestant elite, despite their rhetoric of tolerance and equality, frequently could not embrace the embodied presence of Jews when it came to intimacy in country clubs and other prestigious institutions.[90] But the scene in which Portnoy's representative elite WASP, Sarah Abbott Maulsby, gags on his erect penis—"It's getting big. I'll suffocate," she cries (240)—extends this critique in terms inappropriate for social scientists. "My father couldn't rise at Boston & Northeastern," Portnoy rants, making the point unmistakably, "for the very same reason Sally Maulsby wouldn't deign to go down on me!" (238). By rendering a dynamic of social life in these frankly sexual terms, Roth transforms it into something both comic and resonant. The scene lampoons the discrimination as ridiculous, and, indirectly, it satirizes the tepid protests of the social scientists who had described such racist phenomena in dry language and without capturing the emotional experience of being made to feel socially repulsive. Roth's scene portrays Judeophobia as manifested by American Protestants, with their closed country clubs and preferential promotions, as the ultimate in absurdity—has anyone ever actually been suffocated by an erect penis?—while clarifying just how deeply it hurts to be rejected socially and bodily because of one's Jewishness. Contrary, then, to a feminist cultural historian's reading of Portnoy's emphasis on fellatio as "the height of narcissistic liberation" and "the ultimate replacement for the masturbating hand," in this scene, at least, Roth's representation of oral sex serves to vivify a critique of American social relations.[91]

What *is* true of Portnoy's sex acts is that they are emphatically, uniformly, nonreproductive.[92] Not only is his girlfriend Mary Jane Reed on the birth control pill, but when the two hire an Italian prostitute in Rome, Portnoy insists they educate the woman about contraception and presents her with "a month's supply of . . . Enovid" (140). Tellingly, at the one moment when Portnoy believes he may have reproduced biologically—when, in college, his non-Jewish girlfriend Kay Campbell "misse[s] a period"—Portnoy finds himself insisting that this impending biological reproduction must be cultural, too: "And you'll convert, right?" he asks Kay ("intend[ing] the question to be received as ironic" but admitting that when she demurs, it infuriates him and later that he "never forgave her"; 230–31). This scene suggests that the nonreproductive nature of Portnoy's sexual behavior is anything but incidental; birth control allows him to defer indefinitely the issue of cultural reproduction that bedevils him. One version of the final chapter of *Portnoy's Complaint* that Roth drafted but discarded begins with the words "She's pregnant!"; other drafts dramatically stage the scene in which Portnoy, returned from Israel, is told by Mary Jane that she has missed two periods.[93] That this chapter was discarded as a "false ending" to the novel—which is how it is labeled, in Roth's handwriting, in his archived papers—suggests just how unreproductive Portnoy's sexuality had to be.

This reading helps to explain the importance of impotence and masturbation in *Portnoy's Complaint*. If Portnoy's attraction to *shikses* can be read as the author's insightful and playful commentary on anxieties about the threats to cultural reproduction posed by the lure of America, so too can his impotent, failed attempt to rape an Israeli woman and his infamously enthusiastic masturbation be understood as allegorizing other sociopolitical possibilities.

Portnoy's interactions with Israelis obviously function as a way for Roth to consider the possibilities of American Zionism: no more sympathetically drawn, and no less allegorical than the *shikses*, the Israeli girl he encounters, Naomi, is an "ideological hunk of a girl" (258) and, indeed, more "ideological hunk" than "girl." Within minutes of meeting her, Portnoy is already contemplating marriage (259), parodying the intense attraction of post-1967 Zionism to American Jews, seeming, as it did, to offer a dramatic solution to the instabilities of Jewish identity.[94] Naomi represents Zionism as an ideology Portnoy might embrace, as a strikingly endogamic corrective to his failed attempts at exogamy: she offers the opportunity for him to reproduce Jewishly. "Be my wife," he begs her. "Mother my children" (263). The scribbled notes that Roth scrawled while planning and drafting this novel suggest how deeply the author considered positioning Zionism, as represented by Naomi, as the solution to Portnoy's reproductive anxieties. A snippet in one of Roth's notebooks reads, "ends in Israel—*return*," while another note reads, "In Israel—here don't have to fight the goy. The issue is resolved."[95]

Roth decided that Naomi and Zionism would not be Portnoy's answer, though. At least in this allegorical fiction, Zionism would not be proclaimed the salvation of the American Jew, counter to so much post-1967 ebullience. Finally ready for commitment, Portnoy discovers to his dismay that, aside from Naomi's complete antipathy to his overtures, he "can't get a hard-on in this place": he's "Im-po-tent in Israel" (268). Roth does not leave his readers guessing as to what might cause this case of the "most prevalent form of degradation in erotic life," either, but spells it out as if copying directly from Karl Abraham's 1913 essay "On Neurotic Exogamy."[96] Portnoy reports of Naomi, "in physical type she is, of course, my mother" (259), later calling her a "mother-substitute" and "offspring of the same pale Polish strain of Jews" as "the lady of [his] past," that is, Mrs. Portnoy (266). That Naomi the Zionist resembles (or even "is"!) Portnoy's mother likewise accords well with standard analyses of the role of mothers in American Jewish culture in midcentury. The historian Paula Hyman argues, for example, that American Jewish mothers in the postwar period assumed responsibility for "Jewish survival broadly conceived," and not only because the matrilineal principle meant that they were the only source of Jewish children.[97] Since the Jewish mother had come to be seen as the figure responsible for, and thus representing, the cultural reproduction of Jewishness, an unambiguous embrace of one's Jewish identity in the form of Zionism naturally could be figured by an embrace of one's mother: the endogamic alternative to Portnoy's exogamic misadventures smacks, as endogamy always does, of incest.[98] And, as Freud predicted in the 1912 essay that is the most important explicit intertext of Roth's novel, the "culmination of the Oedipal drama" (266) for Portnoy is not, as in Sophocles's *Oedipus Rex*, copulation with his mother but, as in the cases of Freud's patients, "psychic impotence." Becoming Israeli and embracing Zionism, in this allegory (and not only in this allegory), means forgoing the insider-outsider positioning of diasporic life that has been celebrated by some theorists of Jewishness since at least the early 20th century and accepting instead an incestuous embrace of all-Jewish reproduction.[99] Portnoy cannot do this.

Ruling out both exogamy and endogamy—and concluding on an ambivalently manic note—*Portnoy's Complaint* is notorious for reserving its protagonist one sexual experience that he can enjoy almost unreservedly: masturbation. Extending the allegorical reading of Portnoy's desire for *shikses* and a *sabra*, his masturbation might be read as a path between the Scylla of exogamy/assimilation and the Charybdis of endogamy/Zionism. As one literary scholar has noted (punning perhaps unintentionally), Portnoy's masturbation is "intimately related to incestuous impulses toward his mother and sister"[100]—yet unlike the sex he tries to have with Naomi, which proves impossible because of its incestuous resonances, masturbation remains viable even when it verges on incest, as when Portnoy ejaculates into his sister's bra (22). Portnoy's masturbation, like the fictional ideology Roth named "Diasporism" later in his career, functions by mixing fantasies and unconscious urges both endogamic and exogamic and works for him because it never threatens to lead to reproduction at all.[101] While the text suggests a nascent consciousness of Diasporism in Portnoy—he identifies with Holocaust victims as "Diaspora Jews just like [him]self" (265) and proclaims that he is a "patriot," "only" in a place where he does not "feel at home" (271), a fair description of a Diasporist's sense of location—and while it is easy to hear a masturbating Diasporist manifesto in the offing in Portnoy's speeches ("Just leave us alone, God damn it," he pleads, "to pull our little dongs in peace and think our little selfish thoughts" [122]), it does not seem necessary to rest too much weight on a reading that ultimately just demonstrates that there can be considerably more at stake in Portnoy's compulsive masturbation than in, say, a bawdy teen comedy movie. Roth's later novels treating Zionism and the Diaspora, *The Counterlife* (1986) and *Operation: Shylock* (1993), elaborate his thoughts on these subjects in brilliant detail. Yet it seems worth emphasizing that when A. B. Yehoshua, the Israeli novelist and political activist, proclaimed to an interviewer in March 2003 that "Diaspora Judaism is masturbation," he was echoing the central joke of Roth's most widely read novel.[102]

Mother-Son Incest as Radical Feminist Allegory: *Crackpot*

Rejecting endogamy as incestuous, Portnoy can only masturbate or have fundamentally antiprocreative sex. He reflects, in this sense, and with the sexual frankness made possible by the transformations of U.S. obscenity law, the crisis of Jewish reproduction that terrified American Jewish leaders by the mid-1960s, that intensified in the early 1970s, and that came to dominate the communal agenda for decades to follow. The postwar American Jewish reproduction crisis was not just, as the literary scholar Walter Benn Michaels has remarked, of a different order than the Nazi threat to Jewish survival;[103] it was also, in a sense, real only in the minds of those who feared it. Intermarriage threatens the American Jewish population only if Jews and their non-Jewish partners, and Jewish communal institutions, accede to the notion that intermarried couples cannot raise Jewish children. Some sociologists have more recently argued that intermarriage can create a substantial increase in the Jewish population, if non-Jewish spouses and the children of these marriages are counted as members of the Jewish community. The supposed crisis could be averted, then, simply by thinking differently about Jewish reproduction, as some Jewish institutions and authorities in the United States have done, for one example, by beginning to accept patrilineal as well as matrilineal descent, starting in the mid-1980s. Such alternative thinking about Jewish reproduction was on display, early, in a fascinating novel by the Canadian author Adele Wiseman. In *Crackpot* (1974), Wiseman employs the newly available language of graphic sexuality to articulate a radical vision of Jewish reproduction, largely by embracing as a meaningful allegorical possibility the prospect of mother-son incest that *Portnoy's Complaint*, and other novels of the period, dismissed as an unsettling joke.

In a discussion of Charles Chesnutt's "The Wife of His Youth" and Abraham Cahan's *Yekl*, the influential scholar of ethnic American literature Werner Sollors reads the romantic choices of the fictions' protagonists as representing a contest of "descent" and "consent": will the character choose to align himself with his family history or with the freedom of association made possible in modern America? To make this point, Sollors demonstrates how one of the potential spouses in each of the stories is associated with the protagonist's parents, and in passing, he suggests that "we might have expected Ryder's and Yekl's choice to be one between parent and spouse."[104] Who could argue? It would be a striking fictional effect indeed if Ryder were forced to choose not between his wife and a new girlfriend but between a young woman and his own mother for his sexual and reproductive partner. Jewish protagonists have implicitly faced such choices, between their mothers and *shikses*, certainly—Jackie Robin, in *The Jazz Singer* (1927), is one well-known example—but never had sexual intercourse with a character's mother been a viable narrative possibility. Indeed, it would have been illegal, not to mention deeply unsettling, to represent parent-child incest explicitly when Cahan and Chesnutt were writing or in the *Jazz Singer* or at any time up to 1966. The very term that most succinctly and unflinchingly alludes to such a potential relationship, *motherfucker*, which seems to have originated as African American slang, was among the most proscribed words in the English language and one of the last to become available for literary use.[105] By the late 1960s, though, thanks to the developments in American obscenity law, it had become legal, if not exactly conventional, to describe in explicit terms even such an unusual "libidinal investment" as mother-fucking.[106]

Wiseman's novel goes there, as we will see. Before discussing the scene itself, though, it is worth mentioning that the extraordinary difficulties Wiseman had in placing the book with a publisher reflect the "unsettling" quality of a novel that inverts the Oedipal myth by narrating it from the perspective of the mother, portraying the sexual intimacy between a woman and her son as a profoundly ethical and necessary, if heartbreaking, act.[107] Wiseman conceived the idea for *Crackpot* in 1961, in New York, around the time of the first crucial obscenity cases in both the United States and Canada that heralded the upcoming legal developments, and she drafted the book repeatedly throughout the ensuing decade.[108] She had every reason to be confident that her manuscript would receive sympathetic attention. Her first novel, *The Sacrifice* (1956), a heavily symbolic reworking of Biblical themes and the story of a devout Jewish immigrant to Canada who loses his son and then commits a murder, had been published to critical acclaim in Canada, the United States, and England, generating more prepublication sales, according to one source, than any Canadian novel in history.[109] For that debut, Wiseman won the Governor General's Award for Fiction,

Canada's most prestigious literary prize; was granted residencies at Yaddo and the MacDowell Colony, the two most prominent American artists' colonies; and received a Guggenheim fellowship on the basis of recommendations from a group of Jewish cultural and literary authorities: Saul Bellow, David Daiches, Irving Howe, and Meyer Levin.[110] In the late 1960s, Wiseman's second novel, as she finished it, promised to have just as much potential for critical and marketplace success as her first: early drafts of *Crackpot* had been praised by Margaret Laurence, a major Canadian author, and by Malcolm Ross, one of the country's most famous literary impresarios.[111] Mordecai Richler, who had by then made an international name for himself with such novels as *The Apprenticeship of Duddy Kravitz* (1959) and *Cocksure* (1968), solicited an excerpt from *Crackpot* for a 1970 anthology of contemporary Canadian fiction he edited.[112] Moreover, Wiseman's book was submitted to publishers by perhaps the most prominent literary agent in the United States of that period, Candida Donadio, who represented, among many other clients, Philip Roth, Thomas Pynchon, John Cheever, and Eudora Welty.[113] In short, *Crackpot* was submitted for consideration to publishers with the highest possible literary pedigree. All that notwithstanding, the U.S. publisher of *The Sacrifice*, Viking, rejected *Crackpot* summarily in 1968, and then, over the next several years, no fewer than twenty-five major publishing houses in the United States, Canada, and England also declined to publish the manuscript.[114]

These rejections of a celebrated novelist's sophomore project, while surprising, are not in this case difficult to explain. As Ruth Panofsky and Marcia Mack have pointed out, and as Wiseman herself seems to have realized, *Crackpot* is a radical feminist departure from, and rewriting of, the fairly conventional, patriarchal themes of *The Sacrifice*[115]—and it is much more radically feminist than, for example, Erica Jong's famed *Fear of Flying*.[116] Finally released in 1974 by McClelland and Stewart—then, as now, among the most prestigious of Canadian publishing houses—Wiseman's book received mixed reviews but was celebrated by a few of its early critics as a creative triumph. It was called "one of the more important novels in recent literature," and an early academic respondent characterized the novel as "the most alive, daring, and tempestuously human literary creation in Canadian storytelling."[117] At the same time, *Crackpot* received one scathing review that baldly reflected the reactionary response to Wiseman's book that some of the publishers that rejected it likely had feared. This reviewer, a Canadian academic named Ernest G. Mardon, expressed "horror and disgust" in finding *Crackpot* "pornographic," "a modern Canadian version of the notorious Fanny Hill."[118] That *Crackpot* disturbed a reviewer so deeply testifies to what Tamara Palmer calls "*Crackpot*'s complex and profoundly radical nature," as well as Wiseman's commitment to writing "what was hardest and most important to [her]."[119]

Part of what was "most important" to Wiseman, evidently, was to employ the full expressive range of English, including the language prohibited as obscenity in the United States and Canada until the mid-1960s. In a reminiscence of her childhood, Wiseman makes this clear:

> There were certain words that had such strong feelings attached to them that I had a hard time using them. But I knew that if I was going to be a writer I would have to have the whole world of words at my disposal, in spite of how my upbringing had taught me to feel about them. . . . So I stood in front of the mirror and practised saying "shit" out loud, "shit shit shit," trying not to cringe inside. I still get a little twinge when I hear or use certain words, though publicly I can certainly pass for a familiar.[120]

This description of what Wiseman called her "training" is fascinating as a declaration of the importance of taboo words to a novelist, but the passage also has an uncanny retrospective quality. When Wiseman was a teenager, in the 1940s, it would have been difficult for a young woman even to get her hands on a novel with the word *shit* in it, such as *Call It Sleep* or *Tropic of Cancer*. This passage suggests either that as a child Wiseman had a precociously avant-garde understanding of the literature she would one day write or perhaps that as an adult she wanted to remember herself as always having been committed to obscene modernism.

Wiseman's second novel certainly lives up to that commitment. It turns out, that is, that a dispute about obscenity—a disagreement about how sex can be described in public—motivates the plot of *Crackpot*. The confrontation with authority that pushes the novel's protagonist, Hoda, out of school and into sexual intercourse with a classmate, starting her on the path that leads to prostitution, has almost nothing to do with sex but everything to do with the alleged obscenity of a Jewish story. In the novel's fourth chapter, Hoda's teacher informs the class that, as an exercise in "Oral Expression," each student will present a short speech about "some special aspect of himself that he considered most interesting, like a hobby or a dream or an event that had most affected him."[121] The story Hoda chooses to tell is one that her father recounts to her repeatedly and is the subject of the novel's first chapter. In short, Hoda's father was blind and her mother had a slight hunchback, so the two were married off in their European shtetl according to the folk wisdom that a "black wedding" curries favor with God and can prevent a plague from spreading or a pogrom from starting (24).[122] In Hoda's father's telling, this event and the death in infancy of the couple's first child comprise the family's extraordinary good fortune, as they led to Hoda's birth (14). When her turn in class arrives, Hoda relays this family history without uttering a single taboo word: "You have to get two very poor people who can't help themselves," she explains. "And you have to take them to the graveyard, the Jewish graveyard. . . . And they get married, right there in the graveyard, with everyone watching" (138). From her priggish teacher's perspective, however, Hoda's description is the very definition of obscenity:

> What did [Hoda] mean by "married"? What exactly did she mean? . . . Suddenly [the teacher] knew exactly where Hoda was leading, saw in disgusting detail the whole obscene picture, the wretched couple of cripples copulating in the graveyard while a bearded, black-robed, fierce-eyed rabbi stood over them, uttering God knows what blasphemies. . . . [She] was positively sick to the stomach with the vividness of it. (138)

To describe people "copulating" in "disgusting detail" is precisely, according to a century's worth of legal precedent, to break the law of obscenity. The irony, of course, is that "the whole obscene picture" is not painted by Hoda but supplied by the teacher's imagination, as if to furnish a precise illustration of a point made about obscenity by the free-speech pioneer Theodore Schroeder, that "obscenity and indecency are not sense-perceived qualities of a book, but are solely and exclusively a condition or effect in the reading mind."[123] There is no way that

Hoda could tell her family's story without offending her teacher, that is, if her utterance of the words "very poor people . . . get married" are to be heard as "cripples copulating." Her personal history—not to mention much modern Jewish literature, which repeats the same folk motif—is, by this standard, inevitably obscene. The teacher shames and punishes Hoda for what she has said, and it is in the wake of this fiasco that Hoda has sexual intercourse for the first time as an act of rebellion against her teacher's impossible standards. "To hell with [the teacher]," she thinks. "To hell with any of them who didn't like her. . . . Nobody was going to tell her what to do. If she wanted to she'd even fuck them all!" (150). This sudden appearance of the word "fuck"—referring to sexual intercourse for the first time in the novel—signals that Hoda has undergone a transformation that is at the same time both linguistic and experiential.

Many chapters later, *Crackpot*'s plot climaxes with Hoda's decision to have sex with her son. The boy, David, has been raised in an orphanage. His nickname, Pipick (from the Yiddish for "bellybutton"), derives from his dissevered connection with his mother: having delivered the baby herself, alone in her home, Hoda "gnawed" through the umbilical cord, leaving him with a bellybutton of unusual size and shape (211, 234).[124] Pipick does not know that Hoda, the neighborhood prostitute, is his mother, nor does Hoda realize who Pipick is when he first visits her. They have sex. Pipick, an overexcited virgin, ejaculates prematurely, but he lingers on in Hoda's house after her other customers have left, hoping that she will offer him a second opportunity. As he talks to her, she suddenly realizes that he is the son she left at the orphanage many years earlier. Understanding this, Hoda reacts violently when Pipick tries to initiate sex a second time, begging him not to sleep with her, without letting on what she has realized. Saying "I'm old enough to be your mother" is the closest she comes to revealing their actual kinship, for fear of traumatizing the boy (347–49). Unfortunately, Pipick desperately wants to have sex with her again—he yearns to prove his virility and compensate himself for his earlier embarrassment—and he takes Hoda's rejection as cruelty: "Why don't you tell me, 'You're a freak; I don't want to fuck you!'" he asks her, self-pityingly. "No one wants to fuck a freak, even if he pays you!" (351). Hoda hates to see the boy suffer—she has committed to prostitution in part because of her unwillingness to spurn the advances of lonely men, and she cares more deeply about Pipick's happiness and comfort than anyone else's—and so the novel's crisis finally boils down to this awful dilemma: should she have sex with her son again or not?

As suggested earlier, this dilemma can be read as a radical rewriting of the allegories of assimilation that figure the selection of a sex partner as a symbol of the success or failure of cultural reproduction. The radical twist that Wiseman applies to the traditional allegory is to displace Pipick—the young man, who typically serves as a representative ethnic subject, in much modern fiction, by choosing a sexual partner for himself—from the central role as her narrative's protagonist. She replaces him with his mother, who represents in this allegorical scheme not the ethnic individual but the ethnic community. The book's primary concern is not with David's sexual choices but with Hoda's, and to her, sex is both a means of intense personal connection and a constantly renewable "gift" that she can give to everyone (60). Hoda's approach to sex constitutes a sort of utopian, species-level cosmopolitanism; she embraces anyone who wants to have sex with her in a peaceful and respectful way, whether he is rich or poor, Jew or gentile, healthy or ill.[125] Yet her sexual practices never undermine Hoda's Jewishness: in contrast to the typical hero of a *shikse* narrative—as well as the hypothetical Jew in the Talmud who is rendered physically non-Jewish because of sexual intercourse with a non-Jewish woman—Hoda's Jewishness is simply not vulnerable.[126] This can be understood as a radical recuperation of the matrilineal principle, as the guarantee of the Jewishness of a Jewish woman no matter her choices or behavior. At no moment in the novel is there any suggestion that Hoda could ever be anything other than Jewish. By positioning a Jewish prostitute, with her hundreds of sexual partners, at the center of a sexually allegorical narrative, Wiseman eschews the pernicious either/or logic that propels most male-centered narratives of Jewish exogamy: to wit, either you are a Jew and sleep with a Jew, or you sleep with a non-Jew and are therefore not Jewish. Instead, sex as a metaphor for affiliation in this feminist frame allows for the representative Jew to have multiple, shifting, overlapping, joyful affiliations. And, again, in a brave reimagining of the implications of the matrilineal principle, while Hoda does not know who Pipick's father is—it could be any one of her clients, and in her naiveté she believes that all of them collectively fathered him—there is also no doubt in her or anyone else's mind, in the novel, that Hoda's son, like her, is a Jew.

Hoda chooses to have sex with her own son rather than exclude him, not just once but as often as he likes (352, 366). And the novel endorses, rather than rejects, this decision: in the chapters that follow, Hoda is rewarded with a measure of satisfaction and happiness. The novel's toleration, even endorsement, of mother-son incest demands to be read allegorically, not only because the narrative reflects so powerfully on the Jewish allegorical tradition adumbrated earlier in this chapter, and not simply in response to markers of allegorical intention in the text, but also because studies of human sexuality have shown, Oedipus notwithstanding, that mother-son incest is very rare in practice while father-daughter and sibling incest are relatively common. The rareness of actual, as opposed to imagined, mother-son incest suggests that Wiseman was almost certainly not, in *Crackpot*, responding to a real-life story she had heard (as she responded to a newspaper account of a murder in crafting her first novel, *The Sacrifice*) but rather employing the plot device that best served the narrative, aesthetic, and symbolic requirements of the novel.[127] In *Crackpot*, Wiseman writes back to the wave of Jewish mother jokes and tales of smothering Jewish mothers that crested in the 1960s, and to the related ambivalence at the center of *Portnoy's Complaint*, answering them by following their logic to its conclusion.[128] *Crackpot* embraces the Jewish mother and the Jewish cultural reproduction that she represents.

In doing so, Wiseman's novel diverges sharply from almost all previous literary treatments of incest.[129] If, according to an allegorical reading, David represents the paradigmatic ethnic subject whose choice of exogamy or endogamy stands for the success or failure of Jewish cultural reproduction, Hoda, as his mother, represents what Sollors calls "descent": the traditional Jewish community, which is genealogically and historically Jewish. Such an allegorical scheme is consistent with the representational patterns found in modern Jewish literature and particularly with those of American Jewish culture in the postwar decades.[130] Hoda, as a Jewish mother, embodies Jewish reproduction; she aspires to "achieve a proper, loving friendship with [Pipick] in which she could work for him as she did for Daddy, and teach him their stories, and protect him and help him avoid all those traps that she knew were waiting for him in life" (363). She wants to mother him, to aid his progress, and, crucially, to expose him to the Jewish culture she knows in the form of her father's "stories." The chain of Jewish knowledge dramatized in *Crackpot*, with Jewish culture passing from Hoda's father to Hoda to her son, accords perfectly with the sociocultural pattern in which mothers displaced fathers as the conveyors of Jewish identity in North America after World War II. Simply put, Hoda's being a mother is not at all incidental; if she had been a father, a story about the sexual relationship between her and her child would reflect an entirely different perspective on the possibilities of Jewish continuity.[131] Astonishingly, it is Hoda's sexual connection to her son that allows her to pass on to Pipick her father's stories, which constitute her personal connection to the Jewish past (Pipick "must learn what was important in the stories still," Hoda feels [362]): as one of Wiseman's readers has remarked, "Hoda reclaims her son through incest."[132] In presenting this dynamic, in which mother-son sex is part and parcel of, or at least a resonant symbol for, the potential for cultural reproduction, Wiseman concretizes the challenge of endogamy—that is, the taint of incestuous insularity that marrying in and embracing the culture of one's own group always carries. *Crackpot* declares it an unavoidable necessity for Pipick, or any modern Jew, to follow Freud's advice that in order "to be really free and happy in love" a man must "come to terms with the idea of incest with mother or sister," only slightly modified: in order to be really free and happy as a Jew, a man must come to terms with the idea of incest with his mother or sister, as Alex Portnoy cannot.[133] It is not the "universal siblinghood" that the literary scholar Marc Shell notes is usually symbolized by brother-sister incest that Wiseman proffers as a model for a progressive Jewish community—not, that is, the universalist idea that all humans can be siblings—but rather mother-child incest that allegorizes a particularistic desire for continuity even if it requires some exclusivity and inwardness.

In the novel's dreamlike concluding passage, David reappears to pronounce an obscure but positive judgment on his mother's connection with tradition ("She occupies her past; she inhabits her life," he says [427]) and then to be included in *Crackpot*'s final image of community. Unlike Roth's novel, which ends with Portnoy's alienation and grief and emphasizes the protagonist's alienation, *Crackpot* ultimately focuses on Hoda and on her reconstitution of a Jewish community on her own terms. She has created a community that is neither wholly predicated on descent nor on consent but created through a fluid mixture of affiliations: in Hoda's vague but affirmative vision, Hoda, her father, her son, and her new lover "would all be stirring the muddy waters of the brimming pot together" (427). Hoda's community is not based exclusively on genealogy—indeed, it counters the notion of a racial Judaism, in which identity is determined exclusively by a biological relationship to one's ancestors—but neither does it entirely eschew genealogical relationships. Wiseman's vision, frankly utopian, is of a Jewish community generous and resilient enough not to be troubled by temporary disaffection or wholly dependent on genealogical reproduction but to be open to all those who wish to join it.

This vision of Jewish cultural reproduction parallels others that were being worked out by progressive and countercultural Jews who founded *havurot* (prayer fellowships) in the late 1960s and early 1970s, in the same years that Donadio was shopping Wiseman's novel around to publishers. Arthur Waskow echoed the central tropes of Wiseman's novel in 1971—well before *Crackpot*'s publication, that is—arguing that in the 1960s "the melting pot . . . shattered" and calling for "the building of a new society and the dismantling of the old, with loving care," with "the other peoples of the Earth . . . rising alongside us."[134] The *havurah* movement was a return to Jewish affiliation by young Jews who had been allied with the New Left but disheartened by its antipathy toward Jewish causes and concerns, not least among which was Zionism.[135] Note that Waskow refers to Jews as "us" and to "other peoples" as separate constituencies; his is not an image, as Wiseman's novel is not, of universal siblinghood. As Riv-Ellen Prell observes in her study of the *havurot*, "Havurah members wove together tradition and innovation as essential components of an authentic Judaism," and they shunned simple accounts of Jewishness as passing genealogically from parents to children. Such countercultural Jews "sought their mythological past, one that would inform, though not control, their present and future, . . . [and] yearned for continuity even as they separated themselves from their parents' and grandparents' lives."[136]

Wiseman's novel offers a literary model for how communities such as this might envision and reproduce themselves through its studious attention to Jewish history and theology and its unflagging commitment to the project of rewriting and reshaping Jewish traditions according to its own progressive politics. The following passage describes Hoda's exemplary response to her father's stories, which have stood throughout the novel as her primary connection to the Jewish past and which she begins to listen to again after her sexual encounter with Pipick:

> If she had hoped to hear those stories once again as a child hears, she was disappointed. But she was not aware of such a hope, nor of the disappointment of being barred from a return to innocence. She simply felt the old stories, felt her emptiness filled with resonance, transformed to resonance. She saw the old stories, saw through the old stories, saw beyond the old stories to what the man her father was and what the woman her mother must have been; she heard the stories and knew them all, and gathered them back into herself and knew herself as well, not as she had once known herself, in a sudden, comprehensive flash of revelation, a simultaneity of multiple Hodas, but as she flowed in the sequence of her days. (362)

Eschewing a conservative desire to "hear those stories once again as a child hears," to re-create precisely her past experience or to understand her culture reductively, Hoda seeks a more creative and intense engagement with these narratives. The careful Biblical mimicry of this passage—the repetition and parataxis and the faux-archaic phrasing of "flowed in the sequence of her days," for example—and the emphasis on the repurposing (seeing "through" and "beyond") "old stories" anticipate many of the formal gestures of the second-wave feminist literature and theology produced in the later 1970s, especially as it was undertaken by feminist Jewish women.[137] Tellingly, Wiseman selects the same verb to capture Hoda's newfound comfort in her multiplicity that Robert Greenblatt did, in a polemic on his place in the Jewish counterculture published in 1971: "I am a Jew, an American, a Revolutionary," he wrote. "I am all three at once because each flows out of and merges into one life history."[138] Considering when *Crackpot* was drafted—years before the women's movement garnered national attention in 1969 and 1970 and even before the first countercultural *havurah* was established in 1968[139]—Wiseman's perspicacity is stunning. As a response to crises of "identity and assimilation," that is, to the conflicts between Jews' desires to reproduce Jewishly and to participate fully in non-Jewish social and political communities, Hoda's openness to incest with her son allegorically represents the path pursued by feminists and the countercultural *havurah* movement, but with a more nuanced understanding than her contemporaries manifested of one challenge facing progressive Jews.

Can Jews reproduce—create Jewish offspring—without affirming retrograde, racialist standards of what it means to be Jewish and without isolating the Jewish community from the wider American population and its causes? Yes, *Crackpot* insists, though the book remains adamant through its representation of incest that this communal reproduction will perforce necessitate the uncomfortable demand on individuals to embrace endogamy, to love their own first and best. Wiseman's novel promises that even a Portnoy and a Pipick can find lasting love, as could Arthur Levy and Brudno's David and all the other protagonists of the dozens and dozens of *shikse* novels, but that to do so, they must "come to terms with the idea of incest."

"The Whole World of Words"

The use of graphic sexual allegory to describe dilemmas of cultural reproduction—a woman choking on an erect penis as a symbol of genteel exclusion, or a mother choosing to have sex with her son as a representation of a radical commitment to community—was hardly inevitable, nor was it in any sense necessitated by the transformations in obscenity law that took place in the 1960s. Moreover, such explicit sexual allegories were always just as useful to tell Catholic, African American, or homosexual stories as they were to tell Jewish ones; importantly, the nature of narratives of exogamy, whether graphic or not, is that they are almost always about the relationship between two or more communities. Certainly none of the Jewish lawyers or entrepreneurs who contributed to the dismantling of the Comstock Act did so with the expressed intention of making a book such as *Crackpot* possible. Yet the most committed and insightful of these figures, such as Harriet Pilpel, understood precisely that no one would know exactly what could be done with obscenity until the laws were defeated in court. They may have intuited, too, that dilemmas of reproduction—which, early in the century, had found their paradigms in the challenges facing Jewish immigrants and working women—could be clarified by artists who had at their disposal what Wiseman called "the whole world of words."

4

Seductive Modesty

Censorship versus Yiddish and Orthodox Tsnies

In the late 1980s and 1990s, scholarly treatments of literary censorship in the United States changed in reaction to a series of cultural and political developments. On the one hand, under the Reagan and Bush administrations, artists' work was subject to renewed attempts by the government to suppress sexual explicitness. Robert Mapplethorpe and other artists were attacked by conservative politicians including Jesse Helms, and criminal charges were brought against the curator of a Cincinnati museum for a show of Mapplethorpe's photographs.[1] At the same time, prominent conservative politicians were busy appropriating the free-speech rhetoric of previous generations of liberals and radicals: in a commencement address at the University of Michigan at Ann Arbor in 1991, President George H. W. Bush emphasized that "the freedom to speak one's mind . . . may be the most fundamental and deeply revered of all our liberties." And yet, he went on, "we find free speech under assault throughout the United States, including on some college campuses." The students and faculty in his audience would have recalled that the University of Michigan's speech code had been the subject of a 1989 court battle. Addressing that case, if only obliquely, President Bush suggested that "what began as a crusade for civility has soured into a cause of conflict and even censorship."[2]

That President Bush could position his administration as opposing "censorship," and liberal campus administrators as the new Comstocks, complicated matters for academics who had until then been able to see themselves as opposing censorship *tout court*. Introducing a 1994 collection of essays, the literary scholar Richard Burt explained, "Opposing censorship is generally assumed to be a straightforward matter. . . . The right is for [censorship], the left is against it." "Yet," Burt continued, "many recent events do not resolve themselves easily into neat conceptual oppositions and identities."[3] One way that literary and cultural theorists such as Judith Butler and Stanley Fish reacted to this situation was to eschew any simple notion of censorship as evil and of free speech as unalloyed good.[4] They drew on Sigmund Freud's and Pierre Bourdieu's metaphorical uses of the term *censorship* ("*zensur*" and "*censure*") to refer to, respectively, a process that operates within an individual's psyche or an inevitable effect of social, economic, and linguistic structures.[5] For Butler and especially Fish, censorship operates every time anyone speaks or writes, as forces always regulate expression and a person always chooses to utter specific words and not others.[6] As Fish puts it, "Some form of speech is always being restricted, else there could be no meaningful assertion."[7]

This line of reasoning works, intentionally, to blur the distinction between the formal and legal censorship imposed by states (and other coercive hierarchical institutions) and all the more nebulous regulations of expression that might occur, including self-censorships, market censorship, boycotts, and even the revisions imposed by editors on authors. In the years that followed, such approaches to censorship as a broad category that includes any imposition of aesthetic or cultural limitation became common, even dominant, not only in popular culture and the press (which have always played fast and loose with First Amendment terminology) but also in literary studies. Florence Dore argues in her 2005 study *The Novel and the Obscene*, for example, that modernist authors' "'negative narration' reproduces censorship, renders it symbolic at the very moment of its legal demise."[8] While her readings are compelling, Dore does not always distinguish between "symbolic" censorship and the other, nonsymbolic, kind: in an introductory aside, she treats as an act of censorship (not explicitly a symbolic one) a museum director's decision not to grant Dore permission to reproduce an image from the museum's collection on the cover of her book.[9] If that can be considered censorship, so must every licensing decision, every enforcement of copyright, every editor's suggestion for revision, every proofreader's correction, every choice any individual makes not to sell or read a specific book or to exhibit or watch a particular film.

Bourdieu himself cautioned against blurring the distinctions between real and metaphorical censorships in this way: "The metaphor of censorship should not mislead," he writes in *Language and Symbolic Power*, emphasizing that it is only an analogy to characterize as "censorship," as he does, "the structure of the field itself which governs expression by governing both access to expression and the form of expression," in contrast to the literal understanding of censorship as a "legal proceeding which has been specially adapted to designate and repress the transgression of a kind of linguistic code."[10] The metaphoric censorships addressed by Freud and Bourdieu—and Fish, Butler, Dore, and many others after them—have consequences just as powerful, if not more so, than censorship per se, as Theodor Adorno and Max Horkheimer noted.[11] They surely deserve scholars' attention. But given that we live at a time during which journalists, novelists, and poets continue to be jailed and executed, in which books are being burned by militias, and in which governments (including the U.S. government) continue to determine which words and images can be published through the exercise of police power, it seems an error to conflate all symbolic and noncoercive textual suppressions with *censorship*—which term, after all, has an etymological connection with the exercise of state power.[12] The Roman censor was no self-appointed guardian of morality but a functionary empowered by the government.

This chapter puts forth a different term for the nongovernmental and cultural dynamics through which sexual expression is restrained or suppressed in literature and culture (an alternative to, or subset of, Burt's more general but sympathetic term, "the administration of aesthetics"). The term advanced here for characterizing and analyzing such suppressions of sexual representation—imposed by individual psyches, by social fields, or by markets—is, simply, the same one that Yiddish literary critics typically used to describe the regulation of sexual expression in their cultural field: modesty (in Yiddish, *tsnies* and, in Hebrew, *tzniut*).[13] Using modesty as a frame for reading the regulation of sexual expression in America, this chapter argues that American Yiddish literary modernism, which was virtually never subject to government intervention, presaged the situation of American literature in English after *Memoirs v. Massachusetts* (1966), which established broad First Amendment protections for literature.

The structural parallels between the discourse of literary and cultural modesty that was established in American Yiddish contexts and the new situation of American literature as a whole after the legal transformations of the 1960s and 1970s suggest one explanation for a curious phenomenon that developed simultaneously with the retheorization of censorship by Butler, Fish, and others in the 1990s: that is, the emergence of a widely circulated, popular American discourse of sexual and cultural modesty in which otherwise obscure Orthodox Jewish sexual and behavioral practices could be at least rhetorically embraced by non-Jewish Americans and particularly by political and Christian conservatives and by the mainstream press. Offering a comparative study of two related modesty discourses—early 20th-century Yiddish literary modesty and late 20th-century American cultural modesty as it was rooted in the sources of Orthodox Judaism—this chapter demonstrates that modesty discourses follow from and reflect the diasporization of culture, the uncoupling of cultural production from both the constraints and the opportunities of legal control and state support. What the vogue for Orthodox Jewish ideas about modesty in the 1990s reflects, then, is how much critics of contemporary American culture might learn about their field from attention to the American Yiddish literary culture of the preceding decades.

The Structural Obstacle to Jewish Censorships

Discussing the role of Jews in the development of the U.S. publishing industry, Jonathan Freedman has suggested that "if there is a common denominator . . . linking Horace Liveright, [Emanuel] Haldeman-Julius, Bennett Cerf, and later Jewish publishers like Barney Rosset of Grove Press, it would be a strong antipathy to censorship and a questioning of authority over the dispersion of words, which has been a strong impulse in Jewish culture from the Haskalah forward."[14] While Freedman is certainly correct to note that all of these publishers opposed Comstockery, it does not seem likely that they related to the Haskalah, the Jewish Enlightenment, in parallel ways or, to be more specific, that both the cosmopolitan gadfly Cerf and the entrepreneurial socialist

Haldeman-Julius formed their ideas about censorship based on shared readings of, say, Moses Mendelssohn. As has been noted elsewhere in this book, other American Jews, equally descendants and beneficiaries of the Haskalah, have been vehement in their support of Comstockery; one cannot generalize about the ways in which simply being Jewish will influence the attitudes of an individual American. One might understand the issue a little differently, then, and say that it is not exactly an antipathy to censorship that characterizes so much modern Jewish culture but a structural inability to censor effectively. How can you act as a censor when you do not have access to the state or police power that is necessary to enforce censorship?

One of the key facets of the Jewish Diaspora has been that centralized Jewish authorities have rarely exerted much control over the lives of individual Jews. As the cultural anthropologist Raphael Patai phrases it,

> Judaism has never developed a monolithic structure which could superimpose its authority upon all Jewish communities in the many lands of their diaspora. . . . Jewish doctrine and practice, although derived from one ultimate source, the Bible, differed from place to place, because, lacking a coordinating and sanctifying central authority, their precise formulation was left to local religious leadership.[15]

This aspect of communal organization has served as an obstacle to the imposition of censorships by Jewish authorities. In an admirable study, *Censorship and Freedom of Expression in Jewish History*, the historian Moshe Carmilly-Weinberger notes that in early modern Europe, "there was no single supreme authority whose decisions were accepted by all Jews everywhere in matters of internal censorship." Thus, "if a rabbi in a certain country was moved to ban or forbid the reading of a book, even if he succeeded in persuading other rabbis to join him in this stand, his ban did not automatically apply everywhere."[16] In fact, as Carmilly-Weinberger demonstrates, the *Shulkhan Arukh*—the textual codification of Jewish law produced by Joseph Caro in the 16th century, which is easily the most widely authoritative code of behavior in Ashkenazi Judaism[17]—names a book that is "forbidden for reading on the Sabbath day" and "even on weekdays" because it is filled with "erotic remarks."[18] Yet even this unmistakable attempt to impose textual censorship did not prevent the book in question, Immanuel of Rome's *Makhbarot* (1491), from being permitted and even recommended by other Jewish authorities, such as Rabbi Joseph Delmedigo (1591–1655). "If one rabbi felt free to express a view opposing that contained in the *Shulhan Arukh* itself," Carmilly-Weinberger explains, "that is a clear indication of the degree to which freedom of speech was practiced by the Jews."[19] More precisely, this demonstrates how inimical the structure of the Jewish Diaspora has been to censorship.

This does not mean that Jewish authorities have not *tried* to set limits on speech and writing. On the contrary, a rich *halakhic* tradition prohibits *l'shon hara* (evil speech), including *rekhilut* (gossip) and *nivul peh* (obscenity). In words ascribed to R. Hanan b. Rabbah, the Talmud insists that although everyone knows why "a bride enters the bridal canopy," it is a punishable offense to speak "obscenely" about what follows.[20] Thus, the central text of normative rabbinic Judaism explicitly forbids the graphic representation of sex and commands the use of euphemism. An elaboration of this stance appears in Maimonides's *Moreh nevukhim* (*Guide of the Perplexed*), one of the most influential Jewish texts of the medieval period: "We condemn lowness of speech," Maimonides wrote, and "must not imitate the songs and tales of ignorant and lascivious people."[21] Later rabbinic texts have likewise decried obscene speech as sinful, and dozens of treatises have elaborated on the Jewish ethics of proper and respectful speech and defined sinful self-expression.[22] Nonetheless, especially in the modern period, rabbinic authorities have rarely formally agreed about what constitutes speech worthy of suppression, and so they have rarely possessed the organizational unity necessary to censor.

Even if there have been exceptions and counterexamples in which Jewish communities have succeeded in imposing censorships on Jewish populations—the excommunication of Baruch Spinoza would seem to be the most iconic of these (though note that Spinoza's writings still circulated widely among Jews and influenced their thinking, both in Amsterdam and elsewhere)[23]—the American Jewish public serves as the paradigmatic example of organizational heterodoxy and a lateral, antihierarchical community structure that militates against such enforcement. Jonathan Sarna's *American Judaism*, a broad overview of American Jewish religious history, returns again and again to this as a defining quality of that history from its colonial-era beginnings to the present. Even as latitudinarianism came to typify U.S. Christian churches, Jewish communities were even more fiercely committed to that form of organization, and by the late 19th century, Sarna remarks, "latitudinarianism reigned supreme in Jewish immigrant circles." Because American "courts, for the most part, refused to intervene in internal synagogue affairs," Jewish life in the United States manifested an extraordinary latitudinarianism in contrast even to "the hierarchic British model of Judaism." Thus, Sarna describes as one of the characteristic features of American Jewish life that "no ultimate authority in American Judaism—no rabbi, no court, no lay body—makes religious decisions that are ever broadly accepted as final."[24]

It follows, then, that Jewish institutions in the United States have not tended to be very successful in imposing censorships, despite occasional efforts to do so—because, as the philosopher Horace Kallen once noted, for censorship to be effective, it needs to be unified.[25] One example of how that was impossible for the American Jewish community is that in the 1940s, the editors of the Jewish Publication Society of America were so careful about offending their readers' delicate sensibilities that they asked the Canadian poet A. M. Klein to remove the phrase "nine months" from one of his poems, perceiving that as an overly explicit reference to pregnancy. Similar cuts had been made in Reform and Reconstructionist Passover haggadot, but Klein stood his ground and prevailed.[26] More famously, in 1945, the American Union of Orthodox Rabbis gathered to burn copies of Mordecai Kaplan's Reconstructionist *Sabbath Prayer Book* and "issued a proclamation of excommunication" against him that the leader of the Union said was directed at "all Jewry."[27] These attempted exercises of rabbinic authority illustrated, more than anything else, what one scholar of the Kaplan incident has referred to as rabbis' "impotence"; the Reconstructionist and Reform movements could not suppress the circulation of texts to which they objected any more than the Union of Orthodox Rabbis could compel any American Jews, Orthodox or otherwise, to reject Kaplan's liturgical innovations.[28] Some impositions of censorship have been possible lately within American ultra-Orthodox communities solely because of their hierarchical structures, which concentrate religious and communal authority in the hands of a few rabbis, but even these censorships have rarely been effective outside of small, local communities.

The disagreement between the author Philip Roth and Rabbi Emanuel Rackman, of Congregation Shaaray Tefila in Far Rockaway, New York, about Roth's short story "Defender of the Faith" in 1959 illustrates just how little power rabbinical leaders have wielded over the circulation of texts in the United States.[29] As Roth has recounted, his story about several Jewish soldiers on a base in Missouri occasioned angry letters from a number of Jewish readers when it appeared in the *New Yorker* on March 14, 1959. Roth quotes one letter sent by Rabbi Rackman to the offices of the Anti-Defamation League, beginning, "What is being done to silence [Roth]? Medieval Jews would have known what to do with him."[30] Invoking "medieval Jews"—who could hope to enforce excommunications with at least a little efficacy—Rackman acknowledged his own powerlessness to "silence" Roth, as much as he would have liked to do so. In letters sent directly to Roth, Rackman again acknowledged both his wish to suppress the author's work and his inability to do so, noting that Jews like himself "have neither the economic, political, nor social power to do anything other than scream" in response to publications they find offensive. Roth, too, understood that this was the case. In his own first, unpublished response to Rackman—recall that this preceded the publication of Roth's first book and that the twenty-six-year-old had not yet won the national awards that established him as a literary celebrity—the young author concludes by asserting, "It was presumptuous of you, Rabbi Rackman, to speak of yourself to me as 'a leader of his people.' You are not my leader."[31] Rackman was a respected Jewish clergyman with a national platform, and yet Roth was undeniably correct: Rackman could not do anything to him except send a few hectoring letters—and Roth could still call himself a Jew and be affirmed as such by other American Jews. In this sense, at least, American Jews were not subject to religious communal authority, unlike some of their non-Jewish peers; it would have been somewhat more difficult for an American Catholic, for instance, to deny a bishop's right to call himself "a leader of his people."[32]

Modesty, Not Censorship, in American Yiddish Literature

In the United States, Jews could write and publish what they wanted without worrying about whether a Jewish religious or institutional authority might censure and suppress their work, but of course they were still subject to American obscenity law. However, when American Jews wrote or performed in Yiddish, they could be confident that their government would not censor them. This created a fascinating and unusual situation in which American Yiddish literature circulated among a large, national audience, free from virtually any control by governmental or religious authorities. English literature has always been subject to the law in the United States and England, as French literature has been in France and so on. So, too, was Yiddish literature subject to the law in czarist and Soviet Russia—it was censored intensely and sometimes brutally—as Hebrew literature has been in the State of Israel.[33] It is not unique, but highly unusual, that Yiddish literature has almost never been subject to legal scrutiny in the United States, even though the country has at times been the unquestioned international geographic center for Yiddish authors, publishers, and readers.

The few exceptions, such as they are, prove the rule. Ben-Zion Liber's guidebook *Dos geshlekhts lebn* (*The Sexual Life*) was briefly suppressed by the U.S. Postal Service in 1917. Liber claimed that the text was censored not for its discussions of sexual hygiene but because of its socialist politics, but it seems equally likely that a non-Yiddish-speaking post office employee blanched at the anatomical diagrams of men's and women's genitalia that Liber included as illustrations. In either case, after Liber protested the suppression with an article in the *New Republic*, the Postal Service quickly relented, imposing a few silly emendations on the text and allowing the book to be mailed.[34] A major First Amendment case, *Abrams v. United States* (1919), concerned anarchist pamphlets published in both Yiddish and English, but it is unclear whether those texts would have attracted the attention of the police and been vulnerable to prosecution if they had been distributed only in Yiddish.[35] The same could be said about the role of taboo Yiddish words in the arrests of the comedian Lenny Bruce: while words such as *shmuk* and *putz* were included in some of the charges against him, it is doubtful that he would have been arrested if his act had not included more recognizable English obscenities.[36] Another notorious nightclub comedian performing during Bruce's period of activity, the 1950s and 1960s, Belle Barth, used Yiddish taboo words just as frequently as Bruce but provided fewer of their English equivalents. "A lot of her Rabelaisian words are in Yiddish," one reviewer remarked, noting, however, that "she'll oblige by translating them into English" (though, unlike Bruce, she does not do so on any of the surviving recordings of her act).[37] She was harassed by the police in Los Angeles, Chicago, and Buffalo, but attempts at suppressing her act seem to have been rather halfhearted. In 1958, a Chicago columnist wondered, "What's all the fussin' and shoutin' about Belle Barth? Her night club act is no more risque than those of a couple of headliners who earn more than $5,000 a week," while in Los Angeles, "charges of singing and speaking a lewd, obscene song" in January 1961 were quietly dismissed.[38] The wholesale integration of words such as *shmuk* and *putz* into American slang since the 1950s, denuded of their sexual connotations and of any shock value—they retain their taboo senses only for Yiddish speakers and not at all for non-Yiddish-speaking Americans—reflects just how blasé American authorities have been about the circulation of taboo words in Yiddish.[39]

In fact, the suppression of Yiddish belles lettres seems never to have been mandated or upheld by any U.S. court. Contrary to the facile suggestion of the editors of *The Norton Anthology of Jewish American Literature*, though, that "the First Amendment assured the [Yiddish] press freedom from censorship,"[40] it should be clear by now that the freedom of expression enjoyed by Yiddish writers and publishers in America beginning in the late 19th century was hardly an American norm. Yiddish literary freedom in this arena in the early decades of the 20th century had nothing at all to do with the First Amendment, which did precious little to protect sexually radical American publications in the English language until well into the 1950s.

Indeed, it was clear to translators of Yiddish literature that there was a double standard and that what could be published in Yiddish might occasion legal trouble in English. Thus, Yiddish texts were often bowdlerized upon their translation into English, and they sometimes attracted censorship when they were not sufficiently euphemized. The literary scholar Aviva Taubenfeld has shown, for example, that Abraham Cahan included the taboo English words *hell* and *damn* in the Yiddish version of his first novel, *Yankl der yanki* (serialized from October 18, 1895, to January 31, 1896), while these words do not appear in the English version, *Yekl* (1896).[41] This move demonstrates Cahan's canniness about his audiences; he, or his editors, knew what to expect in these two linguistic markets. Other translators were not always as careful. In 1920, the NYSSV insisted that Lowell Brentano stop distributing a book of translations of David Pinski's Yiddish short stories, *Temptations*, which Brentano had published the previous year, citing "the alleged immorality" of the first three stories. Brentano apparently complied with the request rather than engage in a costly legal defense.[42] Most famously, Sholem Asch's play *Got fun nekome* occasioned no police action in its Yiddish performances in 1907 or 1908, but when it was translated into English as *God of Vengeance* and performed on Broadway in 1923, the producer and all the actors were arrested for immorality.[43] What in a Yiddish text or performance could pass unremarked on by vice societies and postal censors, and unsuppressed by the U.S. police and courts, could stir up considerable trouble when it was translated into English. Why the double standard? The simple explanation is not, of course, that the U.S. government had any special respect for freedom of expression in Yiddish as opposed to its censorious approach to English expression. More simply, it appears that the government did not bother to hire Yiddish-speaking censors.[44]

In the absence of religious and governmental censorship, how did American Yiddish literature develop in terms of its representation of sex? Critics have seemed to disagree in their answers to this question. Isaac Goldberg, a Harvard PhD in modern languages who energetically promoted American Yiddish literature in the first three decades of the 20th century, observed in 1918 that "the theme of sex . . . is treated by Yiddish writers with far greater freedom than would be permitted to their American confrères."[45] By contrast, in 1964 the preeminent modernist poet and critic Yankev Glatshteyn (Jacob Glatstein) called Yiddish "one of the most modest languages in world literature."[46] In a sense, though, both of these knowledgeable critics were correct: limits and restraints were imposed on the representations of sex in American Yiddish literature, and there is not an American Yiddish text that rivals the exuberant explicitness of, say, *Tropic of Cancer* or *Naked Lunch*. There may always have been plenty of titillating *shund*—trashy Yiddish melodrama—on American stages and in the pages of American Yiddish newspapers, but this genre did not generally compete with such modernist works as *Lady Chatterley's Lover* and *Ulysses* in representing sex explicitly or in the use of taboo words. More to the point, *shund* operates under significant constraints imposed by markets.[47] Limits on Yiddish expression in America were imposed not by the government or by vice societies, that is, but by authors, editors, publishers, reviewers, booksellers, and readers, the core participants in the "communications circuit" of literary production, distribution, and consumption.[48] The Yiddish-language cultural sphere roiled with arguments about what constituted acceptable literature, debates just as intense as those taking place in English concerning the status of *Ulysses*, *Howl*, and *Tropic of Cancer*. The crucial difference was that the Yiddish debates took place in newspapers and cafés, not in courtrooms, so their stakes were cultural, not criminal. These debates exemplify how literary and cultural modesty can operate in the absence of state-sponsored censorship.

Sholem Aleichem's pamphlet *Shomers mishpet* (*The Judgment of Shomer*; 1888), a foundational work of Yiddish literary criticism, reflects the self-awareness of an influential Yiddish writer of the difference between national literatures and his own diasporic literature and specifically between literature that was subject to and could avail itself of state power, on the one hand, and that which was outside the jurisdiction of the state, on the other. The pamphlet was likely inspired by the publication, in the "definitive" 1873 edition of Gustave Flaubert's *Madame Bovary*, of the full transcript of the 1857 trial of that novel.[49] Though a work of fiction, the pamphlet takes the form of a trial transcript, "transcribed word for word by Sholem Aleichem." It presents an attack on the most popular Yiddish novelist of the late 19th century, Shomer (Nahum-Meir Shaykevitsh), in which Sholem Aleichem argues through the voice of a prosecuting attorney that Shomer "is not truly a Yiddish writer" and that his work does not merit attention. Sholem Aleichem's selection of a literary trial as the form for his critique is suggestive, especially as the "*nibl pe*" (obscenity) he criticizes in Shomer echoes the accusations of "offenses against public morals" directed against Flaubert and the "obscenity" charges famously made against Charles Baudelaire a few years later.[50] Unlike those cases, of course, as well as the U.S. literary trials of the 20th century, *Shomers mishpet* is only a metaphorical trial. Influential as Sholem Aleichem may have been, unlike Comstock, he had no authority to arrest booksellers or to confiscate and burn copies of Shomer's books. All he could do was attempt to persuade readers, including the editors and booksellers who enabled Shomer's success, to stop buying and reading Shomer's work. Shomer, for his part, dismissed Sholem Aleichem's critique and continued publishing: "You empty critics can say what you want," he wrote, "scream in the streets that my novels are foolish, pass verdicts against me as much as your hearts desire, . . . [but] I will continue to write fairy tales for my readers which, thank God, are helpful to thousands of people."[51] Again, the crucial difference between the trial of Shomer and the trials of Flaubert, Baudelaire, Joyce, Lawrence, and Miller is that no authority was willing or able to enforce the former's "verdict."

In some cases, Soviet and other European governments did stand behind and enforce cultural judgments about Yiddish literature—notoriously, under Stalin, to the point of murder—but in the United States, Yiddish polemicists of all stripes came to recognize that the government would not enforce their cultural judgments. Controversies about Yiddish literary propriety thus remained uniformly outside the purview of American law. As mentioned earlier, the performances of Sholem Asch's *Got fun nekome* in 1907 and 1908 occasioned furious polemics, in which writers declared the play "filthy," "immoral," and "indecent" and even called for police intervention, but none followed. Another contretemps, in 1908–9, focused on the Russian novel *Sanin* and its translation into Yiddish by the novelist Leon Kobrin and serialization in the *Varheyt*, one of New York's daily Yiddish newspapers, but, again, this did not result in the suppression of the newspaper by state authorities.[52] A third well-known debate, in the early 1920s, concerned "*grobe verter un sheyne literatur*" (vulgar speech and belles lettres) in the poetry of Moshe-Leyb Halpern and involved many prominent literary critics—again, without the involvement of the NYSSV or any other government-sponsored mechanism of suppression.[53] Perhaps the most furious such controversy took place in the late 1930s, as Sholem Asch began to publish a trilogy of Yiddish novels dealing sympathetically with the lives of Jesus, Mary, and Paul. Many Yiddish readers were outraged, and Cahan, who had regularly published Asch's work in the *Forverts*, refused to print anything more by the author. As in Sholem Aleichem's attack on Shomer, some of the critiques of Asch even took the form of mock trials in which the author was declared guilty. Yet thanks to the latitudinarianism of the Yiddish literary market and its competitiveness, Asch could simply find an alternative venue for his work, and he soon saw his books in print and on sale despite the opposition.[54]

If not quite rising to the level of the Asch debacle, controversies about literary propriety were so common in Yiddish that they could devolve into absurdity. One critic noticed in 1964 that the writer known in English as Isaac Bashevis Singer railed, in Yiddish, against the filthiness of modern literature under one pseudonym, while under another name he produced precisely the sort of fiction to which his other persona had objected.[55] Such debates were not unique to American Yiddish, but in that demimonde the means of suppression internal to the literary system, including self-censorship, critiques, boycotts, and refusals to publish, were the only forms of suppression available. When it came to American Yiddish, the police, the post office, the courts, and the customs department were not willing or able to intervene.[56]

Glatshteyn's remarks about Yiddish "modesty" can be understood, then, as a polemical attempt to reshape Yiddish literary history, a modern version of Sholem Aleichem's gambit in *Shomers mishpet* that was similarly inspired by literary trials of the day—in Glatshteyn's case, by the American trials of *Lady Chatterley's Lover*, *Howl*, *Tropic of Cancer*, and other books. The crucial feature of Glatshteyn's claim about Yiddish modesty is what it excludes from consideration: while admitting that "Yiddish possesses many 'healthy' vulgar expressions, with sexual insinuations," Glatshteyn goes on to remark that the language "bears simply no vulgar expressions—surely not in the literature—and no writer ventures to break this bridle, except those who are sure that they write in the first place for the translation market."[57] Anyone familiar with American Yiddish literary politics will recognize that Glatshteyn's reference to writers who "write in the first place for translation market" is a dig at Asch and especially Bashevis, who was by the time Glatshteyn's essay appeared famous worldwide because of the English translations of his work. Obviously, there is no truth to the claim that Yiddish literature "bears simply no vulgar expressions." Such a statement about literature is tautological in nature, in that it defines "literature" according to a text's fulfillment of the proposed condition, and in this case the statement is designed to exclude books such as Bashevis's debut novel, *Der sotn in goray* (*Satan in Goray*; 1935), which contains plenty of "vulgar expressions"—and it is also worth noting that Glatshteyn's own published fiction was hardly prim by the NYSSV's standards.[58] Rather than an observation about Yiddish literary history, Glatshteyn's remark is an attempt to redefine Yiddish literature so as to exclude particular writers from consideration within that field.

Like Glatshteyn, polemicists typically invoke modesty—whether literary, cultural, sexual, or in some other form—to normalize and invest symbolic value into particular practices and to characterize other practices as vulgar, abnormal, or distasteful. Such claims, like Glatshteyn's, also tend to obscure their own subjectivity behind an essentialist rhetoric that they often do not seem to recognize comes across as transparently self-serving. Modesty claims are not usually, because of this, particularly persuasive. On the other hand, as Fish argues, there is no way to speak without excluding other utterances, or, as Bourdieu would have it, there is no position to occupy that does not rest on assumptions about what is possible to utter. Everyone, in this sense, has their own ideas about modesty, their own rules of acceptable expression. Indeed, if in Michael Warner's theory of publics, "polite sociability" is necessary for the creation of "a public composed of strangers," then it is in authors' abiding by what they feel to be textual modesty that they assert their relation to a public.[59] In this sense, Glatshteyn had no choice but to operate under his own working definition of Yiddish literary modesty; whether or not one finds his proffered definition compelling, there is no alternative perspective that is not equally subjective.

Even stalwart opponents of censorship must acknowledge that some forms of suppression are inevitable: this is precisely what Freud and Bourdieu, and the 1990s theorists of censorship, demonstrated. And it is what thoughtful advocates of freedom of expression have always admitted. Isaac Goldberg, the critic and translator who noted the freedom of sexual expression enjoyed by Yiddish writers in the 1910s, was an associate of H. L. Mencken's and a stalwart opponent of Comstockery, and yet in his many essays on censorship and obscenity he avoids a utopian demand for the elimination of all suppression. "The Censor," he writes, "may not always be wrong in wishing to do away with the object of his disapproval."

> The wrong lies in his method. He is a King who can do no wrong. His wish must be law. There is no argument; no discussion. There is only obedience.
>
> This is obviously preposterous.
>
> Let him believe what he pleases to believe; let him work in the interests of that belief. But why seek, by law and other compulsion, to tie

> his opponent hand and foot? Why deny to ideas different from his own the right to death—or life—in the open field?[60]

Goldberg's language articulates a distinction between censorship imposed by state power (whether foisted on the public by a "King," metaphorical or real, or by the "law") and the regulation of creative industries by their own practitioners and audiences (who should "work in the interests of [their] belief"). Goldberg's reasonable, if hardly unique, position rejected free-speech absolutism as an impossibly utopian ideal along the lines, more or less, of Fish's arguments in "There's No Such Thing as Free Speech." Latitudinarianism and freedom of expression, as Goldberg understood them, do not mean accepting the equal validity of all positions and beliefs. In fact, he personally admitted to being rather prim and proper about language, acknowledging that he found "it difficult to endure, even from close friends, the type of humor that originates in digestion, elimination and their various functions, and even the common words that describe those functions."[61] Even if his personal modesty tended toward what, by contemporary standards, would seem prudish—and it should be said that even the two volumes of erotic short stories Goldberg wrote for the mail-order erotica dealer Esar Levine, *Sexarians* (1931) and *Madame Sex* (1932), manage to avoid virtually all the taboo words of that era—he understood that one's own personal modesty standards need not be imposed on everyone else through the intercession of government authority. "What we ourselves do not like, we can abstain from," he suggested, "without visiting our fears or our dislikes upon others."[62] He did not see it as an imposition of censorship for cultural professionals to "abstain from" a particular approach to representing sex, if they freely choose to do so.

Irving Howe once remarked on the phenomenon of modern Jews' modesty, noting that "over the centuries the Jews had developed a cultural style encouraging prudishness and self-censorship: there were things everyone knew, had no choice but to know, yet only rarely was it deemed proper to speak or write about them."[63] Howe's passive voice underplays a crucial element of this observation that is, nonetheless, evident in his selection of the term "self-censorship." The people who deemed it proper or improper to "speak or write about" sensitive "things" in modern Jewish culture were typically individual Jews, who made such decisions on the basis of their personal inclinations and principles about propriety, often informed by Jewish traditions, certainly, and other factors in their environments as well as historical contingencies, but outside the coercive imposition of censorships by religious or state authorities.

Modesty and Transgression in Yiddish Modernism

What does textual modesty look like? The modesty of American Yiddish literature has been, like all practices of modesty, variable, historically contingent, and conceptually unstable.[64] How modesty reads on the page varies widely from one author to another, and sometimes from text to text, too. Goldberg recognized this. While he agreed with earlier critics of 19th-century European Yiddish literature that works in that tradition had not tended to devote much attention to representations of sex, he noted that "in the light of later Yiddish fiction we must reform entirely our views of Yiddish sex in art. It may flow deep and strong, as in Pinski; it may seethe and burst all bonds of social restraint, as in Ash [*sic*]; it may turn harsh and brutal, as in Kobrin; it may frisk about and tease, as in [Peretz] Hirschbein; it may blossom as an exotic, as in [Joseph] Opatoshu; but always it is there."[65] Goldberg's characterizations could be debated, of course, and his list could be supplemented with the names of later Yiddish authors, including Bashevis, the poet Celia Dropkin, and the novelist and poet Chaim Grade, who had their own characteristic approaches to the representation of sex that varied in style, tone, and anatomical exactness. Still, the remark reflects a recognition that in American Yiddish literature, just as in any other literary tradition, the representation of sex varies according to authors' individual predilections.

The thorough study of sexual representation in American Yiddish literature that would substantiate this assertion would be the subject for a rather lengthy and valuable book of its own, but what bears addressing, briefly, here is that when Yiddish authors made choices about how to represent sex—whether they were responding primarily to psychological, social, or market cues, or to some combination of them, in making their choices—their representations regularly took forms that resembled those that evolved under legal duress in English. Writers working in Yiddish have often represented sex, that is to say, using euphemism, metonymy, elision, archaism, and lyricism: all the same techniques for avoiding explicitness that American and British authors working in English developed, by necessity, under the coercive influence of obscenity laws.

As an example of his point about the foreignness of "vulgar expressions" to Yiddish literature, Glatshteyn mentions Isaac Meir Weissenberg's one-act play *Dvorele*, which, as Glatshteyn puts it, presents "a moment of sexual unfaithfulness" but does so, he goes on, in such a way that "it would be ridiculed by contemporary American writers as modesty and restraint."[66] The play's avoidance of dirty words cannot be denied, but to characterize Weissenberg's play as modest is, precisely, to suggest how flexible modesty can be. The play centers on the title character, a twenty-two-year-old woman, as she cuckolds her husband. The stage directions indicate a building physical intimacy between Dvorele and her lover, which the audience witnesses in sharp and concrete detail. For example, she removes her *sheytl* (wig) and shows her own flowing hair, a gesture that would be understood in ultra-Orthodox Jewish circles as intensely erotic and as the very definition of sexual immodesty.[67] Then, as her lover declares his desire, she reciprocates with coquetry, and the lover "kisses her neck" and hugs and kisses her generally. Soon "he sits down on the bed with her on his lap"; and, finally, he pulls her into bed with him, kissing her, and turns off the light, which is followed on stage by the sound of "a quiet rustling."[68] Notwithstanding the latitude this leaves for interpretation in performance, the play makes unmistakably clear that Dvorele and her lover are sexually intimate during this moment. Weissenberg does not demand that the actors engage in or visually simulate sex acts—onstage darkness serves as a kind of theatrical elision of visual representation—but the play does direct the actors to provide an aural, if muted, representation of what is unmistakably sexual intercourse, after having visually represented their foreplay.[69] Though it eschews dirty words or the graphic visual representations of sex, some viewers or readers of *Dvorele* would, undoubtedly, find it sexually arousing.

Compare to this the most sexually explicit scene of Sholem Asch's notorious *God of Vengeance*, which Glatshteyn contrasts to Weissenberg as having, with its treatment of "the brothel-theme, . . . scandalized

Yiddish audiences" but which actually employs not less but more elision and euphemism than Weissenberg's *Dvorele*. Asch, like Weissenberg, makes a sexual transgression clear to the audience without representing sexual intercourse overtly. His most explicit stage directions require the actors to embrace and kiss, and he does not use any taboo words. In the scene, a prostitute, Manke, speaks seductively to a virtuous and virginal young woman, Rifkele, but does so with familiar euphemisms:

> We are bride and bridegroom, you and I. We embrace. (*Places her arm around Rifkele.*) Ever so tightly. And kiss, very softly. Like this. (*Kisses Rifkele.*) And we turn so red, —we're so bashful. . . . And then we go to sleep together. Nobody sees, nobody hears. Only you and I. Like this. (*Clasps Rifkele tightly to herself.*) Do you want to sleep with me tonight like this? Eh?[70]

As transgressive as this speech may be in terms of its play with traditional gender norms, it is also noteworthy precisely for how seductively Manke can speak without using any taboo language or explicit sexual display.[71] The terminology of marriage ("bride and bridegroom") and of "sleep," which Manke employs here, is both the most basic and the most unavoidable means by which to allude euphemistically to sex, because it relies on the oldest and most common social structures that acknowledge or allow for sexual activity without explicitly mentioning sex. Asch plays with the ability of modesty itself to reflect and inspire sexual desire: Manke's descriptions of herself and Rifkele as blushing and "bashful" and as being alone ("Nobody sees, nobody hears") all serve to heighten the sense of seduction. There is no denying the sexual charge of Asch's scene—or that it would be, for some audience members, sexually arousing—but it is striking that Asch manages to produce titillating effects precisely through the rhetoric of sexual modesty.

Similar points could be made about other modern Yiddish literature that represents or alludes to sex, from David Pinski's play *Yankl der shmid* and Isaac Bashevis Singer's novel *Satan in Goray* to Celia Dropkin's poems, to fiction written by Sholem Aleichem, Joseph Opatoshu, Leon Kobrin, and Yehoshue Perle.[72] Such texts could and surely did scandalize readers and audiences, but they did so less because they transgressed some standard of sexual modesty that had informed earlier Yiddish literature and more because of the subversive ways in which they engaged and exploited those standards. To phrase this another way, in the spirit of Foucault, sexual transgression and repression require each other. Even when government-empowered censors do not impose sexual repression on a text, authors—under the influence of their own moral and aesthetic programs, as well as the suasion of their editors, publishers, distributors, and audiences—will, invariably, inevitably, eternally, choose to suppress some aspects of sex themselves.

Yiddish Modesty in the American 1960s

There is not much evidence that American writers and critics in the 1960s working in English paid much attention to the ways that sexuality had been handled in American Yiddish literature, but postwar Yiddish writers in the United States were clearly aware of the controversies about obscenity in American law. As mentioned earlier, Glatshteyn was inspired to consider the place of obscenity in the modern Yiddish and Hebrew literary traditions by the American obscenity controversies of the late 1950s and early 1960s. Another example is Chaim Grade's masterful novel *Tsemakh Atlas* (*The Yeshiva*), published in Los Angeles in two volumes, in 1967 and 1968. A philosophically rich historical novel about a yeshiva in prewar Lithuania that distinguished itself in its commitments to Musar—that is, to stringent moral piety and self-denial bordering on asceticism—the book can be understood as linking the ethical and psychological challenges of the 1960s sexual revolution in the United States to a seemingly distant milieu. With stories of teenage boys choosing between obedience to parents and religious leaders, on one hand, or to their sexual urges, on the other—negotiating between faith, intellect, and bodily temptation—Grade reminds us that such conflicts were not unique to the college campuses and suburbs of the postwar United States.

A central episode concerns a controversy over banned books, not entirely unlike the one that was playing out in the American courts during the years Grade drafted his novel. In the second volume of the novel, a heretic attempts to undermine the piety of the students at the Valkenik yeshiva, founded by the title character, by introducing them to "forbidden secular books."[73] He provides them with copies of a book called *Political Economy* and with Charles Darwin's *The Descent of Man*, as well as works of modern Jewish fiction: Mendele Mokher Sforim's reformist *Di kliatshe* (The mare), Zusman Segalowitch's sensationalistic *Di vilde Tsilke* (The wild Tsilke), and a translation of a book by the decadent Italian modernist Pitigrilli, a collection of stories titled *The Chastity Belt*.[74] When the boys' teacher is alerted to the reading his students have been doing, he is appalled: "This wasn't heresy but downright obscenity—pornography" (2:79). The teacher emphasizes the Pitigrilli volume, in particular, and it is worth noting that that book signals its own eroticism, in its title, by a reference to a device designed as a sexual restraint: another instance of the dialectic between transgressive and repressive sexuality. All of the books are regarded as sexual temptations, "worse than the Moabite women who seduced the Israelites in the desert" (2:81). The founder of the yeshiva, Tsemakh Atlas, at first refuses to act to suppress the books, noting that "the students will read these silly stories until they get sick of them, and then they'll return to their Talmuds" (2:84), but this laissez-faire perspective is not shared by his colleagues. Atlas eventually agrees to hire a bricklayer to burn the controversial books. The local population is outraged by this act of suppression—another example, if a fictional one, in which Jews demonstrate their refusal to accept rabbinic edicts—and, what is more, their outrage receives support from the novel's most respected religious thinker, Reb Avraham-Shaye Kosover, whom Grade based on the influential ultra-Orthodox rabbi Avraham Yeshaya Karelitz (1878–1953), known as the *Hazon Ish*. In the novel, Kosover regards Atlas's decision to burn the books as wrongheaded and worse, remarking that "such measures must not be taken against nonbelievers nowadays; it only increases the hatred and obstinacy of the freethinkers." He goes so far as to suggest that "the community *should* replace the destroyed library" (2:137), repurchasing the controversial books for their owners. Confronting Atlas, Kosover tells him that "burning the library books has led to a desecration of God's name" (140); that is, he asserts that according to the system of religious values shared by these characters, Atlas's act of censorship was a grievous sin. Curiously, Grade presents Atlas as a sort of clumsy yeshivish Comstock—or Charles H. Keating, Jr., of the postwar U.S. group Citizens for Decent Literature—and Kosover, sympathetically, as a liberal defender of free expression.

This is just one example of how Grade can be read in *Tsemakh Atlas* to be reminding his readers that the generational conflicts over sexuality taking place in America in the 1960s, of which the debates about Henry Miller and the use of the word *fuck* were subsets, were nothing new: the teenagers and twenty-something yeshiva students whose fates Grade tracks throughout the book, including Chaikl, his own autobiographical avatar, struggle to contain their overwhelming sexual desires given their upbringing in a religious culture that denies them legitimate outlets for it. Grade describes Chaikl, at twenty, "exhausted by forbidden desires, feverish with lust even when he stood over the Talmud" (2:193). His contemporaries either succumb to the sinful act of masturbation, reviling themselves for doing so; or copulate with the first woman who proves willing and then force her to have an abortion; or try not to lose their minds while denying their sexual urges completely. The relevance of the debate in the novel between Kosover and Atlas about the effects of sensational novels on the sexual habits of teenagers to the literary and social debates of the 1960s should be clear. Critics have not appreciated the relevance of Grade's fiction to the time and place in which he was writing, though, even when it appeared in English translation in the 1970s to considerable critical acclaim. Strangely, the 1990s witnessed the presentation of the sexual modesty of Orthodox Judaism to mainstream American audiences as if, contra Grade, the Jewish discourse of sexual modesty could be understood not as a parallel to the efforts at censorship in American culture, in which institutional authorities tried, fruitlessly, to restrain people's sexual desires, but rather as an innovative solution to what was seen as the problem of Americans' increasing freedom to choose their own sexual practices and sexual representations.

Mainstreaming Orthodox Modesty in the 1990s

What is perhaps most fascinating, and most relevant to the current discussion, about the polemics that beginning in 1990 marketed *tzniut* (Jewish modesty) and *taharat hamishpakha* and *niddah* (family purity) to readers beyond the fold of Orthodox Judaism is that they embody the opposite side of the paradox of modesty that we have seen operating in the Yiddish literature of the early 20th century. While texts by Weissenberg and Asch deployed the language of modesty to seductive and arousing effect, these polemical and didactic ones represent sex immodestly in order to advocate for sexual suppression and restraint.

These books—Manis Friedman's *Doesn't Anyone Blush Anymore? Reclaiming Intimacy, Modesty, and Sexuality* (1990), Shmuley Boteach's *Kosher Sex: A Recipe for Passion and Intimacy* (1999), and Wendy Shalit's *A Return to Modesty: Discovering the Lost Virtue* (2000)—should not be confused with the many handbooks and guides to the laws of modesty published during the same period in Hebrew and English for the benefit of Orthodox Jewish readers, such as Rabbi Pesach Eliyahu Falk's *Modesty: An Adornment for Life* (1998).[75] The marketing of the former books make their broader intended audiences clear. They downplay their authors' religious authority, for one thing: Friedman and Boteach are both, like Falk, ordained rabbis, but only Falk includes his rabbinical title on the cover of his book. Friedman, Boteach, and Shalit published with major nonsectarian trade publishers—HarperSanFrancisco, Doubleday, and Touchstone, respectively—that positioned the books as relevant beyond the Orthodox Jewish community. Friedman's book carries a blurb from none other than Bob Dylan, who proclaims that "anyone who's either married or thinking of getting married would do well to read this book," while Shalit's comes with a statement from Robin West, professor at Georgetown Law School, that it is "a book for all of us—feminists, antifeminists, conservatives, and liberals."[76] Such statements are as obviously exaggerated as any other marketing blurbs, but especially when read against the twelve pages of exclusively Hebrew-language *haskamot* (rabbinical endorsements) at the beginning of Falk's book, they vividly illustrate that Friedman, Boteach, and Shalit, along with their publishers, hoped that these works would reach wide American audiences. To some degree, all three did.

These books energetically advocate for Orthodox sexual modesty practices as relevant to all Americans, even if they remain a little cagey about admitting that this is what they are up to. To begin with Friedman, he misleadingly substitutes the term "traditional" when he refers to *haredi* or ultra-Orthodox Jews and their practices, writing, "Traditional Jews lead a modest social life. . . . Men and women who are dating don't touch each other. . . . In a traditional Jewish home, husbands and wives only touch each other in privacy" (67–69). The practices he describes here are not universally accepted among Modern Orthodox, let alone observant Conservative, Reform, or Reconstructionist, Jews, any of whom might reasonably consider themselves "traditional." Friedman sees these Orthodox practices as potentially valuable for both non-Jews and non-Orthodox Jews, remarking that "it's a sensitive, considerate, modest, and healthy way to live" (70). Boteach, for his part, extends that sentiment, presenting the practice of *niddah*, in which a couple "must separate for the five days of menstruation and for seven days thereafter and maintain a strict period of sexual abstinence" (76), as helping to establish the "harmony between the male and female libido" (78) that is necessary for "*any* truly successful marriage" (75, emphasis added). Shalit positions a "*modestynik*"—"a modern single young woman raised in a secular [Jewish] home . . . who . . . starts wearing very long skirts and issuing spontaneous announcements that she is now *shomer negiah*, which means that she isn't going to have physical contact with men before marriage, and that she is now dressing according to the standards of Jewish modesty" (2), or "*tzniut*" (3)—as a model practitioner of the sexual modesty that Shalit advocates for all Americans. Shalit conflates Orthodox Jews' modesty practices with the practices of sexual modesty undertaken by other women, both "Jewish and non-Jewish" (6), without addressing the variations and contradictions between the sexual modesty practices of, say, Orthodox Jews, evangelical Christians, and Muslims. She dedicates some effort to explaining the specifics of Orthodox Jewish modesty practices to her readers, but, like Boteach, she argues for them as being useful not just for Orthodox Jews, citing with palpable relish examples of women who profess not to be Orthodox Jews but for whom the practices of *niddah* or *tzniut* have proven worthwhile (219–21), including one woman whose "reasons for accepting the ancient laws of sexual modesty" she describes as "thoroughly modern" (221). Representing Orthodox Jewish practices as of a piece with Christian and Muslim modesty practices—to which she devotes less specific attention—Shalit describes the attraction of all these practices as resulting from a "universal instinct hidden within us, suppressed sometimes, but always ready to show its face if we would only allow it" (232). Despite being members of a demographic group that is a small fraction even of the American Jewish population, these writers regard *tzniut* as having "universal" applicability.

The deliciously Foucauldian irony of these books is that in order to advance their arguments that Jewish sexual modesty is what contemporary, non-Jewish Americans need as a counter to oversexualized American culture, these authors write about sex—describe graphic, often shocking sex and acts of sexual violence—in ways that demonstrate that there is no standard of Jewish *textual* modesty that even the three of them, let alone all Orthodox Jews or all Americans, could agree on. As evidence that a lack of sexual self-restraint leads to "tragedy," Friedman summarizes the plot of the film *Fatal Attraction* (1987) in detail. What is noteworthy about this is that many modern ultra-Orthodox rabbinic authorities, including Shmuel Wosner, Moshe Feinstein, and Yaakov Yisrael Kanievsky, have declared that watching "*pritzus'dik* [immodest] . . . films" is sinfully immodest and impermissible (which explains why Shalit's own sense of *tzniut* includes not watching R-rated films such as *Fatal Attraction*).[77] Under what circumstances, then, would Rabbi Friedman have sat down to watch *Fatal Attraction*, which includes taboo words, a woman's bare breasts, and several scenes of energetic simulated intercourse? Is his use of the film as a proof text to be taken as implying that watching it might be permissible for his readers?[78]

Boteach, the most popular of these three authors, engages in sensationalistic descriptions of sex that would certainly not be understood as modest by many of his readers, whether Orthodox or not.[79] These range from the quotidian to the grotesque; in *Kosher Sex*, Boteach discusses the difference between the physical contact between a man and woman during penetration when the man's penis is sheathed in a condom and when she wears a diaphragm (141) and references the masochistic practice of "hammer[ing] [one's] scrotum to wood" (136). Boteach seems quite conscious of the irony of this use of sexual sensationalism to promote modesty, and he registers this irony textually. He quotes a rabbinical colleague who once, in Boteach's presence, "launched into a diatribe against rabbis 'who write about immodest subjects like sex and marriage.'" Despite making clear that he understands himself to be the object of this criticism ("I quickly sunk low in my seat to avert the stares," Boteach recalls), he also manages to endorse this rabbi's view of immodesty: "ascetic thinkers are right where they emphasize modesty" (52), he remarks, not making clear how that affirmation jibes with his own text. Indeed, his definition of modesty becomes more convoluted the more one considers it. He tells the story of an Orthodox Jewish man who sought out his counsel because the man's wife had "lost the ability to climax" after giving birth to their first child. "It bothered me," Boteach writes, "that this young man had no modesty. It bothered me that he would compromise his wife's privacy with such abandon" (52), by telling Boteach the story. The contradiction here could not be more glaring: it offended Boteach to encounter this level of disclosure in his office, during an individual's private conversation with a clergyman, but it does not, apparently, bother him to have published the story in a book printed by the thousands and made available to the general public.

The visions of modesty put forth by Friedman and Boteach are, at times, both internally inconsistent and, more generally, inconsistent with those of other Orthodox Jews who write about the subject for general audiences. Shalit is especially self-aware about this and about the paradox that writing about modesty necessitates what others, or she herself, may consider immodesty. When she mentions that as a college student she did not have "sexual intercourse" with her boyfriends, she laments that she cannot think of an appropriately modest euphemism to replace that already euphemistic phrase: "How I wish there were a more elusive way of putting this," she writes (4). She explains, furthermore, that she "would have preferred to avoid" discussing her own sexual experiences entirely but that "it didn't work": "I simply found it impossible to clear up what I perceive to be some central misunderstandings about modesty without, in some cases, getting very specific" (10). The more glaring contradiction, however, is in Shalit's description of other people's sexual experiences: like many antivice crusaders before her, she delights in retelling instances of sexual and violent crime, real or imagined, not excluding gory details. Reading Shalit's book, one encounters boys "brutally raping a retarded girl with a baseball bat" (41), for example, and "boys [who] sodomize girls on the playground" (155) and "sixth-grade girls . . . *forced, one by one, to undergo a genital examination*" (242, quoting *World* magazine). Such anecdotes may be, for different readers, either galvanizing or titillating, and as such, they risk alienating exactly the readers who would be expected to admire Shalit's book. One Amazon review, titled "This book is not G-rated," awards Shalit's book the lowest possible rating and explains:

> I bought this book thinking it was something I could share with my teenage daughter to help reinforce the importance of modesty. What I

> found was alot of sexual content. And after a graphic and very disturbing description of the rape and murder of a young girl (was the author going for shock value[?]) in chapter three I decided that the best place for this book is in the trash.[80]

As if anticipating this critique, Shalit acknowledges in her book's conclusion, "I have defended modesty, essentially, in the most obscene way, but I did it because I had a hunch that this was the only way our culture would ever reconsider it" (243). It is not clear whether this is naiveté or faux-naiveté, but it would be bizarre if Shalit, widely read as she is, were entirely ignorant of the long tradition of Christian antivice crusaders who also "defended modesty . . . in the most obscene way," such as Citizens for Decent Literature, the group founded by Charles H. Keating, Jr., in the mid-1950s, which, as the cultural historian Whitney Strub explains, established itself in national obscenity debates in the 1960s precisely by advancing an "antisex message" through the use of "oversexed rhetoric and imagery."[81]

The internal inconsistencies in these polemics for Jewish modesty as an American virtue say less about the hypocrisy of the individual authors than they do about the prospect of polemicizing for modesty in late 20th-century America generally. In the 1990s, arguments in the United States about "freedom of speech" and "obscenity," however abstract, continued to have at least the potential to be written into law and thus to become binding on Americans, but writers such as Friedman, Boteach, or Shalit who turned to "modesty" as the grounds of their arguments had already, in a sense, conceded courtroom defeat. While the legal scholar and philosopher Anita L. Allen's observation in 2006 that "American laws compel sexually modest behavior" cannot be ignored—not when state and municipal laws "restricting nudity," "prohibiting modes of public undress," and "restricting the time, place, and manner of sexually-oriented public theatrical performances, dancing and touching" continue to be enforced—what Allen neglects to mention is that U.S. statutes do not typically employ the term *modesty* to characterize acceptable conduct.[82] On the contrary, laws prohibit "obscenity," "indecency," or "lewd" behavior or use other synonyms to define criminal sexual excesses, precisely because even the most conservative advocates of modesty recognize that as a negative value (meaning "not obscene"), modesty cannot effectively be written into statutes. A polemic that focuses on modesty tends to be self-defeating not only in its internal contradictions, then, but also in its implicit acknowledgment that state power will not likely enforce its preferences. Like a Yiddish literary critic incensed that this or that writer has disrespected what he considers the essential *tsnies* of the language, the American cultural critic who pleads with readers to be more sexually modest, whether he or she frames that plea as being for the reader's own benefit or for the common good, does so precisely because he or she is operating without state support and without power to enforce his or her tastes through law.

Modesty in Contemporary Representations of Orthodox Jews

Friedman's, Shalit's, and Boteach's pleas for modesty inevitably undermine themselves, especially because they consider textual representation as capable of objectionable obscenity. If they can dramatize the benefits of what they construe as modesty only by contrasting it with immodesty, they must present what they consider immodest to precisely those readers whom they perceive as vulnerable to immodesty: how else will anyone know what to stay away from? Michael Holquist has referred to this as "the paradox of censorship": as David Schearl realizes in *Call It Sleep*, being told not to speak dirty words inevitably makes one think about all the dirty words one knows and must not say; equally, being told to act modestly brings to mind all of the immodest acts from which we must restrain ourselves.[83] This is why a secular work of fiction, using what modesty polemicists call immodesty, can argue for the value of *tzniut* more effectively than the polemicists do.

Shalit's infamous foray into literary criticism—a 2005 essay in the *New York Times Book Review*—is so weak and uninformed a piece of work, and has so effectively been rebutted in print, that it would not be worth mentioning here if it had not disappointingly become a touchstone in a couple of serious scholarly discussions of the representation of Orthodoxy in recent American fiction.[84] Leaving aside Shalit's clumsy central point (that contemporary American fiction represents "deeply observant Jews in an unflattering or ridiculous light"), what is fascinating about the piece is the way that it expands her polemic about modesty to literary representation, especially in her reading of Tova Mirvis's 2004 novel *The Outside World*. Shalit objects, in particular, to a scene in which a young Orthodox couple, at their engagement party, slip outside to share a moment of physical intimacy. The young woman, Tzippy, touches the hand of her fiancé, Baruch; Baruch holds Tzippy's hand in response; then he puts his arms around her as she leans toward him, "their bodies gently pressing against each other."[85] Shalit briefly summarizes the scene in her essay, noting that by touching hands and hugging, the characters are violating the prohibition on premarital physical contact widely upheld in many Orthodox communities—endorsed by the likes of Friedman—and remarks that "it's bad enough that a yeshiva student would embrace a woman not related or married to him, but to do so in public is even worse." Shalit inanely presents this as an example of what she construes as Mirvis's relentless and unstinting exposure of Orthodox hypocrisy. Certainly, one can point to recent literary works—Pearl Abraham's *The Romance Reader* (1995), Shalom Auslander's memoir *Foreskin's Lament* (2007), Judy Brown's young-adult novel *Hush* (2010)—that are, in a variety of different ways, committed to demonstrating the hypocrisies of contemporary ultra-Orthodox communities, especially in their treatments of modesty and sexual ethics.[86] But Mirvis's novel, on the contrary, models a textual *tzniut* that dramatizes Shalit's own contentions about modesty and does so sympathetically.

In the specific scene that Shalit critiques, Mirvis's very next sentence has the young man in question seeing in his mind's eye "the face of his rabbi," onto whom he projects his guilt about his conduct—and then, before the hug between the affianced couple has led to, say, a kiss, "guilt replace[s] desire and he pull[s] away." After this single moment of transgression, Mirvis's couple returns to faithful observance of the prohibition on physical contact, and, after they are married, the novel informs the reader, they dutifully observe the laws of *niddah* (173). Elsewhere in the novel, Mirvis draws on the same literary tools—obscurantism, euphemism, elision—that previous generations of authors have used to avoid explicit descriptions of sex. Early in the novel, when the male protagonist returns to his parents' Modern Orthodox home from his yeshiva in Israel, now newly zealous about religious practice, one of his decisions is to discard "his copies of *Sports Illustrated* (regular and swimsuit)" (36). This is Mirvis's delicate way of suggesting that the character has chosen to stop masturbating, as the *Sports Illustrated* swimsuit issue was, in the period in which Mirvis's novel is set (that is, before widespread adoption of the World Wide Web), one of the more ubiquitous sources of cheesecake photography that could serve as fodder for a heterosexual teenage boy's masturbation fantasies.[87] In a scene that describes the night of the protagonists' wedding, Mirvis carefully avoids a graphic description of their sexual encounter. The closest Mirvis comes to representing their physical sensations sounds quite like the American fiction of the 1920s, shades of Yezierska and Lewisohn: "In the bareness of their skin, they found each other," Mirvis writes, and then—a new paragraph, skipping past the sexual act to its aftermath—"Tzippy fell asleep with the shock that it had happened at all" (177).

In avoiding the representation of intercourse and masturbation through euphemism and elision, *The Outside World* is hardly unique, even if Mirvis's restraint goes considerably further than what one finds in most comparable literary or commercial fiction of the period.[88] Novels published in recent years by Christian and Orthodox Jewish presses tend to treat sex similarly, as do a few contemporary self-identified Orthodox novelists, including Risa Miller and Ruchama King, who publish with nonsectarian presses.[89] Mirvis is worth emphasizing, though, because her books have had broader audiences than these other examples—published by Knopf, still among the most prestigious of American literary houses, *The Outside World* had an announced first printing of seventy-five thousand copies[90]—and because she has thought through the problem of how to represent her characters' sexual experiences from a perspective informed both by Orthodoxy and by contemporary aesthetic and narrative considerations. "In writing *The Outside World*," she explains,

> I wrestled with how explicit to be about sex, and after much writing and rewriting, ultimately felt that further explicitness felt like the sounding of a false note within the narrative voice, inserted for the purpose of exposure (look—*frum* [devout] people having sex!) rather than for literary reasons. For all writers there is this question of allusion versus explicitness, and certainly the pull is in the other direction: to be explicit, to bare all. And yet would this narrative strategy have been the right tone

> for my book? Ultimately is it even the most evocative? Perhaps this [is] the literary equivalent of *shomer negiah* [the prohibition on cross-gender physical contact among the unmarried], in which there is a constant pull between desire and restraint, both of which become sexualized. Should we or shouldn't we? I want to but we shouldn't. Maybe just this once. . . . The very idea of restraint becomes, as it were, a kind of foreplay in this world and I would hope that my book is able to capture some of that dynamic.[91]

To the degree that Mirvis does succeed in capturing this dynamic, she enacts in her novel precisely the insight that led Shalit to embrace *tzniut*: the idea that a restraint of sexual expression serves to heighten sexual sensitivity and arousal, or in Shalit's words, it is a "pulling back, which is the result not of prudery . . . but on the contrary, of intense sexual feeling, of a kind of awe and wonder of where it all will lead" (186). Mirvis understands her restraint of sexual "explicitness" not only as a textual analogy or instantiation of Orthodox practices but, like them, as a means for ratcheting up attention to sexuality (one that ends up sounding not altogether different from the contemporary kinky sexual practice referred to as "chastity play").[92] Continuing the analogy of the textual restraint in her novel to the sexual restraint practiced by Orthodox Jews, Mirvis also notes the way that modesty practices, as she understands them, keep sexuality "absent from the top layer of interaction but oh so tantalizingly present on every other layer. . . . Think about a *frum* wedding. . . . With all the insistence on modesty and privacy, is there any wedding where sex feels more present, and oddly more public, almost bizarrely communal as well?"[93]

One of the sources of the rabbinical prohibition of *nivul peh*, mentioned earlier, is the Talmudic remark, "All know for what purpose a bride enters the bridal canopy, yet against whomsoever who speaks obscenely [thereof], even if a sentence of seventy years' happiness had been sealed for him, it is reversed for evil." This statement is typically adduced as a proof text for the prohibition of sexually explicit speech in traditional Jewish culture, in which the rabbis deliberately repudiate the public discussion of sexual intercourse. Yet Mirvis's remark about a "*frum* wedding" suggests a somewhat different reading, one that would emphasize that "*all know* for what purpose a bride enters the bridal canopy." Surely the rabbis were aware, too, of how sex can be, in Mirvis's words, "absent from the top layer of interaction but oh so tantalizingly present on every other layer." In the Talmud's prohibition of obscene speech, then, it may acknowledge Mirvis's point about textual modesty: not representing sex does not by any means suggest that one is not thinking about it, and indeed, as Friedman, Boteach, and Shalit all emphasize in their calls for modesty, the modesty they call for is, emphatically, just as capable of inciting sexual arousal as obscenity ever has been. In this sense, the interplay between modesty and arousal in the works of Shalit and Mirvis is not entirely different from what Glatshteyn described as the modesty of Weissenberg's *Dvorele* or from the deployment of the language of modesty in the most sensational scene of Asch's *God of Vengeance*: in each case, the author appeals to the reader's or audience member's sexual curiosity through a canny deployment of explicit and nonexplicit references to sexuality. What all these texts also have in common is having been written and circulated in a time, place, and language in which the courts and police would not enforce standards for the representation of sex—that is, censor them. Thus, each of the authors had to establish, according to their own principles, how most effectively to represent sex.

The same can be said of every American literary text published after March 21, 1966, the day the Supreme Court decided *Memoirs v. Massachusetts*. Notwithstanding the step backward that *Miller v. California* represented in 1973 and the creeping reexpansion of obscenity law since the 1980s in fields other than literature, since *Memoirs* there has not been a major risk in the United States that a literary work will be suppressed because of the way it represents sex. There have, of course, still been plenty of boycotts, library and curriculum removals, and acts of market censorship and of self-censorship of texts because of the way they represent sex, as well as literary censorships for reasons other than obscenity, such as libel and copyright. But the crucial and admirable work of organizations such as the Freedom to Read Foundation, which centers on fighting the removal of works deemed inappropriate from libraries, reflects just how much has changed. Whereas in 1948 the Supreme Court had to decide whether the government could legally prohibit the sale of Edmund Wilson's *Memoirs of Hecate County*—and decided that it could be banned, making the book genuinely difficult to find—the case of *Board of Education v. Pico* in 1982 turned on the question of whether school boards could prevent novels such as Kurt Vonnegut's *Slaughterhouse-Five* and Bernard Malamud's *The Fixer* from being available for free to teenagers at their school libraries.[94] Since 1966, in other words, when it comes to sex, for the most part authors in the United States have written what they want to write, publishers have published what they want to publish, booksellers have sold what they want to sell, and readers have read what they want to read, without fear that the consequence would be a court battle or a fine or a prison term. To understand the choices made by a particular author or publisher about the representation of sex in this period, then, it will generally be much more helpful to consider his or her ideas about sexual modesty than it will be to concentrate on "censorship." In this sense, American literature has since 1966 begun to look and act a lot like the American Yiddish literature of the 1920s.

Modesty, Censorship, and the First Amendment

The insight we can glean from American Yiddish literature, as from the literary theorists who reconsidered censorship in the 1990s, is that modesty, individual and changeable as it may be, cannot be done away with. In every representation of sex or refusal to represent sex, some principle of modesty exists in tension with a drive to graphic representation and explicitness. There is nothing wrong with such modesty, in the abstract, and nothing right about it either. It is an expression of an individual's predilections. The most difficult thing about responding to representations of sex is accepting that they matter intensely to us without making the mistaken assumption that others will be affected by them in the exact same way that we will.

This makes it all the more important for critics to distinguish between *modesty* and *censorship*—between limits placed on literary expression by the people who make, market, and consume it and the limits placed on it by governments and other coercive institutions. The former, to the extent that it excludes particular voices from being heard or ideas from being aired, is certainly pernicious, but it is within our power as readers and cultural professionals to resist. When people attempt to shift the grounds of modesty through measures such as boycotts or public denunciations or letter-writing campaigns—whether sympathetically or not—it should be clear at least to anyone who takes the First Amendment seriously that they are not acting as censors (except metaphorically): they are simply expressing themselves. It is when people attempt to pass laws against particular kinds of literary and cultural expression and, in some cases, against sexual behaviors—when they are attempting to enact censorships—that they need to be opposed most unequivocally and forcefully, regarded as contradicting the principle of freedom of expression we derive from the Constitution. To put it another way, everyone in the United States, even if they have the misfortune of not being able to write or read in Yiddish, deserves as much freedom to choose which sexual texts and images they will produce and consume as did the Yiddish-speaking writers, artists, editors, and readers who flourished in the United States in the first half of the 20th century.

Conclusion

Dirty Jews and the Christian Right: Larry David and FCC v. Fox

The gathering with which this book began—the encounter, real and figural, of half a dozen American Jews in a Chicago courtroom in 1961—has its analogue in the structure of this study. Those men found themselves working together to establish the legal right of Chicagoans and other Americans to purchase and read a paperback copy of Henry Miller's *Tropic of Cancer*, the narrator of which claims to "speak like a Jew." It is not clear, though, to what degree, if at all, they regarded their shared Jewishness as relevant to the trial and, in a few cases, whether they even recognized one another as fellow Jews. Similarly, the many authors, publishers, editors, sexologists, birth control activists, lawyers, critics, modesty crusaders, and pornographers whose experiences have been grouped into the preceding chapters would not, in most cases, if magically transported into a seminar room, recognize one another as members of a single ethnic or religious community, either—or at least not as members of a single group in such a way that they would feel more likely to agree or support or sympathize with one another than they would with anybody else.

Nor would many of these figures—or many contemporary American Jews, I suspect—understand themselves as linked through their ethnic or religious affiliations with the "all-Jewish" group of performers who in 2009 collaborated in the production of a video titled *Nice Jewish Girls*, a pornographic anthology in which three hard-core "numbers" are framed by and punctuated with references to Jewish religious ritual. These include intercourse between a young rabbi and his female student, a playfully sadomasochistic lesbian Chanukah candle-lighting ceremony, and the rabbi's ejaculation onto Passover matzoh clenched in two women's teeth.[1] Certainly the progressive academic contributors to a different anthology with the same title, the pioneering collection *Nice Jewish Girls: A Lesbian Anthology* (1982), would be unlikely to find much to embrace as their own in the 2009 video, which, among its other features, presents the standard cooptation of lesbianism for the pleasure of the straight male gaze that has been a regular feature of hard-core pornography throughout its history.[2] Even when Jews use the same words and even when they use those same words for a similar purpose—that is, to signal their desire to undermine, and to reclaim through transformation, a gendered ethnic stereotype—they are infrequently of one mind about how sex should be discussed or represented.

It would certainly be possible to produce a fuller cultural history than has been offered in this book of the roles played by Jews in the representation of sexuality in the United States. Contemplating what that project might look like highlights the impossibility of understanding all these individual Jews as members of a collective. Such a study would have to find a way to treat dozens of pornography performers in the generations before the *Nice Jewish Girls* film, as well as progressive sexual and gender theorists before and after the *Nice Jewish Girls* anthology; antiporn and proporn feminists and campaigners for and against homosexual rights, who would disagree vehemently about the film and the anthology; a number of erotica publishers and pornographers who have not received their fair share of attention here; dozens more novelists, poets, playwrights, cartoonists, filmmakers, lawyers, comedians, and visual artists who intervened influentially in the ways Americans talk about sex; and quite a few unique figures—an "impresaria of striptease" and the "inventor of the monokini," for example—who fit no other general category.[3] No tent could be imagined wide enough to house all such figures, and no single analytic framework could make sense of all of their lives and work. Although there have been plenty of individual American Jews with unclean lips, then, American Jews have not been in any meaningful sense a *people* of unclean lips—no more or less, at least, than they have ever been a people of uniformly clean lips.

In what sense, then, one might ask, has it been productive for this book to yoke a fair number of Americans together so as to consider as interrelated phenomena their responses to sexual anti-Semitism, their pursuits of cultural capital, their rewritings of classic Jewish tropes about reproduction, and their investments in Jewish concepts of modesty?

For one thing, exploring the various ways in which American obscenity debates have been relevant to Jews *as* Jews, as this book has done, allows for the recovery of influential interventions in American literary history that have gone mostly unnoticed. Books about the history of literary obscenity in the United States continue to be produced at a dizzying pace, and scholars in this field might begin to attend as thoughtfully to Jewishness as a potential motivating or complicating factor in an individual's engagements with obscenity as they have to other religious, racial, and ethnic affiliations. Whitney Strub's *Perversion for Profit* (2010) forcefully demonstrates the usefulness of further studies of American obscenity, as it argues persuasively that debates about sexual representation were instrumental in postwar American politics.[4] At the same time, it exhibits how even a punctilious scholar attentive to the effects of Protestant and Catholic affiliations on the people intervening in these debates can avoid Jewishness as a factor in discussions of sexual representation.[5] Strub is hardly unique in this regard. In David Allyn's cultural history of the sexual revolution, *Make Love, Not War* (2000), chapters address the roles played by African Americans, gays and lesbians, and members of the Christian clergy in the developments of the 1960s, but Allyn manages to discuss even *Portnoy's Complaint* for several pages without once noting that it is a fictional tale not just of an American masturbator but also a Jewish one.[6]

By suggesting how Jewishness has mattered to Theodore Dreiser and Horace Liveright and Henry Miller and Harriet Pilpel and Jerome Frank and many other figures who intervened in the treatment of obscenity within the American literary system, this book asserts that Jewishness cannot be relegated to the margins of the history of literary obscenity. It makes the case that scholars of American literature and of the transnational history of literary obscenity need to account for the effect of ethnicity and religion on the choices of all the individuals who have participated in that history, even when doing so brings us into contact with uncomfortable stereotypes, such as the pernicious and still-circulating myth of Jewish hypersexuality.

If this book hopes to demonstrate that scholars of American literary modernism and postmodernism can benefit from attending more thoughtfully to Jewishness, so too does it hope to show that scholars of Jewish literature can benefit from greater attention to American culture—even when its products seem most ephemeral or trivial. Can *The Harrad Experiment* or *Nice Jewish Girls* find a place on the bookshelf next to the Song of Songs and the erotic Hebrew poetry of Golden Age Spain? For Americanists, Jewish or not, who grew up during the heyday of postmodernism, this question does not even need to be asked, but for some traditional scholars of a two-thousand-year-old textual tradition rich with theological, political, and aesthetic complexities, just about anything American is already a little suspect as a kind of low culture, if not precisely, or not anymore, as the output of a *trayfe medine* (nonkosher country), which is how some European Jews regarded the United States in the late 19th and early 20th centuries. One impetus of the readings here has been to demonstrate that the distinction between high and low culture is just as unstable in modern Jewish literary history as it has been shown to be in postmodern literary history more generally: this book has argued that even literary obscenity—textual representation that is excessive, gratuitous, unsacred—can be understood as a meaningful avenue through which modern writers and thinkers, such as Philip Roth and Adele Wiseman, grapple with traditional Jewish concerns. Ideas about Jewish modesty derived from Orthodox religious tradition resonate in American popular culture, too, in ways that make debates about American obscenity, in part, about *halakha* (Jewish religious law). It is revealing that over the years some American observers have placed the Talmud—in which, famously, a student spies on his teacher having sex and characterizes that act of observation as Torah—into the same category as Lew Rosen's enticing illustrations of naked women: the category of the obscene.[7] The constitutional doctrine that protects Americans' right to read and sell the Talmud today, without bowdlerization of its sometimes frank treatments of human sexuality, is the same one that protects *Tropic of Cancer* and, for that matter, the *Nice Jewish Girls* film. That fact does not imply that anyone must juxtapose such texts or that doing so will always be productive or that anyone should conflate the very different circumstances from which such texts emerge, but this book has argued that it can be meaningful to think about classic and modern Jewish texts and modern American ones as being deeply in conversation with one another.

* * *

Like many phenomena that responsible scholars have avoided discussing, the relationship between Jews and obscenity—the rich history that this book has only begun to sketch—has surfaced insistently, if inconsistently, in American popular culture. When the comedian Sarah Silverman alluringly calls herself a "dirty Jew" in her 2005 performance film *Jesus Is Magic*[8] or when a glossy, hipster-oriented magazine called *Heeb* celebrates Jewish pornographers and pornographic performers, it would seem to suggest that there are some Jews comfortable enough in the United States that they can laugh at, and even ironically recuperate, the stereotype of Jewish hypersexuality.[9] Even Alexander Portnoy's idea that the typical American Jewish man has a tendency to say "*shit* and *fuck* a lot" has, in the 21st century, become an occasion for celebration.[10] For evidence of this, see the finale of the third season of Larry David's television show *Curb Your Enthusiasm*, first aired on November 17, 2002, which culminates in an impressive barrage of taboo words. The episode centers on the grand opening of a restaurant in which David's fictional character, also called Larry David, has invested. In the middle of the meal, the chef, who suffers from Tourette's syndrome and cooks in an open kitchen, involuntarily shouts a string of taboo words: "Fuck-head, shit-face, cocksucker, asshole, son-of-a-bitch." A strained silence descends, and David recalls a group of high school students he saw earlier in the episode who had all shaved their heads in solidarity with a classmate undergoing chemotherapy. He decides to act on the students' example, showing his support for the chef by mimicking his behavior, bellowing, "Scum-sucking, motherfucking whore!" David's assembled friends and loved ones follow suit: "Cock, cock, jism, grandma, cock. . . . Bum, fuck, turd, fart, cunt, piss, shit, bugger, and balls. . . . Dammit, hell, crap, shit. . . . Fellatio, cunnilingus, French kissing, rim job." David's father on the show, played by the veteran comedian Shelley Berman, chimes in to add a set of Yiddish taboo words—"*Shmuk, putz, tukhis-lekher*"—to the episode's catalog of obscenities before the camera zooms in on David's satisfied face, and the episode comes to an end.[11] David and the episode's director, Robert Weide, were almost certainly thinking of Lenny Bruce's use of taboo words when they planned and shot this memorable scene, but the climactic collocation of taboo words also parallels Henry Roth's *Call It Sleep*, which builds to a similar crescendo.[12]

Like Roth's, the *Curb* episode's climax presents a blending of obscene voices, a chorus of profane American speech. The difference is that what in 1935 was shameful, vulgar, and legally risky—a cacophony that could be unified and rendered valuable only through the techniques of high modernism—recurs in *Curb* as sweet, harmonious, inclusive cable TV comedy. What could be less threatening than Berman, at the age of seventy-six, calling out "*tukhis-lekher*" (ass-licker) to nobody in particular? And what could be more fun, the scene implies, than having a good reason to yell out some dirty words in public? Obscenity figures here as pleasure and as a rallying point around which a community—not an exclusively Jewish one but one in which Jews are the most prominent and vocal members—coheres. Way back in 1982, the novelist, publisher, and theologian Arthur A. Cohen predicted this, noting insightfully that "the real curse in a sanitized culture . . . would be 'clean Jew.' I would be insulted by being thought now a clean Jew."[13] The corollary to this insight is that it seems nowadays that lots of Jews are more than happy to be called dirty.[14]

Are Jews any different, in this regard, than other Americans in the 21st century? No, and maybe yes. No in the sense that the number of American media outlets in which one can be sure not to encounter what U.S. law once proscribed as obscene is small and shrinking. Thanks to the decisions in *FCC v. Fox* in 2009 and 2012, broadcast television and terrestrial radio still operate under rules, established in *FCC v. Pacifica* in 1978, that force them to euphemize and "bleep" dirty words;[15] but books, newspapers, magazines, cable TV, satellite radio, websites, and podcasts generally do not. In the latter categories, there are, of course, many publications and producers and channels that forswear taboo language—but doing so regularly looks silly and often occasions derisive, sometimes even self-mocking, commentary.[16] The use of taboo language no longer seems to constrain a product's marketability at all, either: a book called *On Bullshit* was a best-seller in 2005, and in 2010, an upbeat pop song titled "Fuck You," by Cee Lo Green, was a massive chart-topping hit. The mobile Internet has meanwhile achieved what generations of pornographers never dared to dream: nearly ubiquitous, on-demand access to a stunningly extensive library of explicit sexual photographs and videos. There is nothing to indicate that American Jews are any more or less the beneficiaries or victims of these circumstances than anyone else in the United States.

Yet, at the same time, censoriousness persists. Strub describes how as access to the World Wide Web spread in the 1990s, so did efforts to expand "governmental moral surveillance." With the Communications Decency Act (1996), the Child Pornography Prevention Act (1996), the Child Online Protection Act (1998), and the PROTECT Act (2003), as well as a host of local prosecutions, antipornography lawmakers and lobbyists have attempted to exert control of visual and textual representations of sexuality on the Internet.[17] In likely unintentional homage to the rhetorical techniques of Anthony Comstock, who titled one of his most widely read books *Traps for the Young*, these bills—struck down repeatedly in the 1990s as unconstitutional but passed under George W. Bush and then upheld by the Supreme Court—have emphasized the notion that children are threatened by the availability of sexually explicit materials and then also included broad, vague language that allows for criminal charges to be brought even in cases in which no children have been involved.[18] The enforcement of such laws has stretched beyond the Internet to a variety of offline media, while in recent years Internet powerhouses such as Facebook and Apple have established their own draconian and often absurd policies for suppressing sexual expression.[19] At the same time, as mentioned earlier, the decisions in the *FCC v. Fox* cases in 2009 and 2012 have reinforced the mandate of the Federal Communications Commission to levy huge fines on broadcasters that allow even "fleeting" obscenities to air—a dirty word tossed off, spontaneously, during a live broadcast—while cases such as *Bethel v. Fraser* (1986) and *Morse v. Frederick* (2007) have made clear that in or near American public schools, First Amendment protection cannot be guaranteed to sexual innuendo, no matter how silly ("I know a man who is firm—he's firm in his pants, he's firm in his shirt, his character is firm . . ."), nor to drug references, no matter how incoherent ("Bong Hits 4 Jesus").[20]

What bears emphasizing in this study is the degree to which these recent efforts to suppress and criminalize explicit sexual representation and taboo language on the Internet, in the media, and in public schools mirror previous censorship attempts, beginning with Comstock's original crusade, in being understood by many of their leaders as a Christian project. The Nebraska Democrat James Exon, who sponsored the Communications Decency Act in 1995, for one example, opened the congressional debate about the act by repeating a prayer offered earlier by the televangelist Dr. Lloyd John Ogilvie, then serving as Senate chaplain, who had asked "Almighty God, Lord of all life," to "give us wisdom to create regulations that will protect the innocent."[21] Exon was reported at the time of those debates, by the Associated Press, as having told a reporter that he appreciated the help of Enough Is Enough, an antipornography group, in "laying the groundwork for compromise between Christian conservatives and pro-business Republicans" in support of the act, and the congressman also highlighted the conservative Christian support for his proposal by introducing letters of support from the Christian Coalition and the Family Research Council (an organization advocating "a Christian worldview") into the congressional record.[22]

The contemporary Christian Right has a much more complex and self-conscious relationship with American Jews than its 19th-century predecessors did, and its leaders typically, if not universally, deemphasize Jewish difference—and the efforts still regularly being made by missionary groups to convert Jews to Christianity—in the hopes of attracting Jewish support.[23] It is not surprising, then, that recent antipornography campaigns have welcomed with open arms any Jews with compatible ideas, such as Wendy Shalit; have sought out Jews to sit on their boards; and have universally avoided emphasizing that many Jews are among those who oppose their efforts.[24] But there have nonetheless been occasional moments when hints of the anti-Semitism of historical Comstockery have been perceivable in contemporary antiobscenity discourse.

Writing for the majority in the 2009 *FCC v. Fox* decision, for example, Justice Antonin Scalia made an odd remark about the relative use of taboo language among Americans of different backgrounds. He was rebutting a point from a dissenting opinion about how "small-town broadcasters" would suffer unduly under the court's decision, because it would necessitate their purchase of expensive equipment to bowdlerize fleeting expletives during live broadcasts. These "small-town broadcasters" would not suffer, Scalia countered, because their "down-home local guests probably employ vulgarity less than big-city folks" and the "foul-mouthed glitteratae from Hollywood."[25] Vulgar use of taboo words, Scalia declared, is a "big-city," "Hollywood" problem, rather than one affecting "down-home," "small-town" Americans. Scalia did not, of course, go so far as to suggest that the demographic group most insistently associated both with "big-city" life and with "Hollywood"—Jews—tend to speak more obscenely than other Americans, but if he had wanted to, he could not have a better illustration of his hypothesis than *Curb Your Enthusiasm*'s fictional Larry David, a Hollywood insider whom it would be difficult to imagine setting foot even momentarily outside his metropolitan habitat. The actual celebrities whose speeches occasioned the case, Cher and Nicole Ritchie, are not Jewish, but Scalia's quip relies on some old stereotyped associations. Recall that Telemachus Timayenis fulminated against the Jews who spew "filthy expressions and obscene words" and whose "number is daily increasing . . . in every one of the large cities in America"[26] or that John Sumner, somewhat savvier, argued that the nation's "literati" should be considered "abnormal" and thus unsuited to testify as to literary merit in obscenity cases (though, as noted in chapter 1, the judge in the relevant case, who was Jewish, took exception to Sumner's insinuations).[27] The feminist scholars Janet Jakobsen and Ann Pellegrini have argued, in reference to Scalia's remarks in his dissent in *Romer v. Evans*, that "the anti-Semitic resonances of Scalia's rhetoric are not incidental features of his argument" but demonstrate that the "traditional sexual mores" Scalia defends are specifically Christian ones. Like Jakobsen and Pellegrini, I would not go so far as to accuse Scalia of deliberate anti-Semitism, but it is worthwhile to note the ways in which his discourse slips into "a shared—and largely unconscious—cultural logic": in this case, an unfounded assumption about who favors the use of taboo language and who does not.[28]

The persistence of emphatically Christian campaigns against obscenity, and the vague, recrudescent sense promulgated by such campaigns, if indirectly, that the people using obscenity are not sufficiently Christian or American, may help to explain why, in a media environment in which the representation of sex and the use of taboo words is increasingly mainstream—in which it is entirely obvious to comedians of all backgrounds that the use of obscenity is a sure way to get a laugh, so obvious in fact that one might think it is a little hacky to do so—brilliant performers such as Larry David and Sarah Silverman continue not only to assert their Jewishness emphatically, in virtually every one of their performances, but also to glory in and glorify the use of taboo language.[29] Especially because the Christian Right of the late 20th and early 21st centuries has gone to such lengths to demonstrate that Jews should not feel excluded from its initiatives, identifying oneself as a "dirty Jew" in the 21st century has become attractive as a means for signaling one's opposition not just, in general, to the banalities of a "sanitized culture," as Arthur A. Cohen remarked in the early years of the Reagan administration, but also to what has become in the ensuing decades the country's most powerful social, religious, and politically reactionary movement.

* * *

If the rise of the Christian Right and its opposition to obscenity is one reason obscenity can be meaningful to Jews today, it is hardly the only one—and, more to the point, it is not the same one that made obscenity meaningful to American Jews in the 1890s or 1920s or 1960s. This book has argued that taboo words and explicit representations of sex were meaningful to American Jews during the 20th century, but they were meaningful in contingent and historically specific ways. In fact, most of the dynamics studied in the preceding chapters no longer apply. Contrary to the beliefs of the writers and theorists discussed in chapter 1, we now know that pornotopias are not often idyllic once they collide with reality, and progressive sexual attitudes are not always a cure for anti-Semitism. Unfortunately for cultural entrepreneurs and artists who want to use obscenity to acquire cultural capital, such as those discussed in chapter 2, saying "shit" and "fuck" no longer seems all that daring or avant-garde: to get noticed for taboo language now, one has to find a clever way of revivifying it, as in *Curb Your Enthusiasm* or the already legendary three-minute scene from David Simon's television opus *The Wire*, in which two detectives investigate a crime scene speaking only the word "fuck" and its variants.[30] Though it remains popular to do so, no longer is there much frisson to be had by rewriting traditional rabbinical tropes in sexually graphic terms, as chapter 3 argued that Philip Roth and Adele Wiseman did. On the other hand, debates about modesty, as discussed in chapter 4, continue to crop up, even more insistently, as the unfettered sharing of social media continues to expand. But even if one can also hear echoes of late 19th-century antiobscenity crusades in the cries of those who are fighting to purify the Internet today, much more has changed in the way American Jews relate to obscenity than has stayed the same.

It is impossible to predict how future debates about obscenity in the United States—for example, the debate, already begun but due for greater attention, about the perniciousness of laws that were designed to protect children and teenagers from sexual predation but that have ended up, too often, tarring innocent people as sex criminals and limiting the freedom of artists—might involve American Jews, for better and worse.[31] That is as it should be: the story of American obscenity and the story of American Jews remain unfinished and will continue to develop. What this book has argued is simply that as we consider those stories in the 20th century, when they were central to the development of American literature, we cannot understand them separately.

NOTES

Notes to the Introduction

1. A detailed account of the trial, and events leading up to it, can be found in Hoke Norris, "'Cancer' in Chicago," *Evergreen Review* 6 (July–August 1962): 40–66. See also Edward de Grazia, *Girls Lean Back Everywhere: The Law of Obscenity and the Assault on Genius* (New York: Random House, 1992), 371–83.
2. Charles Rembar, *The End of Obscenity: The Trials of "Lady Chatterley," "Tropic of Cancer," and "Fanny Hill"* (New York: Random House, 1968), 114.
3. De Grazia, *Girls Lean Back Everywhere*, 325.
4. On Haiman's biography, see the Franklyn S. Haiman Papers, 1927–2003, at Northwestern University Archives. For Gertz's account of the trial, see Elmer Gertz, *A Handful of Clients* (Chicago: Follett, 1965), 229–304. On Gertz's childhood in a B'nai B'rith orphanage in Cleveland, see his memoir, "Poor Little Orphan," *Panorama* (January 1935): 6–7; as an adult, among many other affiliations, Gertz served as president of the Greater Chicago Council of the American Jewish Congress. Rosset's father was Jewish, and his mother was an Irish non-Jew; he identifies himself as Jewish in Neil Ortenberg and Daniel O'Connor's biographical documentary film *Obscene: A Portrait of Barney Rosset and Grove Press* (New York: Arts Alliance America, 2009). Ellmann's father, James Isaac Ellmann, was a lawyer and justice of the peace in Highland Park, Michigan, who had also served as president of the Jewish Community Council of Detroit; see the Ellmann Family File in the Rabbi Leo M. Franklin Archives, Bloomfield, Michigan. On the Epstein family, see Mark Bauman, *Harry H. Epstein and the Rabbinate as Conduit for Change* (Rutherford, NJ: Fairleigh Dickinson University Press, 1994).
5. Henry Miller, *Tropic of Cancer* (New York: Grove, 1961), 187, 3.
6. Circumcision was understood by both Jews and non-Jews in the ancient world to be the primary marker of Jewish difference. As Peter Schäfer reports, the Roman satirist Rutilius Namatianus referred to "the *obscena gens* ('obscene, filthy people') of the Jews 'that shamefully cuts off the genital head' (*quae genitale caput propudiosa metit*), that is, practices circumcision." Peter Schäfer, *Judeophobia: Attitudes toward the Jews in the Ancient World* (Cambridge: Harvard University Press, 1998), 102. As early as the 5th century, then, many centuries before the "reinvention of obscenity" that brought that concept to bear on the culture of early

modern Europe—see Joan DeJean, *The Reinvention of Obscenity: Sex, Lies, and Tabloids in Early Modern France* (Chicago: University of Chicago Press, 2002)—Jews were already regarded as an "obscene people." Aside from circumcision, the characteristics ascribed to Jews by Romans and early Christians that contributed to this perception included their alleged sexual aggression and theological comfort with both marriage and polygamy. In one poem, quoted by Schäfer, that is revealing in its portrait of specifically Jewish sexual aggression, Martial criticizes a Jewish colleague who has seduced his own young lover: "even though you were born in Jerusalem itself, / you bugger my boy, circumcised poet" (96). On the topic of marriage, meanwhile, Justin Martyr attacked Jewish polygamy and the license that the Torah's narratives offered for men's lust: "If anyone see a beautiful woman and desire to have her, they quote the doings of Jacob," he complained. Justin Martyr, "Dialogue with Trypho, a Jew," in Rev. Alexander Roberts and James Donaldson, eds., *Anti-Nicene Christian Library*, vol. 2 (Edinburgh: T. and T. Clark, 1868), 85–278 (quote on 269). Moreover, according to the eighteenth demonstration of Aphrahat, written in 4th-century Persia, some Jews attempted to convince early Christians to eschew celibacy: "I have written to you, my beloved ones, on the issue of virginity and sanctity," Aphrahat explained, "because I heard of a Jew who embarrassed one of our brethren of our community and said to him: 'You are impure because you take no wives, whereas we who procreate and increase the world are holy and excellent.'" Quoted in Isaiah M. Gafni, "The Institution of Marriage in Rabbinic Times," in David Kraemer, ed., *The Jewish Family: Metaphor and Memory* (New York: Oxford University Press, 1989), 20. Publius Cornelius Tacitus effectively captured the spirit of these views in his description of Jews as "prone to lust," and Augustine concurred in his characterization of "the Jews" as "indisputably carnal." Shaye J. D. Cohen, *The Beginnings of Jewishness: Boundaries, Varieties, Uncertainties* (Berkeley: University of California Press, 1999), 43; Daniel Boyarin, *Carnal Israel: Reading Sex in Talmudic Culture* (Berkeley: University of California Press, 1993), 1.

7. A number of medieval and early modern *Judensau* drawings and relief sculptures represent Jews as sexually perverse—suckling from and fornicating with pigs—and Debra Higgs Strickland argues that depictions of other unclean animals, including hyenas, in medieval English illustrated bestiaries likewise conveyed a "charge of Jewish sexual perversity." Strickland, "The Jews, Leviticus, and the Unclean in Medieval English Bestiaries," in Mitchell B. Merback, ed., *Beyond the Yellow Badge: Anti-Judaism and Antisemitism in Medieval and Early Modern Visual Culture* (Leiden: Brill, 2007), 203–32. See also Isaiah Shachar, *The Judensau: A Medieval Anti-Jewish Motif and Its History* (London: Warburg Institute, 1974).
8. On the democratization of the media in this period, see Paul Starr, *The Creation of the Media: Political Origins of Modern Communications* (New York: Basic Books, 2004), 233–66. On the more specific link made by anti-Semites of Jewish greed to lust and sexual abnormality in this period, see Allison Pease, *Modernism, Mass*

Culture, and the Aesthetics of Obscenity (New York: Cambridge University Press, 2000), 3, 22, 86.

9. Édouard Drumont, *La France juive: Essai d'histoire contemporaine* (Paris: C. Marpon and E. Flammarion, 1886), 2:458. For a brief description of Timayenis's career, see Jacob Rader Marcus, *United States Jewry, 1776–1985* (Detroit: Wayne State University Press, 1989), 170.
10. Telemachus T. Timayenis, *The Original Mr. Jacobs* (New York: Minerva, 1888), 288–89. For the corresponding passage, see Drumont, *La France juive*, 2:456.
11. Timayenis, *Original Mr. Jacobs*, 280–81.
12. Nicola Beisel, *Imperiled Innocents: Anthony Comstock and Family Reproduction in Victorian America* (Princeton: Princeton University Press, 1997), 25–33, 45.
13. "Comstock and the Courts: How a Director of the Vice Society Gave Anthony Away," *Boston Daily Globe* (January 21, 1880): 2. For a plausible anecdote sympathetic to Comstock's pursuit of a Jew who "was found to be employing a dozen or more girls and boys, of from twelve to fifteen years of age, to make articles of a vile sort"—condoms, other birth control devices, or dildos, presumably—in the early 1870s, and in which Comstock triumphs over "a certain Hebrew society" that attempts to protect the alleged offender, see C. G. Trumbull, *Anthony Comstock: Fighter* (New York: Fleming H. Revell, 1913), 115–27.
14. *Christianity Practically Applied: The Discussions of the International Christian Conference Held in Chicago, October 8–14, 1893, in Connection with the World's Congress Auxiliary of the World's Columbian Exposition and under the Auspices and Direction of the Evangelical Alliance for the United States* (New York: Baker and Taylor, 1894), 416.
15. *Rosen v. United States*, 161 U.S. 29 (1896), Transcript of Record, 16.
16. Ibid., 14.
17. *Rosen*, 161 U.S. at 31.
18. Lewis Rosenthal, *America and France: The Influence of the United States on France in the Eighteenth Century* (New York: Holt, 1882). Biographical information on Rosen can be found in Isaac Markens, *The Hebrews in America: A Series of Historical and Biographical Sketches* (New York: Published by the author, 1888), 244–45.
19. Lew Rosen, *Grisette: A Tale of Paris and New York* (New York: John Delay, 1889). One critic called the book "a graphic sketch of a Parisian cocotte," but another opined that "whatever may have been the morals of his heroine, Lew Rosen most certainly has treated them in a subtle, successful way. The story of Grisette is told with happy tact, with consommate [*sic*] skill, with successful avoidance of the many pitfalls which this subject lays for the unsuspecting novelist." "Literature," *San Francisco Chronicle* (June 30, 1889): 7; *Book Chat* 4:5 (May 1889): 135.
20. "News and Notes," *The Writer* 3:8 (August 1889): 191.
21. Markens, *Hebrews in America*, 244–45; Lew Rosen, "Masks and Faces," *National Police Gazette* (December 6, 1890): 2.
22. *Rosen*, Transcript, 17.

23. In the trial of David Gordan for publishing an obscene poem in 1927 (discussed later), one of the judges pointed out that Gordan's original name was Goronefsky, and another remarked, "it is too bad we cannot sentence you to Russia." This was not just wishful thinking: in a contemporaneous case, the U.S. government actually did deport a Jewish immigrant from the United States for publishing obscenity. She was a Polish Jewish woman named Chava Zlotchever, who had lived in the United States since 1912 and in the 1920s operated a tea house in Greenwich Village under the names Eve Adams and Evelyn Addams. In June 1925, she was accused of "tak[ing] girls into her apartment, serv[ing] them drinks, and within a short space of time [she] had the girls stripped a lying on her bed where she practiced her habits as a conenlinguist [*sic*]." She also privately published a book called *Lesbian Love* that police called "indecent." She was sentenced to "an indeterminate term in the Penitentiary" and deported in December 1927. "Eve Addams' Ring of Rich Cultists," *Variety* (July 28, 1926): 37; "Sworn Statement of Mr. Jay Fitzpatrick," Ellis Island, June 23, 1925. Thanks to Steven W. Siegel of the Jewish Historical Society of New York for sharing materials on Zlotchever with me. Almost three decades later, Senator Estes Kefauver, in the subcommittee hearings on pornography he organized in 1955, "wondered out loud," as one newspaper account put it, "just how valid [Samuel] Roth's citizenship was." James Desmond, "Dirty-Pix Probers Entangle Three," *New York Daily News* (June 1, 1955), reproduced in Jay A. Gertzman, *Bookleggers and Smuthounds: The Trade in Erotica, 1920–1940* (Philadelphia: University of Pennsylvania Press, 1999), 278.
24. Rosen's column ran weekly from December 1895 to January 1902.
25. "On the Watch Tower," *Bookseller and Newsman* 14:6 (June 1897): 33.
26. *Rosen* was explicitly upheld as precedent, for example, as late as *Hamling v. United States*, 418 U.S. 87 (1974). On the place of *Rosen* in the development of American obscenity law, see Frederick Schauer, *The Law of Obscenity* (Washington, DC: Bureau of National Affairs, 1976), 19–20.
27. Gertzman, *Bookleggers and Smuthounds*, 28–29.
28. See Neil Pearson, *Obelisk: The History of Jack Kahane and the Obelisk Press* (Liverpool: Liverpool University Press, 2007). Edward Titus, the first publisher to print D. H. Lawrence's unexpurgated *Lady Chatterley's Lover* in Paris, is briefly mentioned by name in a list of Miller's Jewish associates in the first pages of *Tropic of Cancer* (3).
29. *Burstyn v. Wilson*, 343 U.S. 495 (1952), *Freedman v. Maryland*, 380 U.S. 51 (1965), *Mishkin v. New York*, 383 U.S. 502 (1966), *Ginzburg v. United States*, 383 U.S. 463 (1966), *Ginsberg v. New York*, 390 U.S. 629 (1968), *Cohen v. California*, 403 U.S. 15 (1971), *Miller v. California*, 413 U.S. 15 (1973). For discussions of these cases, see Schauer, *Law of Obscenity*; and de Grazia, *Girls Lean Back Everywhere*.
30. Forrest Bailey to Wellman, March 31, 1927, quoted in Samuel Walker, *In Defense of American Liberties: A History of the ACLU* (New York: Oxford University Press, 1990), 83; Whitney Strub, *Perversion for Profit: The Politics of Pornography and the Rise of the New Right* (New York: Columbia University Press, 2010), 49.

31. Hearings before the Select Committee on Current Pornographic Materials, House of Representatives, 82nd Cong., 1952, 342, quoted in David Allyn, *Make Love, Not War: The Sexual Revolution: An Unfettered History* (Boston: Little, Brown, 2000), 61.
32. Walker, *In Defense of American Liberties*, 301–2, 312. The specific appeal of the legal profession to American Jews—which has been discussed in such studies as Jerold Auerbach's *Rabbis and Lawyers: The Journey from Torah to Constitution* (Bloomington: Indiana University Press, 1990)—does not, as far as I can tell, offer much in the way of explanation for the differing priorities of Jewish and liberal Protestant lawyers in the 1920s. Surely the liberal Protestant founders of the ACLU felt themselves to be just as committed to the Constitution's protection of free speech as their Jewish peers; where they differed was specifically on the strategic question of whether obscenity cases should be taken on.

    On Hays, see his *Let Freedom Ring* (New York: Boni and Liveright, 1928), *Trial by Prejudice* (New York: Covici, Friede, 1933), and *City Lawyers: The Autobiography of a Law Practice* (New York: Simon and Schuster, 1942). For Ernst, see his *To the Pure . . . : A Study of Obscenity and the Censor* (New York: Viking, 1928), *Censorship: The Search for the Obscene* (New York: Macmillan, 1964), and his memoirs, *The Best Is Yet* (New York: Harper, 1945) and *So Far So Good* (New York: Harper, 1948). Recent studies of Ernst's career include Brett Gary, "'Guessing Oneself into Jail': Morris Ernst and the Assault on American Obscenity Law in the 1930s," in Loren Glass and Charles Francis Williams, eds., *Obscenity and the Limits of Liberalism* (Columbus: Ohio State University Press, 2011), 50–68; and Joel Matthew Silverman, "Pursuing Celebrity, Ensuing Masculinity: Morris Ernst, Obscenity, and the Search for Recognition" (PhD diss., American Studies, University of Texas at Austin, 2006).
33. In addition to the books listed in the previous note, see Ephraim London's anthology *The World of Law* (New York: Simon and Schuster, 1960) and Martin Garbus's memoirs *Ready for the Defense* (New York: Farrar, Straus and Giroux, 1971) and *Traitors and Heroes: A Lawyer's Memoir* (New York: Atheneum, 1987). In the 1950s and 1960s, Pilpel wrote a regular column for *Publisher's Weekly* on legal issues, including obscenity.
34. See *People v. Viking Press, Inc.*, 147 N.Y. Misc. 813 (Magistrate's Ct. 1933). On Greenspan and the Wall Street Synagogue, see Marvin Greisman, "The Orthodox Spirit of Wall Street since 1929," *Downtown Express* 18:9 (July 22–28, 2005).
35. Perlman (1887–1952) had served as a Republican New York State congressman from 1920 to 1927, and among his philanthropic involvements in the Jewish community, he had served as vice president of the American Jewish Congress and president of Beth Israel Hospital in New York. See Kurt F. Stone, *The Congressional Minyan: The Jews of Capitol Hill* (Jersey City, NJ: Ktav, 2000), 376–77.
36. On Frank, see Robert Jerome Glennon, *The Iconoclast as Reformer: Jerome Frank's Impact on American Law* (Ithaca: Cornell University Press, 1985). An excellent source for understanding Frank's Jewish identity and how he felt it influenced

his politics is "Red, White, and Blue Herring," *Saturday Evening Post* (December 6, 1941): 9. Before his legal career, Frank harbored literary inclinations of his own. He reviewed books and befriended authors including Sherwood Anderson and Sinclair Lewis. He wrote two-thirds of a novel himself that he submitted to Houghton Mifflin; the editors feared that one chapter of the novel would lead to its suppression in Boston, presumably by the Watch and Ward Society on the grounds of obscenity. Frank decided not to complete or publish the book for fear that doing so would jeopardize his legal career. See the transcripts of interviews with Frank, conducted between 1950 and 1952, in the Oral History Collection of Columbia University, 1:6–7.

37. *Big Table, Inc., v. Schroeder*, 186 F. Supp. 254 (N.D. Ill. 1960). On this trial, see de Grazia, *Girls Lean Back Everywhere*, 343–65.
38. On the attacks on Fortas, see Strub, *Perversion for Profit*, 125–29, and on Brennan's role in building coalitions on the court and developing doctrinal solutions to First Amendment problems, see de Grazia, *Girls Lean Back Everywhere*, 398–416, 434–43.
39. When Senator Estes Kefauver convened a congressional committee to address "obscene and pornographic literature and juvenile delinquency" in 1955, the committee examined some entrepreneurs, such as Samuel Roth and Edward Mishkin, whose cases were thereafter considered by the Supreme Court, but a handful of the others, including Al Stone, Louis Shomer, and Arthur Herman Sobel, never achieved that degree of notoriety. See Strub, *Perversion for Profit*, 25–27; and Senate Committee on the Judiciary, *Obscene and Pornographic Literature and Juvenile Delinquency: Interim Report of the Subcommittee to Investigate Juvenile Delinquency* (Washington, DC: GPO, 1956).
40. Andrea Friedman argues convincingly in her study of obscenity activism, *Prurient Interests: Gender, Democracy, and Obscenity in New York City, 1909–1945* (New York: Columbia University Press, 2000), "Rabbis entered into anti-obscenity activism in the attempt to counter Christians' perceptions of Jews as a different, alien, and more primitive people, by demonstrating that they shared the 'Christian' morals of their Protestant and Catholic brethren and by trying to control the behavior of other Jews" (141). Felicia Herman dramatizes and elaborates on Friedman's point in the context of film-industry reform in "American Jews and the Effort to Reform Motion Pictures, 1933–1935," *American Jewish Archives Journal* 53:1–2 (2001): 11–44. See also Leigh Ann Wheeler, *Against Obscenity: Reform and the Politics of Womanhood in America, 1873–1935* (Baltimore: Johns Hopkins University Press, 2004), 170–71. One can see how these attitudes were manifested in a 1918 Rosh Hashana sermon by a Louisiana rabbi, Maximilian Heller, who fulminated, "In the name of Judaism . . . I deem it my duty to denounce this irreligion of a pleasure-mad generation; it is not only pleasure and pastime and unwholesome excitement which must not figure as serious ends of life; but even to be happy and to make others happy, be that achievement ever so desirable, even this is not the end and aim of human existence." Heller, "The Religion of

Having a Good Time," a sermon in the collection of the American Jewish Historical Society, 4.

Major cases in which Harry Kahan testified for the prosecution included *Doubleday v. New York* (1948) and *Winters v. New York* (1948). For details about his earlier activities as an antivice crusader, see Thomas C. Mackey, *Pursuing Johns: Criminal Law Reform, Defending Character, and New York City's Committee of Fourteen, 1920–1930* (Columbus: Ohio State University Press, 2005), 48–49; Burton William Peretti, *Nightclub City: Politics and Amusement in Manhattan* (Philadelphia: University of Pennsylvania Press, 2007), 32, 40–44; and Rachel Shteir, *Striptease: A History* (New York: Oxford University Press, 2005), 102.

On Harry Loeb, see Strub, *Perversion for Profit*, 138–41. For Kristol's antipornography argument, see Irving Kristol, "Pornography, Obscenity, and the Case for Censorship," *New York Times Magazine* (March 28, 1971): 24. For Andrea Dworkin's most influential texts, see Andrea Dworkin, *Pornography: Men Possessing Women* (New York: Putnam, 1981); and Andrea Dworkin and Catharine MacKinnon, *Pornography and Civil Rights: A New Day for Women's Equality* (Minneapolis: Organizing Against Pornography, 1988). On Reisman's activities, see Isabel Wilkerson, "Witness in Obscenity Trial Calls Explicit Photographs 'Destructive,'" *New York Times* (October 5, 1990); and Dagmar Herzog, *Sex in Crisis: The New Sexual Revolution and the Future of American Politics* (New York: Basic Books, 2008), 20, 70–71.

41. See Norris, "'Cancer' in Chicago," 60–61.
42. Some of the more noteworthy work in this field, not already cited, includes Paul S. Boyer, *Purity in Print: The Vice Society Movement and Book Censorship in America* (New York: Scribner, 1968); Gay Talese, *Thy Neighbor's Wife* (New York: Doubleday, 1980); Walter Kendrick, *The Secret Museum: Pornography in Modern Culture* (New York: Viking, 1987); Florence Dore, *The Novel and the Obscene: Sexual Subjects in American Modernism* (Stanford: Stanford University Press, 2005); Celia Marshik, *British Modernism and Censorship* (New York: Cambridge University Press, 2006); Loren Glass, "Redeeming Value: Obscenity and Anglo-American Modernism," *Critical Inquiry* 32:2 (Winter 2006): 344; Collette Colligan, *The Traffic in Obscenity from Byron to Beardsley: Sexuality and Exoticism in Nineteenth-Century Print Culture* (New York: Palgrave Macmillan, 2006); Loren Glass, "#$%^&*!?: Modernism and Dirty Words," *modernism/modernity* 14:2 (April 2007): 209–23; and Loren Glass and Charles Francis Williams, eds., *Obscenity and the Limits of Liberalism* (Columbus: Ohio State University Press, 2011).
43. Strub, as one example, emphasizes the interventions of the Christian Right in debates about pornography and obscenity—documenting how Charles Keating's Citizens for Decent Literature, founded by "a Catholic man in a heavily Catholic town," succeeded by "graft[ing] a nominally secular and respectably legalistic rhetoric onto the existing language of sin, damnation, and authoritarianism" that had been established by previous generations of explicitly Catholic antivice groups (*Perversion for Profit*, 87, 84). Yet Strub almost never mentions the

Jewishness of many of the Jewish participants in the debates about pornography he covers.

44. De Grazia, *Girls Lean Back Everywhere*, 226.
45. David Hollinger, *Science, Jews, and Secular Culture: Studies in Mid-Twentieth Century American Intellectual History* (Princeton: Princeton University Press, 1996), 11.
46. Hugh Hefner, "The Playboy Philosophy," *Playboy* 11:1 (January 1964): 62.
47. Ruth K. Westheimer and Jonathan Mark, *Heavenly Sex: Sexuality in the Jewish Tradition* (New York: NYU Press, 1995), 5, 11.
48. Nathan Abrams, "Triple-exthnics," *Jewish Quarterly* 196 (Winter 2004). In a later essay, Abrams admits to having "perhaps naively and uncritically accept[ed] . . . unconfirmed statements" by the blogger Luke Ford about the prominence of Jews in contemporary pornography, statements that were probably themselves drawn from such sources as Daniel Shocket's "Did You Know Most Male Porn Stars Are Jewish?," originally published in *Samantha Fox's X-Rated Cinema* in 1984 and reprinted in *Shmate* 21–22 (Spring 1989): 33–35. Abrams aptly describes the parallel weaknesses ("inaccuracies," "no consideration that Jews in porn do not represent their religious/ethnic group," and so forth) of treatments of the subject by both boosters and bigots. See Nathan Abrams, "Kosher Beefcakes and Kosher Cheesecakes: Jews in Porn—An Overview," in Abrams, ed., *Jews and Sex* (Nottingham, UK: Five Leaves, 2008), 177–88.
49. Hollinger, *Science, Jews, and Secular Culture*, 11. The most notable exception is Gertzman's *Bookleggers and Smuthounds*.
50. Hollinger, *Science, Jews, and Secular Culture*, 13.
51. Even Gayatri Chakravorty Spivak, who popularized the idea of "strategic essentialism," famously blanched, back in 1993, at the way it had become a "union ticket for essentialism" and said she has "given up on" the phrase. Sara Danius and Stefan Jonsson, "An Interview with Gayatri Chakravorty Spivak," *boundary 2* 20:2 (1993): 35.
52. For some of the more compelling and provocative contributions to this growing literature, see Howard Eilberg-Schwartz, *God's Phallus and Other Problems for Men and Monotheism* (Boston: Beacon, 1994); Boyarin, *Carnal Israel*; Daniel Boyarin, *Unheroic Conduct: The Rise of Heterosexuality and the Invention of the Jewish Man* (Berkeley: University of California Press, 1997); Moshe Idel, *Kabbalah and Eros* (New Haven: Yale University Press, 2005); Naomi Seidman, *A Marriage Made in Heaven: The Sexual Politics of Hebrew and Yiddish* (Berkeley: University of California Press, 1997); Riv-Ellen Prell, *Fighting to Become Americans: Jews, Gender, and the Anxiety of Assimilation* (Boston: Beacon, 1999); and Paula Hyman, *Gender and Assimilation in Modern Jewish History: The Roles and Representations of Women* (Seattle: University of Washington Press, 1995). Edited collections also continue to proliferate in this field; earlier examples included Howard Eilberg-Schwartz, ed., *People of the Body: Jews and Judaism from an Embodied Perspective* (Albany: SUNY Press, 1992); and Jonathan Magonet, ed.,

Jewish Explorations of Sexuality (Providence, RI: Berghahn Books, 1995), while recent additions have included Nathan Abrams, ed., *Jews and Sex*; and Danya Ruttenberg, ed., *The Passionate Torah: Sex and Judaism* (New York: NYU Press, 2009).

53. David Biale, "Confessions of an Historian of Jewish Culture," *Jewish Social Studies* 1:1 (Autumn 1994): 40–51.
54. David Biale, *Eros and the Jews: From Biblical Israel to Contemporary America* (New York: Basic Books, 1992), 205. Interestingly, Biale notes that the chapter on the United States was an afterthought, suggested by his editor (xi).
55. Jonathan Sarna, "The Cult of Synthesis in American Jewish Culture," *Jewish Social Studies* 5:1–2 (Autumn 1998–Winter 1999): 52–79.
56. The case of David Gordan (a.k.a. Gordon), mentioned briefly in an earlier note, furnishes a stunning example of how vehement this rejection of America could be. Gordan published a poem, "America," in the "New Magazine" section of the *Daily Worker* (March 12, 1927): 2, while still a student at DeWitt Clinton High School. The poem pulls no punches in its rejection of American values: "America is a land of censored opportunity / Lick spit; eat dirt. / There's your opportunity / . . . Hell, / America, / You can't be liked, spreading hot-air stink. / You're everything, aren't you, America? / Of course. / You're even a neat whore house / . . . A fleshy woman / To make you feel you're giving away your life water / For a healthy bastard." Gordan was charged with publishing an obscene poem under the Comstock Act. According to the *New York Times*, the police "denied that the economic views of the editors had anything to do with the case," insisting that this was purely a case of literary obscenity. Gordan received a sentence of thirteen months in the New York City Reformatory. While an appeal was pending, Gordan received a scholarship to the University of Wisconsin. He spent a year in Madison but had to leave the school in April 1928 to serve out his sentence. A campus protest followed, and Gordan was released after thirty-five days in jail, though the parole board emphasized that its decision did not contradict the original verdict, affirming again Gordan's guilt in "writing a very bad and vulgar piece of poetry" and threatening harsh consequences if he wrote any more obscene poems. See "Poem in Red Paper Is Called Indecent," *New York Times* (April 1, 1927): 13; "Red Poet Gets 13 Months," *New York Times* (June 11, 1927): 34; "Young Poet Freed By Parole Board," *New York Times* (May 11, 1928): 21.
57. Gertzman, *Bookleggers and Smuthounds*.
58. The mistakes that can be made in this vein are illustrated by John Murray Cuddihy's *The Ordeal of Civility* (New York: Basic Books, 1974), a fascinating and influential but flawed book. Cuddihy suggests, for one example, that the clash between Abbie Hoffman and Judge Julius Hoffman can be reduced to a confrontation between "the socially unassimilated Eastern European Jew versus the assimilated German Jew who 'passes' among the *goyim*" (191), doing no favors to either of those complex figures by reducing them to stereotypes. For an apt critique of Cuddihy and his source material, see Boyarin, *Unheroic Conduct*, 39–51.

59. See *B. Yeb.* 49a. Thanks to Rabbi Joseph Telushkin, who suggested the relevance of this source to my approach.
60. Keith Allan and Kate Burridge, "Taboos and Their Origins," chap. 1 in *Forbidden Words: Taboo and the Censoring of Language* (New York: Cambridge University Press, 2006), 23. For Tacitus's statement—about books "which, while it was dangerous to procure them, were anxiously sought and much read"—see *The Annals of Tacitus*, ed. Alfred John Church and William Jackson Brodribb (New York: Macmillan, 1906), 277.
61. Reichenbach's story is not true—the painting's obscenity was adjudicated in Chicago before it ever aroused controversy in New York, and while Comstock complained about the print, he never took any action against it. For Reichenbach's version, see his *Phantom Fame: The Anatomy of Ballyhoo* (New York: Simon and Schuster, 1931), 103–4. For the real controversy over the painting, in Chicago—and not in New York, where Reichenbach claims to have participated—see "When Is Art Art? When Wicked?," *Chicago Daily Tribune* (March 14, 1913): 3; "September Morn Pits Her Beauty against Censors," *Chicago Daily Tribune* (March 21, 1913): 1. Comstock did complain about the painting, but he did not attempt to arrest the art dealer; see "Comstock Dooms September Morning," *New York Times* (May 11, 1913): 1; and "Wearies of Waiting a Comstock Arrest," *New York Times* (May 15, 1913): 7.
62. Esar Levine to Nellie Harris, June 6, 1930 (?), Frank Harris and Arthur Leonard Ross Papers, Syracuse University, quoted in Gertzman, *Bookleggers and Smuthounds*, 66.
63. On Flynt, see Larry Flynt with Kenneth Ross, *An Unseemly Man: My Life as Pornographer, Pundit, and Social Outcast* (Los Angeles: Dove Books, 1996); for Damiano, see Fenton Bailey and Randy Barbato's documentary *Inside Deep Throat* (Universal Studios, 2005). See also Gertzman, *Bookleggers and Smuthounds*, 289. Eric Schlosser's useful if breezy account of Reuben Sturman's activities in the pornography industry emphasizes this point; Sturman was Jewish and perhaps the most successful distributor of pornography in America for a decade or so, but his approach to his work does not seem to have been any different from those of Michael Thevis, Robert DiBernardo, Harry Virgil Mohney, and other non-Jewish pornography distributors of his era. See Schlosser, "An Empire of the Obscene," in *Reefer Madness: Sex, Drugs, and Cheap Labor in the American Black Market* (Boston: Houghton Mifflin, 2003), 109–210.
64. Researchers have noted that "swearing is frequently one of a small set of speech functions—'automatic speech'—selectively preserved in the severely aphasic patient," suggesting that the use of expletives may be produced in an area of the brain separate from the one that handles most other language production and that swearing in moments of pain or surprise may not be subject to conscious control. See D. Van Lancker and J. L. Cummings, "Expletives: Neurolinguistic and Neurobehavioral Perspectives on Swearing," *Brain Research Review* 31 (1999): 84.

65. Al Goldstein and Josh Alan Friedman, *I, Goldstein: My Screwed Life* (New York: Thunder's Mouth, 2006), 2.
66. In the novel, Roth's protagonist, Nathan Zuckerman, introduces himself to strangers as "the pornographer Milton Appel," impersonating a respected Jewish literary critic who has attacked Zuckerman's fiction and questioned his commitments. Roth does not attempt to disguise that he has based Appel on Irving Howe, who published attacks on Roth's midcareer work, as many scholars have noted. It is equally transparent, though less remarked on, that the dialogue about pornography that Zuckerman-as-Appel spews so enthusiastically derives from three days Roth spent observing and interviewing Goldstein, as reported in Goldstein's autobiography. Philip Roth, *The Anatomy Lesson*, in *Zuckerman Unbound* (New York: Farrar, Straus and Giroux, 1985), 600, 590, 597.
67. Indeed, *Screw* regularly presented aggressive critiques of local and national political figures; Talese rightly praises its "scathing and scatological editorials" (*Thy Neighbor's Wife*, 230).
68. David Lance Goines, *The Free Speech Movement: Coming of Age in the 1960s* (Berkeley, CA: Ten Speed, 1993), 480–508.
69. Ibid., 489, 490. "Most of us thought the whole thing was silly, not political," another member of the movement recalls. Jo Freeman, *At Berkeley in the Sixties: The Education of an Activist, 1961–1965* (Bloomington: Indiana University Press, 2004), 235.
70. *Cohen*, 403 U.S. at 26.
71. Goines, *Free Speech Movement*, 508.
72. The formulation "Jews as Jews" here deliberately echoes Hannah Arendt's "The Jew as Pariah," in *The Jew as Pariah*, ed. Ron H. Feldman (New York: Grove, 1978), 68.
73. In a recent study of "the complex negotiations required to produce African American texts through a predominantly white publishing industry," John K. Young treats, by way of introduction, the example of Richard Wright's *Native Son* and its bowdlerization—particularly the removal of Wright's representation of masturbation—by the Book of the Month Club. Young, *Black Writers, White Publishers: Marketplace Politics in Twentieth-Century African American Literature* (Jackson: University Press of Mississippi, 2006), 13–19. It is worth noting that because Young is attentive to the ways in which African American literary texts are the product of complex negotiations between African American writers and their white publishers, he finds it relevant to mention—in passing, surely, but more responsibly than most studies of American Jewish literature—the key roles played by Jewish publishers in the development of modern American literature (7–8). Another example: editors at Doubleday were responsible for "the outright bowdlerization" of a "graphic lesbian affair" in Chester Himes's novel *If He Hollers Let Him Go*. See Lawrence Jackson, "'Saying Things on Paper That Should Never Be Written': Publishing Chester Himes at Doubleday," *American Literary History* 23:2 (2011): 295.

74. De Grazia, *Girls Lean Back Everywhere*, 379.
75. Gertz, *Handful of Clients*, 246.
76. Norris, "'Cancer' in Chicago," 64–65.
77. Karl Shapiro, introduction to Miller, *Tropic of Cancer*, xv, xix; Gertz, *Handful of Clients*, 241, 274–75.

Notes to Chapter 1

1. Granich was then known for a couple of plays on Jewish themes staged by the Players, but he later became famous as Mike Gold, a founding editor of the *New Masses* and author of the novel *Jews without Money*. See Mike Gold, "The Dreiser I Knew," in *The Mike Gold Reader* (New York: International, 1954), 159–64.
2. On Dreiser's representations of Jews and personal relationships with Jews, see Donald Pizer, *American Naturalism and the Jews* (Urbana: University of Illinois Press, 2008), 31–49.
3. H. L. Mencken to Theodore Dreiser, December 20, 1916, in *Dreiser-Mencken Letters: The Correspondence of Theodore Dreiser and H. L. Mencken, 1907–1945*, ed. Thomas P. Riggio, 2 vols. (Philadelphia: University of Pennsylvania Press, 1986), 1:285.
4. Tom Dardis, *Firebrand: The Life of Horace Liveright* (New York: Random House, 1995), 81.
5. Fanny Butcher, "Tabloid Book Review," *Chicago Daily Tribune* (October 5, 1919): D5.
6. Theodore Dreiser, *The Hand of the Potter* (New York: Boni and Liveright, 1918). Further citations of this source are given parenthetically in the text.
7. On these stereotypes, see Sander Gilman, *The Jew's Body* (New York: Routledge, 1991); and George Mosse, "Race and Sexuality: The Role of the Outsider," in *Nationalism and Sexuality: Respectability and Abnormal Sexuality in Modern Europe* (New York: Howard Fertig, 1985), 133–53. On the "Jew as savage," see Derek Penslar, *Shylock's Children: Economics and Jewish Identity in Modern Europe* (Berkeley: University of California Press, 2001), 38–42.
8. Gilman, *The Jew's Body*, 115–16.
9. Ellen Schiff, "Shylock's *Mishpocheh*: Anti-Semitism on the American Stage," in David A. Gerber, ed., *Anti-Semitism in American History* (Urbana: University of Illinois Press, 1986), 88. See also Sol Liptzin, *The Jew in American Literature* (New York: Bloch, 1966), 159–60.
10. For another example, in "The Dreiser I Knew," Mike Gold calls the play "an unforgettable plea for understanding of the mentally sick" (161). Pizer notes that most contemporary objections to the play did not concentrate on its representation of Jews but on its representation of sexuality (*American Naturalism and the Jews*, 33). See also Jean Jaffe, "Dreiser Wants to Know More about Us: The Famous Novelist Asks Questions about the Jews—and Answers Some," *The Day* (April 13, 1924), reprinted in Donald Pizer, ed., *Theodore Dreiser: Interviews* (Urbana: University of Illinois Press, 2004), 95–97.

11. Walter Kendrick, *The Secret Museum: Pornography in Modern Culture* (New York: Viking, 1987), 24.
12. William Sanger, *History of Prostitution* (New York: Harper, 1858), 35–40.
13. Edmond Dupouy, "Prostitution in Antiquity," *Cincinnati Lancet Clinic: A Weekly Journal of Medicine and Surgery* 35 (August 31, 1895): 226.
14. George Kibbe Turner, "The Daughters of the Poor," *McClure's* 34:1 (November 1909): 45.
15. Edward Bristow, *Prostitution and Prejudice: The Jewish Fight against White Slavery* (New York: Schocken Books, 1983), 4.
16. A clear example is Swiss scientist Auguste Forel's *The Sexual Question: A Scientific, Psychological, Hygienic and Sociological Study for the Cultured Classes*, English adaptation by C. F. Marshall (New York: Rebman, 1908), in which Forel notes that Jews' "sexual appetites are generally strong" and that "their sexual life is also influenced by the mercantile spirit, and we find them everywhere connected with the traffic of women and prostitution" (189).
17. Telemachus Timayenis, *The American Jew: An Exposé of His Career* (New York: Minerva, 1888), 81, 87.
18. Ibid., 87.
19. For histories and analyses of the Frank case, see Leonard Dinnerstein, *The Leo Frank Case* (New York: Columbia University Press, 1968); and Paul Jeffrey Melnick, *Black-Jewish Relations on Trial: Leo Frank and Jim Conley in the New South* (Jackson: University Press of Mississippi, 2000).
20. H. Rider Haggard, *Benita: An African Romance* (New York: Cassell, 1906), 292, 237. On fears of mesmerism as a means of sexual control, see Daniel Pick, *Svengali's Web: The Alien Enchanter in Modern Culture* (New Haven: Yale University Press, 2000), 92–111.
21. Reginald Wright Kauffman, *House of Bondage* (New York: Grosset and Dunlap, 1910), 20, 68. Hardly a literary masterpiece, Kauffman's novel nonetheless went through sixteen printings in just two years and was translated into French, German, Swedish, Finnish, and Japanese. See Laura Hapke, *Girls Who Went Wrong: Prostitutes in American Fiction, 1885–1917* (Bowling Green, OH: Bowling Green State University Popular Press, 1989), 4, 122.
22. Though first translated to English in 1890, *Nana* reached many more American readers in a 1922 edition, with a preface by Burton Rascoe, published by Alfred A. Knopf, which is quoted here in a reprint edition (Mineola, NY: Dover Thrift Editions, 2007), 73.
23. Edith Wharton, *The House of Mirth* (New York: Scribner, 1905), 255, 410.
24. For a thoughtful reading of Rosedale's character, see Meredith Goldsmith, "The Year of the Rose: Jewish Masculinity in *The House of Mirth*," *Modern Fiction Studies* 51:2 (Summer 2005): 374–92.
25. Such stereotypes were not uniquely the province of non-Jewish writers, either, of course. Somewhat later, Ben Hecht's notorious *A Jew in Love* describes Jo Boshere as a "dark-skinned little Jew" whose sexual attention to his wife resembles "that of

a rapist" and whose pursuit of sexual affairs outside his marriage Hecht describes in such a way as to link him to one of the most well-known monsters of late 19th-century literature: "Although he began each of his wooings with passionate, rapist pretenses," Hecht's narrator notes, "his ardor in this direction was no more than a mask for his real purpose which was that of a deeper and more inner seduction, a Dracula-like hunger for the life blood of his victim." In Hecht's novel, the sexually aberrant Jew figures as a lusting monster with supernatural powers of coercion and seduction. Ben Hecht, *A Jew in Love* (New York: Covici Friede, 1931), 3, 10, 17.

26. John Efron, *Medicine and the German Jews* (New Haven: Yale University Press, 2001), 155. Charcot noted in 1888, "Nervous illnesses of all types are innumerably more frequent among Jews than among other groups" (J. M. Charcot, *Leçons du Mardi à la Salpêtrière* [Paris: Progrès médical, 1889], 2:11–12, quoted in Efron, *Medicine and the German Jews*, 157), while his student Richard von Krafft-Ebing remarked more broadly, "Very often religious inclination is itself a symptom of an originally abnormal character or actual disease, and, not infrequently, concealed under a veil of religious enthusiasm there is abnormally intensified sensuality and sexual excitement that lead to sexual errors that are of etiologic significance" (Krafft-Ebing, *Text Book of Insanity* [Philadelphia: F. A. David, 1905], 143, quoted in Efron, *Medicine and the German Jews*, 155). Efron describes Freud as having "supplanted degeneration theory with a universalistic explanation of neuropathologies that stressed the role of environment and sexuality in their acquisition" (ibid., 157). See also Sander Gilman, *Difference and Pathology: Stereotypes of Sexuality, Race, and Madness* (Ithaca: Cornell University Press, 1985), 150–62. Jonathan Freedman suggests that, like Freud, Caesare Lombroso and Max Nordau also "sought to shift the burden of degeneracy" away from Jews and Jewishness and onto "other forms of causation and consequence," as part of an "anti-anti-Semitic agenda." Freedman, *The Temple of Culture: Assimilation and Anti-Semitism in Literary Anglo-America* (New York: Oxford University Press, 2000), 125–26.

27. Toby Gelfand, "Sigmund-sur-Seine: Fathers and Brothers in Charcot's Paris," in Toby Gelfand and John Kerr, eds., *Freud and the History of Psychoanalysis* (Hillsdale, NJ: Analytic, 1992), 51, quoted in Efron, *Medicine and the German Jews*, 157.

28. *United States v. One Book Called "Ulysses,"* 5 F. Supp. 182 (S.D.N.Y. 1933).

29. Neil Davidson, *James Joyce, "Ulysses," and the Construction of Jewish Identity: Culture, Biography, and "the Jew" in Modernist Europe* (Cambridge: Cambridge University Press, 1998), 11.

30. This discussion is, of course, just a very brief summary of a complex subject. A good introduction to the issues, detailing Joyce's reliance on Krafft-Ebing, is Robert Byrnes, "Bloom's Sexual Tropes: Stigmata of the 'Degenerate' Jew," *James Joyce Quarterly* 27:2 (1990): 303–23. See also Marilyn Reizbaum, *James Joyce's Judaic Other* (Stanford: Stanford University Press, 1999); and Ira Nadel, *Joyce and the Jews: Culture and Texts* (Basingstoke, UK: Macmillan, 1989).

31. Compare to "Beautiful Make-Up of Women Caused Swartz to Lose Mind," *Atlanta Constitution* (July 19, 1912): 4.

32. On the addition of these speeches at a late stage in the play's composition, and on Dreiser's sources, see Keith Newlin and Frederick E. Rusch, introduction to *The Collected Plays of Theodore Dreiser*, ed. Newlin and Rusch (Albany, NY: Whitston, 2000), xxix–xxx.
33. Dreiser's *The Bulwark*, not published until 1944 but conceived in 1914, features a non-Jewish young man "cursed with an overwhelming hunger for physical sex gratification," demonstrating that Dreiser did not ascribe this characteristic particularly to Jews. See Newlin and Rusch, introduction to *Collected Plays of Dreiser*, xxiv. Similarly, Dreiser's *The Financier*, written not long before *The Hand of the Potter*, features "Judge Rafalsky, a meditative and yet practical man of Jewish extraction but peculiarly American appearance" whose somewhat unconventional sexual behavior mirrors that of the book's solidly American protagonist, Frank Cowperwood. Cowperwood's extramarital affair becomes an element in his trial for "semi-legitimate financial subtlety." In this context, Dreiser mentions that Rafalsky sympathizes with Cowperwood because of "a similar event in his own life in so far as a girl was concerned." Dreiser, *The Financier* (New York: Meridian, 1995), 351–54.
34. See Ludwig Lewisohn, "Drama: Year's End," *The Nation* 113:2947 (December 28, 1921): 762–63. Notable among the other supportive reviews was Abraham Cahan's, in the *Forverts* (December 4, 1921): 4; on Cahan's reaction, see Pizer, *American Naturalism and the Jews*, 34–35. On Lewisohn's career generally, see Julian Levinson, *Exiles on Main Street: Jewish American Writers and American Literary Culture* (Bloomington: Indiana University Press, 2008), 56–75; and Ralph Melnick, *The Life and Works of Ludwig Lewisohn*, 2 vols. (Detroit: Wayne State University Press, 1998).
35. Ludwig Lewisohn, *The Island Within* (New York: Harper, 1928), 175.
36. Ludwig Lewisohn, *Stephen Escott* (New York: Harper, 1930), 106. Under an 1813 statute that remained virtually "unchanged for 150 years," "only proof of adultery justified a full divorce" in New York, and people guilty of adultery were prohibited from remarrying "during the lifetime of the 'innocent' spouse." Hendrik Hartog, *Man and Wife in America: A History* (Cambridge: Harvard University Press, 2000), 72.
37. "'Ella' and Some Other Recent Works of Fiction," *New York Times* (March 9, 1930): 67.
38. Ludwig Lewisohn, *An Altar in the Fields* (New York: Harper, 1934), 268.
39. Lewisohn, *Stephen Escott*, 131–32.
40. Ludwig Lewisohn, *Mid-Channel* (New York: Arno, 1975), 112; Lewisohn, *Island Within*, 180, 185.
41. Nathan G. Hale, *Freud and the Americans: The Beginnings of Psychoanalysis in the United States, 1876–1917* (New York: Oxford University Press, 1971), 44. On such archiving practices, see Kendrick, *Secret Museum*.
42. Lewisohn, *Island Within*, 285.
43. Otto Rank, "The Essence of Judaism," in Dennis B. Klein, ed., *The Jewish Origins of the Psychoanalytic Movement* (New York: Praeger, 1981), 171. More obliquely, of

course, this comparison should call to mind Otto Weininger's *Sex and Character* (London: Heinemann, 1906). On Rank's reversal of Weininger, see Sander Gilman, "Otto Weininger and Sigmund Freud: Race and Gender in the Shaping of Psychoanalysis," in Nancy A. Harrowitz and Barbara Hyams, eds., *Jews and Gender: Responses to Otto Weininger* (Philadelphia: Temple University Press, 1995), 112.

44. Lewisohn, *Altar in the Fields*, 273.
45. Sigmund Freud, "'Civilized' Sexual Morality and Modern Nervousness" (1908), in *Collected Papers*, vol. 2, trans. Joan Rivière (New York: Basic Books, 1959); Rank, "Essence of Judaism," 117. See *Stephen Escott*, for example, in which one of Lewisohn's characters paraphrases Freud in asserting that "all creative idealisms are in large measure . . . the sublimations of a repressed and curbed and temporarily defeated appetite" and that "curbing and defeating is integral to the kind of civilization we want" (208). On the friendship between Lewisohn and Rank, see Melnick, *Life and Works of Ludwig Lewisohn*, 600.
46. Lewisohn, *Altar in the Fields*, 259.
47. Ibid., 270–71, 296, 305, 311.
48. Aside from Lewisohn's assiduous biographer Ralph Melnick, Werner Sollors is the only contemporary critic who seems to have read Lewisohn's fiction of this period; see Sollors, "Freud, Marx, Hard-Boiled," in *Ethnic Modernism* (Cambridge: Harvard University Press, 2008), 113–27. On Dreiser's anti-Semitic turn, see Pizer, *American Naturalism and the Jews*.
49. For a study of how American responses to Nazism informed postwar liberalism more generally, see Kirsten Fermaglich, *American Dreams and Nazi Nightmares: Early Holocaust Consciousness and Liberal America, 1957–1965* (Lebanon, NH: Brandeis University Press / University Press of New England, 2006).
50. Dagmar Herzog, *Sex after Fascism: Memory and Morality in Twentieth-Century Germany* (Princeton: Princeton University Press, 2005), 19–27.
51. Alfred Kinsey, *Sexual Behavior in the Human Male* (Bloomington: Indiana University Press, 1998), 389, 485.
52. For an example of Jewish opposition to Kinsey, see "Young Israel Holds Kinsey Publicity Detrimental to Public Morals," *Jewish Telegraphic Agency* (September 1, 1953). On the other hand, Jews supported and helped to popularize sexology in the postwar United States, even before Dr. Ruth Westheimer became indelibly associated with the public airing of sex therapy in the 1980s. The First Amendment lawyer Harriet Pilpel, for example, who is discussed in more depth in chapter 3, won the Kinsey Institute the right to import sexually explicit photographs for inclusion in its archives; the case is *United States v. 31 Photographs*, 156 F. Supp. 350 (S.D.N.Y. 1957); for Pilpel's account of the case, see "But Can You Do That? Federal Court Makes Important Ruling in Kinsey Case," *Publisher's Weekly* (November 25, 1957): 29–30. Nat Lehrman, the editor of *Playboy* responsible for the magazine's trailblazing coverage of human sexuality in the 1960s, helped to popularize the work of Masters and Johnson, with a respectful May 1968

interview in *Playboy* and a book he edited, called *Masters and Johnson Explained* (Chicago: Playboy, 1970); on Lehrman's career, see Josh Lambert, "My Son, the Pornographer," *Tablet* (February 24, 2010). Albert Ellis's books, discussed later in the chapter, are also important examples.

53. See Jay Gertzman, *Bookleggers and Smuthounds: The Trade in Erotica, 1920–1940* (Philadelphia: University of Pennsylvania Press, 1999), 135–36. For an overview of book burning in Jewish culture, see Stephen Whitfield, "Where They Burn Books," *Modern Judaism* 22:3 (2002): 213–33.
54. Herzog, *Sex after Fascism*, 28.
55. Lucy Dawidowicz, "Smut and Anti-Semitism," in *The Jewish Presence: Essays on Identity and History* (New York: Holt, Rinehart, and Winston, 1978), 221.
56. George Steiner, for another example, in an argument with the publisher Maurice Girodias that took place in the pages of *Encounter* and the *Times Literary Supplement* in 1965 and 1966, insisted that "there are definite links between the history of modern totalitarianism and the present abundance and sadistic character of erotica." Letter to the editor, *Times Literary Supplement* 3352 (May 26, 1966): 475. Or, as Steiner put it in an earlier essay, "The novels . . . shout at their personages: strip, fornicate, perform this or that act of sexual perversion. So did the S.S. guards at rows of living men and women. The total attitudes are not, I think, distinct." George Steiner, "Night Words: High Pornography & Human Privacy," *Encounter* (October 1965): 14–19 (quote on 18). The insistence on a conceptual overlap between Nazism and pornography has been taken furthest by Andrea Dworkin, who used the phrase "concentration camp pornography" in her testimony before the Attorney General's Commission on Pornography on January 22, 1986, reprinted in Dworkin, *Letters from a War Zone: Writings, 1976–1987* (London: Secker and Warburg, 1988), 276–307. In her later book *Scapegoat: The Jews, Israel, and Women's Liberation* (New York: Free Press, 2000), Dworkin remarks, "For the Nazis pornography was a verb. They were always doing it no matter what they were doing" (167).
57. On the newspaper's coverage of the Holocaust, see Laurel Leff, *Buried by the Times: The Holocaust and America's Most Important Newspaper* (New York: Cambridge University Press, 2005).
58. "93 Choose Suicide before Nazi Shame," *New York Times* (January 8, 1943): 8.
59. A recently published prayer book, for example, refers to "a story of a group of religious young women in Warsaw who were selected by Germans for immoral purposes and who committed suicide rather than submit to immorality." See Simon Posner, ed., *The Koren Mesorat Harav Kinot* (Jerusalem: Koren/OU Press, 2010), 372.
60. For a series of detailed discussions of the sexual crimes committed by Nazis against Jewish women, see Sonja M. Hedgepeth and Rochelle G. Saidel, eds., *Sexual Violence against Jewish Women during the Holocaust* (Lebanon, NH: Brandeis University Press / University Press of New England, 2010).
61. Judith Tydor Baumel and Jacob J. Schacter, "The Ninety-Three Bais Yaakov Girls of Cracow: History or Typology?," in Jacob J. Schacter, ed., *Reverence,*

Righteousness, and Rahamanut: Essays in Memory of Rabbi Dr. Leo Jung (Northvale, NJ: Jason Aronson, 1992), 127.

62. See Hillel Bavli, "*Igeret tishim v'shalosh ha'na'arot*," *Ha'doar* 22:12 (January 22, 1943): 186; Bavli, "The Letter of the Ninety-Three Maidens," *Reconstructionist* 9:2 (March 5, 1943): 23; Alter Abelson, "The Ninety-Three Women Martyrs," *Jewish Forum* 26:4 (May 1943): 84; Eugene Weintraub, "The Ninety-Three," *Opinion* 13:8 (June 1943): 6–7.
63. Ka-Tzetnik 135633, *House of Dolls*, trans. Moshe M. Kohn (New York: Simon and Schuster, 1955), 204.
64. Ibid., 202–3.
65. Two compelling readings of the novel and film are Alan Rosen, "'Teach Me Gold': Pedagogy and Memory in *The Pawnbroker*," *Prooftexts* 22:1–2 (2002): 77–117; and Julian Levinson, "The Maimed Body and the Tortured Soul: Holocaust Survivors in American Film," *Yale Journal of Criticism* 17:1 (2004): 141–60.
66. Edward Lewis Wallant, *The Pawnbroker* (New York: Harcourt, Brace and World, 1961), 168–69.
67. Thanks to Kerry Wallach for help with the German.
68. Sidney Lumet, dir., *The Pawnbroker* (1964; DVD, Republic Entertainment, 2003).
69. Meyer Levin, "Out of the Depths of Nazi Bestiality," *New York Times* (May 8, 1955), BR4.
70. For this marketing, see advertisements in the *New York Times* (May 1, 1955): BR23, and (June 5, 1955): BR32. *House of Dolls* has been taken for a factual account both in Israel, where it has reportedly been included in educational curricula as a historical source, and in the United States. A *Washington Post* report from 1955 about a discussion of the book by the B'nai Israel Sisterhood implies that readers took the female protagonist to be the author of the text; see "Sisterhood Hears about House of Dolls," *Washington Post* (October 11, 1955): 31. A more recent example is that Dee L. Graham, Roberta K. Rigsby, and Edna I. Rawlings misconstrue the text as having been published in 1983 and as the actual diary of the character Daniella, in *Longing to Survive: Sexual Terror, Men's Violence, and Women's Lives* (New York: NYU Press, 1995), 90–91.
71. Quoted in advertisement in the *New York Times* (June 5, 1955): BR32.
72. For a detailed history of the film's production and reception, see Leonard J. Leff, "Hollywood and the Holocaust: Remembering *The Pawnbroker*," *American Jewish History* 84:4 (1996): 353–76.
73. Federal Communications Commission, "Memorandum Opinion and Order in the Matter of WPBN/WTOM LICENSE SUBSIDIARY, INC.," January 14, 2000.
74. One reason this argument should not be blithely accepted is that it tends to open the door to a depressing exploitation of Holocaust imagery for the purpose of justifying titillation. That is one way, at least, to read such phenomena as the Israeli *stalagim*, Hebrew-language pornography pulp novels published in the early 1960s featuring American soldiers sexually abused and tortured by female Nazi guards (on which, see Amit Pinchevski and Roy Brand, "Holocaust Perversions: The Stalags

Pulp Fiction and the Eichmann Trial," *Critical Studies in Media Communication* 24:5 [2007]: 387–407); the genre of Holocaust sexploitation films, which include *Love Camp 7* (1969), *Ilsa, She-Wolf of the SS* (1974) (on which, see Lynn Rapaport, "Holocaust Pornography: Profaning the Sacred in *Ilsa, She-Wolf of the SS*," *Shofar* 22:1 [2003]: 53–79), and *Nazi Love Camp 27* (1977); and a similar set of films with higher production values and fewer hard-core pornographic elements, including Liliana Cavani's *The Night Porter* (1974). *Ilsa* exemplifies the ways in which the notion of compulsory witnessing can easily be appropriated even by generic pornography; it begins with the claim that it is "based upon documented fact" and "historically accurate" and has been presented in "the hope that these heinous crimes will never occur again." In *Sex Drives: Fantasies of Fascism in Literary Modernism* (Ithaca: Cornell University Press, 2002), Laura Frost attends thoughtfully to the association of sexual deviance and fascism, both in literary modernism and in texts such as *Ilsa* and *The Night Porter*, and in concluding, she sympathetically remarks that while "in the discourse of deviant fascism, sexuality is an index of truth, an essential indicator of ideology," it may finally not be "really advantageous to make sexual 'abnormality' equivalent to genocide. . . . The contemporary focus on fantasy and sexual deviance as the primary root of violence is a smoke screen for more difficult and complicated political and social problems" (159).

75. Mark Shechner, *After the Revolution: Studies in the Contemporary Jewish American Imagination* (Bloomington: Indiana University Press, 1987), 91–101.
76. For the most recent biography of Reich, see Christopher Turner, *Adventures in the Orgasmatron: How the Sexual Revolution Came to America* (New York: Farrar, Straus and Giroux, 2011).
77. Wilhelm Reich, *The Sexual Revolution: Toward a Self-Regulating Character Structure* (New York: Farrar, Straus and Giroux, 1974), 15; Reich, *The Mass Psychology of Fascism* (New York: Farrar, Straus and Giroux, 1970), 31, 75, 84.
78. Myron Sharaf, *Fury on Earth: A Biography of Wilhelm Reich* (New York: St. Martin's, 1983), 166.
79. On Mailer's Reichian phase, see Mary Dearborn, *Mailer: A Biography* (Boston: Houghton Mifflin, 1999), 116; on Bellow's, see James Atlas, *Bellow: A Biography* (New York: Random House, 2000), 164–65; on Ginsberg's, see Bill Morgan, *I Celebrate Myself: The Somewhat Private Life of Allen Ginsberg* (New York: Viking, 2006), 80–86.
80. "Symposium: The Jewish Writer and the English Literary Tradition," *Commentary* 8 (1949): 213–14. On Rosenfeld's fascination with Reich, see Steven Zipperstein, *Rosenfeld's Lives: Fame, Oblivion, and the Furies of Writing* (New Haven: Yale University Press, 2009), 116–21.
81. Reich, *Sexual Revolution*, 262.
82. Mikita Brottman, *Funny Peculiar: Gershon Legman and the Psychopathology of Humor* (Hillsdale, NJ: Analytic, 2004), 1.
83. Gershon Legman, *Love & Death: A Study in Censorship* (1949; repr., New York: Hacker Art Books, 1963), 10.

84. Ibid., 12, 13.
85. Ibid., 93, 95.
86. Carolyn Dean, *The Fragility of Empathy after the Holocaust* (Ithaca: Cornell University Press, 2004), 128–31.
87. See "La psychopathologie des bandes dessineés," *Les temps modernes* 31 (May 1948); "Le bitch-heroine," *Les temps modernes* 58 (August 1950); "The Best Books I Read This Year—Twelve Distinguished Opinions," *New York Times* (December 4, 1949): BR4. Leslie Fiedler borrowed Legman's title for his own classic work of cultural criticism, *Love & Death in the American Novel* (New York: Criterion Books, 1960), and called Legman's book "an indignant pamphlet . . . directed against the sadist travesties of women and the celebration of violence on all levels of our culture" (328).
88. See David Rabban, *Free Speech in Its Forgotten Years* (New York: Cambridge University Press, 1997), 126–28.
89. Kenneth Ira Kersch, *Freedom of Speech: Rights and Liberties under the Law* (Santa Barbara, CA: ABC-CLIO, 2003), 20–21.
90. Ernst Freund, *The Police Power: Public Policy and Constitutional Rights* (Chicago: Callaghan, 1904), 12.
91. Ibid., 11; see also 220–25. Freund was by no means a radical on the question of obscenity, at this stage in his career; he acknowledged that while "religion and speech and press are primarily free," they still should be "subjected to restraints in the interest of good order and morality"—and he somewhat naively (or Pollyannaishly) observed that "very little difficulty has so far been encountered in the mutual adjustments of these interests" (11).
92. Ibid., 502.
93. See Freund's articles "The Debs Case and Freedom of Speech," *New Republic* (May 3, 1919): 13–15; and "Freedom of Speech and Press," *New Republic* (February 16, 1921): 344–46.
94. Ernst Freund to Zechariah Chafee, Jr., August 19, 1919, Zechariah Chafee, Jr., Papers, Harvard Law School Library, Box 14, Folder 26, quoted in Rabban, *Free Speech in Its Forgotten Years*, 303.
95. *People v. Viking Press, Inc.*, 147 N.Y. Misc. 813 (Magistrate's Ct. 1933).
96. See Oscar I. Janowsky, *The Jews and Minority Rights (1898–1919)* (New York: Columbia University Press, 1933).
97. Jo Sinclair, *Wasteland* (Philadelphia: Jewish Publication Society, 1987), 156. Warren Hoffman offers a thorough and relevant reading of *Wasteland* in which he explains that the novel's protagonist learns "to embrace his Jewish American identity by seeing it as part of a larger spectrum of marginalized subjectivities that include African Americans and gays and lesbians." Warren Hoffman, *The Passing Game: Queering Jewish American Culture* (Syracuse: Syracuse University Press, 2009), 90–105 (quote on 92).
98. Sinclair, *Wasteland*, 153.
99. William Carlos Williams, introduction to *Howl and Other Poems*, by Allen Ginsberg (1956; repr., San Francisco: City Lights, 2000), 8.

100. Obviously this was not the last time that the experience of homosexuals in the United States and the experience of Jews under the Third Reich were compared in this way. Ben Furnish mentions Harvey Fierstein's *Torch Song Trilogy*, Martin Sherman's *Bent*, and Larry Kramer's *The Normal Heart* as plays that articulate a similar "gay-Jewish analogy." Ben Furnish, "'It's Both Hot and Incredibly Innocent': A Century of Sex on the American Jewish Stage," in Nathan Abrams, ed., *Jews and Sex* (Nottingham, UK: Five Leaves, 2008), 150–61 (quote on 156).
101. Jerome Frank, "Red, White, and Blue Herring," *Saturday Evening Post* (December 6, 1941): 83.
102. *United States v. Roth*, 237 F.2d 796 (2d cir. 1956), available at https://bulk.resource.org/courts.gov/c/F2/237/237.F2d.796.387.24030_1.html.
103. *Roth v. United States*, 354 U.S. 476, 477 (1957).
104. *Roth*, 354 U.S. at 512.
105. Charles Rembar, *The End of Obscenity: The Trials of "Lady Chatterley," "Tropic of Cancer," and "Fanny Hill"* (New York: Random House, 1968), 119. Justice Douglas, dissenting in *Roth*, anticipated this argument: "Any test that turns on what is offensive to the community's standards is too loose, too capricious, too destructive of freedom of expression to be squared with the First Amendment. Under that test, juries can censor, suppress, and punish what they don't like, provided the matter relates to 'sexual impurity' or has a tendency 'to excite lustful thoughts.' This is community censorship in one of its worst forms." *Roth*, 354 U.S. at 512.
106. Rembar, *End of Obscenity*, 122.
107. *Memoirs v. Massachusetts*, 383 U.S. 413 (1966).
108. Rembar, *End of Obscenity*, 169.
109. Martin Garbus, *Traitors and Heroes: A Lawyer's Memoir* (New York: Atheneum, 1987), xiii–xv.
110. American Jews have not uniformly felt themselves to be excluded minorities, of course. Many of the American Jewish critics and scholars who have forthrightly advocated censorship, such as Irving Kristol and Harry Clor, have done so by implicitly or explicitly claiming an affinity with the values of the American majority and insisting that those majoritarian values deserve legal protection. See, for examples, Kristol, "Pornography, Obscenity, and the Case for Censorship," *New York Times Magazine* (March 28, 1971): 24; and Harry Clor, *Obscenity and Public Morality: Censorship in a Liberal Society* (Chicago: University of Chicago Press, 1969). This attitude is captured well in the testimony that the American Jewish writer Leon Uris gave at a Los Angeles trial of Miller's *Tropic of Cancer*. "We have codes that we live by," Uris testified. "They were started in Mount Sinai, and we have traditions of ethics. . . . I believe we have a right to defend ourselves against this type of garbage [Miller's book] the same way we would any other ordinary criminal or any pervert walking the streets of Los Angeles. I think we have a community duty to defend ourselves against this type of thing." Asserting that "traditions of ethics" unite all Americans—and claiming that these ethics "started in Mount Sinai," rather than, say, with the Sermon on the Mount—Uris identifies

himself as part of a majority, as a member of a putative Judeo-Christian "we" with a "community duty" to uphold its values. Quoted in Stanley Fleischman, "Obscenity and Witchcraft," *Wilson Library Bulletin* (April 1965): 642. An embrace of censorship seems eminently reasonable coming from a member of the majority, concerned with preserving that group's status and values. A more recent, nuanced, and formidable elaboration of the arguments made earlier by Clor, Kristol, and Uris can be found in Rochelle Gurstein's *The Repeal of Reticence: A History of America's Cultural and Legal Struggles over Free Speech, Obscenity, Sexual Liberation, and Modern Art* (New York: Hill and Wang, 1996). An able and resourceful historian, Gurstein sounds very much like her predecessors—and she quotes Kristol and Clor approvingly—in her calls for "judgment and taste" and in her lamentation of "the impoverishment of our public conversation and the debasement of our common world" (304, 261). Her concern with changing cultural standards is certainly sympathetic, but her assumption that all Americans agree about what sort of discussions should be made public seems to underestimate the cultural and intellectual diversity that exists in the United States.

111. "*Naked Lunch* on Trial," in *Naked Lunch*, by William Burroughs (1959; repr., New York: Grove, 1987), xxx.
112. On the novel's success and influence, see David Allyn, *Make Love, Not War: The Sexual Revolution: An Unfettered History* (Boston: Little, Brown, 2000), 71–84.
113. Robert H. Rimmer, *The Harrad Experiment* (New York: Bantam, 1966), 1. Further citations of this source are given parenthetically in the text.
114. Richard Fairfield, "Harrad West," *Modern Utopian* (Winter 1969): 146, quoted in Linda Grant, *Sexing the Millennium: Women and the Sexual Revolution* (New York: Grove, 1994), 165.
115. Linda Williams, *Hard Core: Power, Pleasure, and the "Frenzy of the Visible,"* expanded paperback ed. (Berkeley: University of California Press, 1999), 34–57.
116. Rimmer's Yiddish is frequently erroneous; *landsleyt* is the standard term for "countrymen."
117. Robert H. Rimmer, "Loving, Learning, Laughter & Ludamus: The Autobiography of Robert H. Rimmer," in *The Harrad Experiment*, 25th anniversary edition (Buffalo, NY: Prometheus, 1990), 291–324 (quotes on 313, 314).
118. Robert H. Rimmer to Douglas M. Black, Doubleday, October 1, 1959, Robert Rimmer Papers, Mugar Memorial Library, Boston University.
119. Rimmer, "Loving, Learning," 292.
120. Ibid., 314–15.
121. Allyn, *Make Love, Not War*, 74; Robert H. Rimmer, *The Harrad Letters to Robert H. Rimmer* (New York: Signet, 1969), 41.
122. Joseph Shoben, "Readings," *Change in Higher Education* 1:3 (1969): 46.
123. Robert H. Rimmer to Scott Meredith, December 15, 1959, Robert Rimmer Papers, Mugar Memorial Library, Boston University.
124. Victor Frankl, *Man's Search for Meaning* (Cutchogue, NY: Buccaneer Books, 1992), 116.

125. Edward Hoffman, *The Right to Be Human: A Biography of Abraham Maslow* (Los Angeles: Jeremy P. Tarcher, 1988), 2, 153.
126. Albert Ellis with Debbie Joffe Ellis, *All Out! An Autobiography* (Amherst, NY: Prometheus Books, 2010), 246; Albert Ellis, *Sex without Guilt* (New York: Lyle Stuart, 1958), 176.

Notes to Chapter 2

1. Roth journal, Berg Collection, New York Public Library, quoted in Steven G. Kellman, *Redemption: The Life of Henry Roth* (New York: Norton, 2005), 114.
2. "To Pass on 'Ulysses,'" *New York Times* (August 30, 1933): 16.
3. Kellman, *Redemption*, 88–89. Roth discusses Joyce and *Ulysses* frequently in his tetralogy *Mercy of a Rude Stream* (New York: St. Martin's, 1994–1998), the four volumes of which are titled *A Star Shines over Mt. Morris Park* (vol. 1), *A Diving Rock on the Hudson* (vol. 2), *From Bondage* (vol. 3), and *Requiem for Harlem* (vol. 4). Further citations of these sources are given parenthetically in the text, by volume and page number. On *Ulysses*, see particularly 3:61–77. Roth also regularly discussed Joyce's influence in interviews; see, for example, Bonnie Lyons, "Interview with Henry Roth," *Studies in American Jewish Literature* 5:1 (1979): 50–58.
4. For discussions of the trial, see Paul Boyer, *Purity in Print: The Vice-Society Movement and Book Censorship in America* (New York: Scribner, 1968), 252–59; Edward de Grazia, *Girls Lean Back Everywhere: The Law of Obscenity and the Assault on Genius* (New York: Random House, 1992), 20–39; and Elizabeth Landenson, *Dirt for Art's Sake: Books on Trial from "Madame Bovary" to "Lolita"* (Ithaca: Cornell University Press, 2007), 78–106. For further detail, see also Michael Moscato and Leslie LeBlanc's *The United States of America v. One Book Entitled "Ulysses" by James Joyce* (Frederick, MD: University Publications of America, 1984), which provides a selection of documents and commentaries on the case. For the censorship of *Ulysses* more generally, see Paul Vanderham, *James Joyce and Censorship: The Trials of "Ulysses"* (New York: NYU Press, 1998).
5. Michel Foucault, *History of Sexuality, Volume 1: An Introduction* (New York: Pantheon, 1978), 7.
6. Celia Marshik, *British Modernism and Censorship* (Cambridge: Cambridge University Press, 2006), 4.
7. See also Allison Pease, *Modernism, Mass Culture, and the Aesthetics of Obscenity* (Cambridge: Cambridge University Press, 2000), 71; and Pascale Casanova, *The World Republic of Letters*, trans. M. B. DeBevoise (Cambridge: Harvard University Press, 2004), 293.
8. On this group, see Jonathan Freedman, *The Temple of Culture: Assimilation and Anti-Semitism in Literary Anglo-America* (Oxford: Oxford University Press, 2000), 168–75; and Charles Madison, *Jewish Publishing in America: The Impact of Jewish Writing on American Culture* (New York: Sanhedrin, 1976), 246–85.
9. This account is drawn from Tom Dardis, *Firebrand: The Life of Horace Liveright* (New York: Random House, 1995), 3–44 (quotes on 8, 9).

10. H. L. Mencken to Theodore Dreiser, September 2, 1920, in *Dreiser-Mencken Letters: The Correspondence of Theodore Dreiser and H. L. Mencken, 1907–1945*, ed. Thomas P. Riggio, 2 vols. (Philadelphia: University of Pennsylvania Press, 1986), 2:385, quoted in Dardis, *Firebrand*, 79.
11. George Doran—a Canadian-born, New York–based publisher with an increasingly conservative outlook in the 1910s, who remarked that while he was "less puritan than Doubleday, [he] was not broad enough for Knopf"—refused Lawrence's *The Rainbow* (1915), despite the acclaim for *Sons and Lovers* (1913). Lawrence's "art took the form of the vulgar nudity of intellectualism," Doran later wrote, congratulating himself on his refusal. George Doran, *Chronicles of Barabbas* (New York: Holt, 1935), 83, 285, quoted in John Tebbel, *Between Covers: The Rise and Transformation of Book Publishing in America* (New York: Oxford University Press, 1987), 146, and in de Grazia, *Girls Lean Back Everywhere*, 69. Huebsch published *The Rainbow* after expurgating it without Lawrence's consent, and he distributed the book gingerly so as to avoid the attention of the NYSSV (de Grazia, *Girls Lean Back Everywhere*, 70).
12. Adele Seltzer to Dorothy Hoskins, January 15, 1923, in *D. H. Lawrence: Letters to Thomas and Adele Seltzer*, ed. Gerald M. Lacy (Santa Barbara, CA: Black Sparrow, 1976), 254, quoted in de Grazia, *Girls Lean Back Everywhere*, 79.
13. See, e.g., "Vice Society Assails Book," *New York Times* (August 21, 1916): 20.
14. See, e.g., "Authors Oppose 'Vicious' Society," *Los Angeles Times* (October 1, 1916): III:21.
15. Boyer, *Purity in Print*, 100–102.
16. The bill would establish that a book should not be judged as a whole but that any line or paragraph considered in isolation could render an entire book obscene; that "filthy" and "disgusting" books were obscene even if they were not sexual in their nature; that all obscenity cases would have to be tried by juries and not decided by judges; and that expert testimony, from literary scholars or psychologists, for example, would never be admissible in such trials. Ibid., 104–5.
17. Henry W. Boynton, "Native vs. Alien Standards," *Independent* 110 (March 17, 1923): 192; Mary Austin, "Sex in American Literature," *Bookman* 57 (June 1923): 391.
18. Horace Liveright, "The Absurdity of Censorship," *Independent* (March 17, 1923): 92–93.
19. Boyer, *Purity in Print*, 105; "Censoring Books Again," *New York Times* (February 27, 1923): 18; "Advertising Bad Books," *New York Times* (March 15, 1923): 18.
20. "Rabbi Wise Scores Book Censorship," *New York Times* (April 23, 1923): 19.
21. "Liveright Quits Other Publishers," *New York Times* (June 15, 1923): 6.
22. Search-Light [Waldo Frank], "One Hundred Percent American," *New Yorker* (October 10, 1925): 9–10.
23. Liveright's publishing house was owned, at least on paper and at least until 1924, by his wife, Lucille Elsas, whose father founded the International Paper Company; see Dardis, *Firebrand*, 37, 209, 224. Cerf bought into Liveright's company and later founded Random House, using some of the $125,000 he inherited at the age of

sixteen from his grandfather Nathan Wise, who owned the Metropolitan Tobacco Company. See Bennett Cerf, *At Random: The Reminiscences of Bennett Cerf* (New York: Random House, 1977), 3, 11, 27, 29. Barney Rosset "fought the bans in court with his own money"; though his Grove Press struggled financially in its early years, Rosset had "inherited enough money"—"over a million"—from his father, "a Russian Jew" and "wealthy bank president," to stay afloat. Gerald Jonas, "The Story of Grove," *New York Times Magazine* (January 21, 1968).

24. They were, for example, being largely excluded from the most prestigious Ivy League universities, which were among the most prominent sites of aristocratic retrenchment in the United States. See Jerome Karabel, *The Chosen: The Hidden History of Admission and Exclusion at Harvard, Yale, and Princeton* (New York: Houghton Mifflin, 2005).
25. Leo Hamalian, "Nobody Knows My Names: Samuel Roth and the Underside of Modern Letters," *Journal of Modern Literature* 3 (1974): 890.
26. Samuel Roth, "Editor's Note," in Roth, ed., *New Songs of Zion: A Zionist Anthology* (New York: Judean, 1914), 64.
27. Lithmus, "America and Europe," *Menorah Journal* 6:4 (April 1920): 116–20.
28. Louis Untermeyer, "Sweetness and Light," *Dial* 68:4 (April 1920): 530.
29. On Frank, Lewisohn, Yezierska, and their moment, see Julian Levinson, *Exiles on Main Street: Jewish American Writers and American Literary Culture* (Bloomington: Indiana University Press, 2008).
30. For biographical sketches of Samuel Roth that dismiss his Zionist poetry in a line or two, see Gay Talese, *Thy Neighbor's Wife* (Garden City, NY: Doubleday, 1980), 92–111; and Hamalian, "Nobody Knows My Names." For a thorough study of Roth's poetry, see Jay Gertzman, "The Promising Jewish Poetry of a Pariah," *Studies in American Jewish Literature* 28 (2009): 55–72.
31. Roth's daughter, Adelaide Kugel, offers her perspective on the controversy in "'Wroth Wrackt Joyce': Samuel Roth and the 'Not Quite Unauthorized' Edition of *Ulysses*," *Joyce Studies Annual* 3 (Summer 1992): 242–48.
32. "Roth's Magazine Accused," *New York Times* (March 10, 1927): 2.
33. Waverly Root, "The King of the Jews," *transition* 9 (December 1927): 178–84. Root accuses Roth of plagiarizing Yiddish poets, a claim I have not been able to verify. While claiming to be "no anti-Semite," Root does note, for example, that "Galicia is reputed to produce probably the lowest recognizable specimens of the human race extant" (180).
34. Richard Aldinton to James Joyce, March 10, 1927, in *Richard Aldington: An Autobiography in Letters*, ed. Norman T. Gates (University Park: Pennsylvania State University Press, 1992), 79.
35. In *Jews Must Live: An Account of the Persecution of the World by Israel on All the Frontiers of Civilization* (1934; repr., Birmingham, AL: National States Rights Party, 1964), which continues to be made available by anti-Semitic websites on the Internet, Roth insists that "all the evils of [his] life had been perpetrated by Jews" and describes whom he resents in particular: "the Jews whose machinations had three

times sent me to prison" and "that clique of Jewish journalists which built up about my name the libel that I was unfair to the authors of the books I published" (12). As a result, Roth says he has become a "Jew who has been brought to the point where he so loathes his people that he thinks in terms of their destruction" (17).

36. Roth, *Jews Must Live*, 197, quoted in Jay Gertzman, *Bookleggers and Smuthounds: The Trade in Erotica, 1920–1940* (Philadelphia: University of Pennsylvania Press, 1999), 253. For the traditional source, see *M. Avot* 15.
37. Casanova, *World Republic of Letters*, 334–36; see also Freedman, *Temple of Culture*.
38. Leviticus 20:17 explicitly states the prohibition of sex between a brother and his sister, and though it does not refer to that act as a "תּוֹעֵבָה," which is the most familiar Hebrew term translated as "abomination"—used, for example, a few verses earlier, in an infamous verse about homosexuality—but as "חֶסֶד," which can be translated as "disgrace, shame, abomination." See "חֶסֶד," in Reuben Alcalay, *The Complete Hebrew-English Dictionary* (Bridgeport, CT: Prayerbook / Hartmore House, 1974), 796.
39. For a complementary discussion of "the range of connections Roth makes" in *Mercy of a Rude Stream* "between writing, sex, guilt, and Jewishness," see Alan Gibbs, "Ira Stigman's 'Jewish Salami': Sex and Self-Hatred in the Works of Henry Roth," in Nathan Abrams, ed., *Jews and Sex* (Nottingham, UK: Five Leaves, 2008), 138–49 (quote on 138).
40. On the uses of African dialect in American modernism, see Michael North's *The Dialect of Modernism: Race, Language, and Twentieth-Century Literature* (New York: Oxford University Press, 1994).
41. Roth repeatedly returns to economic and alchemical metaphors for describing this process, noting that "all those myriad, myriad squalid impressions he took for granted, all were convertible from base to precious, from pig iron to gold ingot" (3:75) and that "sordidness and Jew-baiting, penury and persecution, one's own enormities, one's own callousness and cowardice, everything was convertible to universal literary currency" (3:145).
42. "Trove," *The Oxford English Dictionary Online*, 2nd ed. (1989).
43. In a sense, then, Roth fulfilled the prediction F. Scott Fitzgerald had made, unsympathetically, several years earlier, that soon "the novel of the Jewish tenement block will be festooned with wreaths from 'Ulysses' and the later Gertrude Stein." F. Scott Fitzgerald, "How to Waste Material: A Note on My Generation," *Bookman* 63 (May 1926): 262–63.
44. On Jews, violins, and high culture—including treatments of Wagner and Elman—see Sander Gilman, "Einstein's Violin: Jews and the Performance of Identity," *Modern Judaism* 25:3 (2005): 219–236; and Leon Botstein, "German Jews and Wagner," in Thomas S. Grey, ed., *Richard Wagner and His World* (Princeton: Princeton University Press, 2009), 151–200.
45. Loren Glass, "#$%^&*!?: Modernism and Dirty Words," *modernism/modernity* 14:2 (April 2007): 210.

46. James Gordon Frazer, *The Golden Bough* (New York: Macmillan, 1928), 224. For the most explicit reading of Roth's novel as having been informed and influenced by Frazer, see Mary Edrich Redding, "Call It Myth: Henry Roth and *The Golden Bough*," *Centennial Review* 18 (Spring 1974): 180–95.
47. Sándor Ferenczi, *Sex in Psychoanalysis* (Boston: Gorham, 1916), 134–35.
48. Henry Miller, *Tropic of Cancer* (New York: Grove, 1961), 258.
49. Compare, also, Mikhail Bakhtin's contemporaneous essay "Discourse in the Novel" (1934–35; in Mikhail M. Bakhtin, *The Dialogic Imagination: Four Essays*, trans. Caryl Emerson and Michael Holquist [Austin: University of Texas Press, 1981], 259–422), in which Bakhtin describes "the novelistic hybrid, . . . [i.e.,] an artistically organized system for bringing different languages in contact with one another, a system having as its goal the illumination of one language by means of another" (361), and asserts that "the novel must represent all the social and ideological voices of its era" (411).
50. Henry Roth, *Call It Sleep* (1935; repr., New York: Noonday, 1991), 49, 60, 151. Further citations of this source are given parenthetically in the text. David's aunt's remark echoes the ubiquitous Yiddish jeer "Gay kakn afn yam" (go shit on the ocean).
51. Hana Wirth-Nesher, afterword to Roth, *Call It Sleep*, 448.
52. Kellman, *Redemption*, 75; see also Roth, *Mercy*, 3:202–3. The title character of Abraham Cahan's *Yekl* (New York: Appleton, 1896), a Jewish immigrant, struggles with this particular aspect of American speech; see 4, 7, and 11. This speech impediment is not uniquely Jewish, of course; Roth also mocks the speech of a non-Jewish teacher in a similar way—"shtand up, shit down"—in *Mercy* (4:187). For the origin story of the modern term *shibboleth*, in which a mispronunciation of the *s* and *sh* sounds was used to distinguish Jews from non-Jews, see Judges 12:6.
53. H. W. Boynton, "The Story of a Ghetto Childhood," *New York Times* (February 17, 1935): BR7.
54. Fred A. Roth, "Roth's *Call It Sleep*," *Explicator* 48:3 (Spring 1990): 219.
55. Morris Dickstein, "Memory Unbound," *Threepenny Review* (Summer 2007), http://www.threepennyreview.com/samples/dickstein_su07.html.
56. "Shitten" here seems to be a hybrid Yiddish-English coinage that connects the English verb *shit* and the typical Yiddish infinitive suffix, *n*, approximating both the meanings "to shit" and "shitting." David might also be saying "no good, shit on them!" Or, since *shitn* in Yiddish means "to pour (dry material)," David might have some other, more obscure bilingual meaning of this phrase in mind.
57. Unlike other novels of the period—even John Dos Passos's similarly heteroglossic *USA* trilogy, which reproduces only the first and last letters of taboo words, separated by what Allen Reade calls "the euphemistic dash"—the typographical poetics of *Call It Sleep* would have made it difficult to expurgate. The representations of English and other languages in *Call It Sleep* and Roth's enthusiastic use of all the available typographical symbols for conveying the movements of consciousness (including dashes, spaces, and italics to render breaks, pauses, and

emphases in thought) may have made any typographical bowdlerizations appear to be part of a character's speech or consciousness and not a publisher's imposition. Allen Walker Read, "An Obscenity Symbol," *American Speech* 9:4 (December 1934): 278n. 82.

58. While in an important sense Roth relies in this scene on the Biblical promise of purification and redemption through the prophetic call, I contend that it is not the authority of Judaism or Christianity or ancient prophecy per se that makes the imagery from Isaiah 6 meaningful within *Call It Sleep* but its appropriateness as source material within modernist practice. Roth sought out Isaiah as a myth that he could use, as Joyce had used *The Odyssey* and Eliot material from *The Golden Bough*. The simplest evidence that Roth was not interested in Isaiah itself is that in Roth's many autobiographical reflections on his literary education and the composition of *Call It Sleep*, he does not dwell at any length on the impact that reading Isaiah, or other Biblical texts, had on him. He concentrates instead on the transformative power of Joyce and Eliot. For a thoughtful consideration of the "Jewish American 'prophetic mode,'" though, see Levinson, *Exiles on Main Street*, 192–200.

59. On this debate, see, for example, Tom Samet's 1975 essay "Henry Roth's Bull Story: Guilt and Betrayal in *Call It Sleep*" (*Studies in the Novel* [Winter 1975]: 569–83), which summarizes the "unanimous agreement among critics," including Rideout, Fiedler, Ferguson, Allen Guttman, and Lyons, who "argue that *Call It Sleep* traces a movement from terror and alienation to tranquility and reconciliation" (569–70), before articulating his own contention that "David's moments of illumination are essentially bogus" (570) and that the novel "witnesses neither transfiguration nor redemption, but strategic retreat" (581). Samet is joined in his minority position by Gary Epstein in "Auto-Obituary: The Death of the Artist in Henry Roth's *Call It Sleep*," *Studies in American Jewish Literature* 5:1 (1979): 37–45, and by Gert G. Buelens in "The Multi-voiced Basis of Henry Roth's Literary Success in *Call It Sleep*," in Winfried Siemerling and Katrin Schwenk, eds., *Cultural Difference and the Literary Text: Pluralism and the Limits of Authenticity in North American Literature* (Iowa City: University of Iowa Press, 1996), 142–50.

60. Kellman's biography of Roth argues that two factors militated against the success of *Call It Sleep* upon its original publication in the mid-1930s: the reduction in book sales generally during the Depression and a relative indifference to writing on Jewish themes at that time. Neither of these arguments is entirely convincing. Many writers made their reputations in the 1930s, and *Call It Sleep* itself managed to sell well enough that its publisher proudly advertised in the *New York Times* that the novel was "selling 600 weekly." *New York Times* (April 7, 1935): BR23. Kellman's point about the virtual mania for all things Jewish in 1964 cannot be gainsaid, but plenty of books on Jewish subjects were written and published in the 1930s to general acclaim: two years after *Call It Sleep* appeared, for example, Jerome Weidman had a best-seller with *I Can Get It for You Wholesale* (1937), which was so popular that it occasioned a quick sequel. On the other hand,

Kellman's explanations for Roth's inability to publish a novel in the following decades, including his ambivalent engagements with Communism and his ongoing sexual shame, are quite plausible. Kellman, *Redemption*, 141–49.

61. Kellman mistakenly dates Woolsey's *Ulysses* decision to 1932 (*Redemption*, 88) and does not mention the affirmation by Hand, thus unintentionally obscuring the relevance of these decisions to the reception of Roth's novel.
62. *United States v. One Book Entitled "Ulysses" by James Joyce*, 72 F.2d 705 (2d Cir. 1934).
63. For an explicit comparison to *Ulysses* in an early review, see John Chamberlain, "Books of the Times," *New York Times* (February 18, 1935): 13.
64. Boynton, "Story of a Ghetto Childhood."
65. Ibid.
66. For a discussion of Perkins, obscenity, and American modernism, see Glass, "#$%^&*!?."
67. Max Perkins to Elizabeth Lemmon, July 29, 1935, quoted in A. Scott Berg, *Max Perkins: Editor of Genius* (New York: Dutton, 1978), 280.
68. Quoted in Rochelle Gurstein, *The Repeal of Reticence: A History of America's Cultural and Legal Struggles over Free Speech, Obscenity, Sexual Liberation, and Modern Art* (New York: Hill and Wang, 1996), 210.
69. See, e.g., Marie Syrkin, "The Cultural Scene: Literary Expression," in Oscar Janowsky, ed., *The American Jew: A Composite Portrait* (New York: Harper, 1942), 101–2; James T. Farrell, *Literature and Morality* (New York: Vanguard, 1947), 152; Irving Howe, "The Stranger and the Victim," *Commentary* (August 1949): 149. In 1956, Leslie Fiedler wrote that "to let another year go without reprinting it would be unforgivable"; Fiedler, "The Most Neglected Books of the Past 25 Years," *American Scholar* 25 (Autumn 1956): 486.
70. See de Grazia, *Girls Lean Back Everywhere*, 209–42.
71. For the testimony, see Charles Rembar, *The End of Obscenity: The Trials of "Lady Chatterley," "Tropic of Cancer," and "Fanny Hill"* (New York: Random House, 1968), 98. On Kazin's knowledge of *Call It Sleep*—and his use of it as a model for *A Walker in the City*, whether consciously or not—see Levinson, *Exiles on Main Street*, 164.
72. See Matthew Frye Jacobson, *Roots Too: White Ethnic Revival in Post–Civil Rights America* (Cambridge: Harvard University Press, 2006), 171–75.
73. This fact was mentioned in the oral arguments of *Cohen v. California*, 403 U.S. 15 (1971).
74. Names for the genre of literary comic books have proliferated since the 1980s: "art comics," "adult comics," "alternative comics," "graphic narrative," "graphic fiction" and "sequential art" are a few of the more or less reasonable suggestions that have not caught on widely; "graphic novel" is the awkward one that has stuck. Without ignoring the manifest problems with this term, this chapter employs the term *graphic novels* to refer to literary comic books (and not to the manga, superhero adventures, and other genre fiction also widely marketed under that rubric), in

part because it argues that the use of "graphic" sexual content was crucial to their development. On "sequential art," see Will Eisner, *Comics and Sequential Art* (Tamarac, FL: Poorhouse, 1985); and Scott McCloud, *Understanding Comics: The Invisible Art* (Northampton, MA: Kitchen Sink, 1993), 2–23. For "art comics," see Douglas Wolk, *Reading Comics: How Graphic Novels Work and What They Mean* (New York: Da Capo, 2007), 29–36. For "graphic narrative," see Hillary Chute, "Comics as Literature: Reading Graphic Narrative," *PMLA* 123:2 (March 2008): 453. For "graphic fiction," see Ivan Brunetti, ed., *An Anthology of Graphic Fiction, Cartoons, and True Stories* (New Haven: Yale University Press, 2006), 10. For "adult comics," see Roger Sabin, *Adult Comics: An Introduction* (New York, London: Routledge, 1993). For "alternative comics," see Charles Hatfield, *Alternative Comics: An Emerging Literature* (Jackson: University Press of Mississippi, 2005). The problems with the term *graphic novel* are discussed at some length in most of these sources, most insightfully by Wolk and Hatfield.

75. In Japan, France, and Belgium, comic books had been taken seriously much earlier. Manga has been widely read by and marketed to adults since the decades after World War II; in the mid-1980s, the circulation of a biweekly manga magazine for adults was reported to be more than a million, and there were eighteen monthly magazines for adult women readers. Frederick L. Schodt, *Manga! Manga! The World of Japanese Comics* (Tokyo: Kodansha, 1986), 13, 17. On the development of album comics for adults in France and Belgium, see Bart Beaty, *Unpopular Culture: Transforming the European Comic Book in the 1990s* (Toronto: University of Toronto Press, 2007), 24–27.
76. Mark McGurl, for example, remarks in passing on "the importance of major historical reference in the recent rise of the graphic novel to artistic respectability, whether it be Art Spiegelman's highly reflexive *Maus* (1986) or Marjane Satrapi's *Persepolis* (2001) or even Alan Moore's *Watchmen* (1986–87)." McGurl, *The Program Era: Postwar Fiction and the Rise of Creative Writing* (Cambridge: Harvard University Press, 2009), 447n. 61.
77. Pascale Casanova defines *littérisation* as "any operation . . . by means of which a text . . . comes to be regarded as literary by the legitimate authorities" (*World Republic of Letters*, 135–36).
78. This notion can be traced as far back as the pronouncement by Pope Gregory the Great, around the year 600 CE, that "what writing presents to readers, this a picture presents to the unlearned who behold, since in it even the ignorant see what they ought to follow; in it the illiterate read." St. Gregory the Great, "Book 11, Epistle 13," in Philip Schaff and Henry Wace, eds., *A Select Library of Nicene and Post-Nicene Fathers of the Christian Church*, 2nd series, vol. 13 (New York: Christian Literature Company, 1898), 53. Lawrence G. Duggan traces this dictum's remarkable acceptance throughout the ensuing centuries and assesses its validity, concluding that "Gregory and his many disciples erred in regarding art as the book of the illiterate," in "Was Art Really the 'Book of the Illiterate'?," *Word & Image* 5:3 (July–September 1989): 227–51 (quote on 251). That notion persisted

into modernity; Rudolphe Töpffer noted in 1845 that "the picture story appeals mainly to children and the lower classes" (Töpffer, *Enter the Comics*, trans. and ed. Ellen Wiese (Lincoln: University of Nebraska Press, 1965), 3, quoted in McCloud, *Understanding Comics*, 201). Similar ideas circulated during the first popularization of comic strips in America; see "A Crime against American Children," *Ladies' Home Journal* (January 1909): 5; and "The Comic Supplement," *Outlook* (April 15, 1911): 802. The recent *Norton Anthology of Children's Literature* explains that narratives "in which pictures dominate the verbal text . . . are the form of literature that more than any other is designed specifically for children." Jack Zipes et al., introduction to "Picture Books," in *The Norton Anthology of Children's Literature: The Traditions in English* (New York: Norton, 2005), 1051. The visual nature of cinema was also seen as making it a dangerously powerful medium for children, in the early years of the motion-picture industry; see Lee Grievson, *Policing Cinema: Movies and Censorship in Early-Twentieth-Century America* (Berkeley: University of California Press, 2004), 64.

79. For demographic studies demonstrating widespread adult readership of comic strips, see Ian Gordon, *Comic Strips and Consumer Culture, 1890–1945* (Washington, DC: Smithsonian Institution Press, 1998), 89.

80. Eisner, *Comics and Sequential Art*, 141. On the postwar comics scare, which concerned the relationship between comics and "juvenile delinquency" (and in which defenders of comics almost never attempted to suggest that comics might have a readership other than children), see Whitney Strub, *Perversion for Profit: The Politics of Pornography and the Rise of the New Right* (New York: Columbia University Press, 2010), 15–21; Amy Kiste Nyberg, *Seal of Approval: The History of the Comics Code* (Jackson: University Press of Mississippi, 1998); and David Hajdu, *The Ten-Cent Plague: The Great Comic Book Scare and How It Changed America* (New York: Farrar, Straus and Giroux, 2008).

81. Lawrence W. Levine, *Highbrow/Lowbrow: The Emergence of Cultural Hierarchy in America* (Cambridge: Harvard University Press, 1988), 231.

82. Michele Gorman, "What Teens Want," *School Library Journal* (August 1, 2002), http://www.schoollibraryjournal.com/article/CA236064.html.

83. Random House publishes a guide to *Maus* "for high school teachers," while other guides recommend the book for middle school students (see, e.g., Bucks County Free Library, "Teaching Resources for Art Spiegelman's *Maus: A Survivor's Tale*, One Book / One Bucks County 2005," http://www.buckslib.org/OneBook/Maus/unit1.htm). Spiegelman was anxious about the possibility that his work would be thought of as children's culture. He has recalled, "I read an interview with Steven Spielberg that he was producing an animated feature film entitled *An American Tail*, involving a family of Jewish mice living in Russia a hundred years ago named the Mousekawitzes, who were being persecuted by Katsacks, and how eventually they fled to America for shelter. . . . I was appalled, shattered. . . . I went sleepless for nights on end, and then, when I finally did sleep, I began confusing our names in my dreams: Spiegelberg, Spielman." Lawrence Weschler, "Art's Father, Vladek's

Son," in *Shapinsky's Karma, Bogg's Bills, and Other True-Life Tales* (San Francisco: North Point, 1988), 56–57, quoted in Michael G. Levine, "Necessary Stains: Spiegelman's *Maus* and the Bleeding of History," *American Imago* 59:3 (Fall 2002): 330.

84. Note, for example, that Stephen Weiner, a children's librarian who has written enthusiastically about *Contract* and *Tantrum* in two book-length surveys of the graphic novel field, strongly recommends *Maus* but not the two graphic novels under discussion here when he contributes to the *English Journal*, which is aimed at an audience of "English language arts teachers in junior and senior high schools and middle schools." Weiner, "Show, Don't Tell: Graphic Novels in the Classroom," *English Journal* 94:2 (November 2004): 114–17.
85. "Graphic," Draft Additions June 2003, *The Oxford English Dictionary Online*. The term was often used to refer to novels with sexually explicit content: in 1879, the *Washington Post* reported that the Russian government objected to Ivan Turgenev's "graphic novels." See "Personal," *Washington Post* (July 2, 1879): 2. *Graphic novel*, in this historical usage as a noun with a modifying adjective, differs grammatically from the contemporary use of the term as a compound noun, of course, but for whatever reason, many people continue to recall the older or more literal sense of the phrase when they hear about graphic novels today, especially because of the powerful contemporary association of the word *graphic* with its occasional prefix *porno-*. Both librarian Aviva Rothschild and editor Charles McGrath have reported such confusion; Rothschild writes, "When I told noncomics readers that I was compiling a bibliography of graphic novels, the invariable response was, 'You're doing a bibliography of pornographic fiction?'" Rothschild, *Graphic Novels: A Bibliographic Guide to Book-Length Comics* (Westport, CT: Libraries Unlimited, 1995), xiii. McGrath's anecdote is very similar: "When I mentioned to a friend that I was working on an article about graphic novels, he said, hopefully, 'You mean porn?'" McGrath, "Not Funnies," *New York Times Magazine* (July 11, 2004). Art Spiegelman plays with this confusion in his remark, "Personally, I always thought that Nathanael West's *Day of the Locusts* was an extraordinarily graphic novel"—referring, presumably, to West's attention to classical painting and illustration as well as to the book's gruesome scenes of violence and sex. Quoted in Sabin, *Adult Comics*, 235. Such misunderstandings amuse comics readers because publishers have successfully marketed superhero tales, memoirs, and historical fiction as graphic novels but only in rare cases erotica or pornography.
86. *Memoirs v. Massachusetts*, 383 U.S. 413 (1966). For an overview of these developments, see Rembar, *End of Obscenity*.
87. *Ginsberg v. New York*, 390 U.S. 629 (1968).
88. "Pornography and Common Sense," *Los Angeles Times* (March 3, 1978): C4.
89. *FCC v. Pacifica Foundation*, 438 U.S. 726 (1978); in oral arguments, Joseph A. Marino, speaking for the FCC, emphasized that the fact that children were in the audience was "at the heart of the commission's decision." *Pinkus v. United States*, 436 U.S. 293 (1978).

90. Henry Raymonts, "Fig Leafs for Children Irk Librarians," *New York Times* (June 27, 1972): 34.
91. Perry Nodelman, "Of Nakedness and Children's Books," *Children's Literature Association Quarterly* 9:1 (Spring 1984): 28.
92. Eisner regularly told a story about what happened when Brentano's bookstore shelved *Contract* alongside reprints of newspaper comic strips in 1978. A father complained to the manager, "You have a comic book that shows a naked lady in with the *Beetle Bailey* books! . . . I don't want my kid being exposed to that kind of stuff." Bob Andleman, *Will Eisner: A Spirited Life* (Milwaukee: M Press, 2005), 292. A precedent for the treatment of sex in Eisner's early work, as David Beronä has demonstrated, can be found in the "wordless novels" of the 1930s and 1940s. Beronä, "Breaking Taboos: Sexuality in the Work of Will Eisner and the Early Wordless Novels," *International Journal of Comic Art* (Spring–Summer 1999): 90–103.
93. Steven Marcus coins "pornotopia" and defines it at length, elaborating on its timeless and placeless character as well as the plenitude that characterizes it: "Pornotopia is literally a world of grace abounding to the chief of sinners. All men in it are always and infinitely potent; all women fecundate with lust and flow inexhaustibly with sap or juice or both. Everyone is always ready for anything, and everyone is infinitely generous with his substance." Marcus, *The Other Victorians: A Study of Sexuality and Pornography in Mid-Nineteenth-Century England* (New York: Basic Books, 1966), 268–74.
94. The distinction here, between pornotopic representations and sexual realism, uncomfortably echoes the one made by Eberhard and Phyllis Kronhausen in *Pornography and the Law: The Psychology of Erotic Realism and Pornography* (New York: Ballantine Books, 1959), between "pornography" and "erotic realism." The Kronhausens wrote their book during the early years of the liberalization of U.S. obscenity law, as they phrase it, "to define more clearly what 'hard core obscenity' or pornography actually consists of in order to make it possible for the courts to apply the standards upheld by the United States Supreme Court" (22)—or, in other words, to make clear to judges which works of literature should be censored. It is unfortunate that they were willing to concede that "pornography," of which "the main purpose is to stimulate erotic response in the reader" (18), should be subject to censorship, especially because they defined as obscene works that represented defloration, incest, "profaning the sacred," and homosexuality. The tendency to realism rather than pornotopic representations in Eisner and Feiffer suggests how much they, as authors, may have assimilated a distinction like the Kronhausens' and used it to distinguish their own graphic novels from earlier pornographic comics.
95. Will Eisner, *The "Contract with God" Trilogy* (New York: Norton, 2006), 175.
96. Ibid., 111.
97. Jules Feiffer, *Tantrum* (New York: Knopf, 1979), 7.
98. Ibid., 165.
99. Levine, *Highbow/Lowbrow*, 234.

100. Will Eisner, "Keynote Address, Will Eisner Symposium," *ImageTexT: Interdisciplinary Comics Studies* 1:1 (2004), http://www.english.ufl.edu/imagetext/archives/v1_1/eisner/index.shtml.
101. "The comic strip is no longer a comic strip but in reality an illustrated novel. It is new and raw just now, but material for a limitless, intelligent development. And eventually, and inevitably, it will be a legitimate medium for the best of writers and artists." Dated as having been written in 1942, this statement is quoted in Jon B. Cooke, "Blithe Spirit," *Comic Book Artist* 2:6 (November 2005): 4–5. Many decades later, Eisner repeated the point: "I don't want my work to be bought because it's a graphic novel. I want it to be bought because it's a piece of literature—visual literature or graphic literature, maybe. But I want it to be thought of as literature." David Hajdu, "Good Will," *Comic Book Artist* 2:6 (November 2005): 30.
102. Two sets of notes for lectures, both dated "'79," beginning "All my life victim" and "The cartoon is different," Box 56, Jules Feiffer Papers, Manuscript Division, Library of Congress, Washington, D.C.
103. Tebbel, *Between Covers*, 381.
104. Stephen Steinberg, *The Academic Melting Pot: Catholics and Jews in American Higher Education* (New York: Transaction, 1977), 122.
105. Hajdu, "Good Will," 31.
106. In a useful history of the period, Gerard Jones notes that "rough-edged Jewish kids knew they had a steep hill to climb if they wanted to become 'high-class' illustrators" for magazines and advertising agencies, "not only because of editors' prejudices but also because of the costs of the training, studio lighting, and live models needed for that perfect sheen." Jones, *Men of Tomorrow: Geeks, Gangsters, and the Birth of the Comic Book* (New York: Basic Books, 2004), 135. This was true for writers, too. Stan Lee puts it this way: "When I entered the comics field in 1940, comics were not held in high regard at that time—and that's putting it mildly. Not wanting my name to be sullied by them, I used the pen name of Stan Lee, leaving Stanley Martin Lieber for the great novel to come." Lee, foreword to *Disguised as Clark Kent: Jews, Comics, and the Creation of the Superhero*, by Danny Fingeroth (New York: Continuum, 2007), 10. Feiffer recalls, "One's ambitions were to break into the field through comics, move on to newspaper strips, and then ideally go into magazine illustrations for *The Saturday Evening Post* or *Esquire*." Jon B. Cooke, "Jules Feiffer: His Early Years with Will Eisner," *Comic Book Artist* 2:6 (November 2005): 117.
107. Pierre Bourdieu, *The Field of Cultural Production: Essays on Art and Literature* (New York: Columbia University Press, 1993), 67.
108. Eisner recalled of the mid-1970s, "By then, I had a few coins in my pocket and so I was able to afford to spend the whole year doing something without worrying about whether or not I'm going to have enough bread to eat. So I decided I would start what I later called a 'graphic novel.'" Jon B. Cooke, "Will Eisner: The Creative Life of a Master," *Comic Book Artist* 2:6 (November 2005): 43. On "literary access," see Richard Brodhead, *Cultures of Letters: Scenes of Reading and*

Writing in Nineteenth-Century America (Chicago: University of Chicago Press, 1993).

109. Gottlieb has recalled coming up with a book idea in the mid-1970s: "I thought, I am a Jew who knows nothing about Jewishness. I grew up in an atheist household; I never attended anything. I thought that Chaim [Potok] could write a very popular and useful book that might instruct someone like me." The result was Potok's *Wanderings* (1978), and Gottlieb's comment reflects not only his Jewish self-awareness but also his sense of the marketability in the late 1970s of a book about Jewish culture. "Robert Gottlieb: The Art of Editing," in Philip Gourevitch, ed., *The Paris Review Interviews*, vol. 1 (New York: Picador, 2006), 349.
110. See David Finn, "An Interview with Oscar Dystel," *Move Magazine* 10 (2006), http://www.ruderfinn.com/move/issue-10/the-fragility-of-democracy.html.
111. In an interview, Goldfine said, "[These were] all experiences which I went through growing up as a Jew in New York City." Telephone interview with the author, August 29, 2008.
112. In one of the first published reviews of *Contract*, Dennis O'Neil compared the book to "the stories of Bernard Malamud, Philip Roth, and Isaac Singer [*sic*]." O'Neil, "Winners and Losers: Harsh Memories from Will Eisner," *Comics Journal* 46 (May 1979): 52–53. In a review in the *Times Literary Supplement*—which had previously reviewed nine of Feiffer's books—Russell Davies compared *Tantrum* not just to Kafka but also to Philip Roth's *The Breast* and to Woody Allen's movies. Davies, "The Cradle Falls," *Times Literary Supplement* (May 16, 1980): 552.
113. Harvey Pekar, "The Young Crumb Story," *American Splendor* 1:4 (October 1979): n.p.
114. Crumb noted in 1985 that "most comic specialty shops won't even carry books like *American Splendor*. Why should they? 'Adults' never go in such places, and so the 'adult' comics just sit there taking up space on the shelf." See R. Crumb, introduction to *American Splendor: The Life and Times of Harvey Pekar*, by Harvey Pekar (Garden City, NY: Doubleday, 1986). The collection, described on its back cover as "the first literary comic book," was reviewed, for example, by Michiko Kakutani: "Picasso's Documented Imagination," *New York Times* (May 26, 1986): 13.

Notes to Chapter 3

1. For an example of the complexity of reproduction in rabbinic literature, see the Talmudic debate as to whether a non-Jew who has had children before his conversion to Judaism has already fulfilled the commandment to reproduce. Is the command to reproduce commanding biological or cultural reproduction, or some combination of both? *B. Yevamot* 62a. The anthropologist Harvey E. Goldberg offers a set of provocative observations and hypotheses about the links between biological and cultural reproduction in "Torah and Children: Symbolic Aspects of the Reproduction of Jews and Judaism," in *Judaism Viewed from Within and from Without: Anthropological Studies* (Albany: SUNY Press, 1987), 107–30. For a focused sociological study of the complexities of reproduction in one

contemporary Jewish community, see Susan Martha Kahn, *Reproducing Jews: A Cultural Account of Assisted Conception in Israel* (Durham: Duke University Press, 2000). The work of Pierre Bourdieu is frequently concerned with "reproduction strategies" attended to in terms of their complex and deeply intertwined social, cultural, and biological factors; see, for example, *Distinction: A Social Critique of the Judgment of Taste*, trans. Richard Nice (Cambridge: Harvard University Press, 1984).

2. Comstock Act, chap. 258, 17 Stat. 598 (1873).
3. See Andrea Tone, *Devices and Desires: A History of Contraceptives in America* (New York: Hill and Wang, 2001), 3–25; Nicola Beisel, *Imperiled Innocents: Anthony Comstock and Family Reproduction in Victorian America* (Princeton: Princeton University Press, 1997).
4. The outing of abortionists as Jews was common in the press of the time, as if the act of changing one's name was, in and of itself, an indicator of criminality. For example, the *New York Times* noted that "'Dr. ASCHER,' alias 'Rosensweig,' of South Fifth-avenue, below Amity-street, claims to be a Russian, but his voice has the twang of a German Jew." "The Evil of the Age," *New York Times* (August 23, 1871): 6. For other examples, see Beisel, *Imperiled Innocents*, 45.
5. On the poverty of immigrants on the Lower East Side of New York, see Gerald Sorin, *A Time for Building: The Third Migration, 1880–1920* (Baltimore: Johns Hopkins University Press, 1992), 70–73.
6. Rabbinic authorities have differed on the questions of when and in what forms birth control is permissible. See David M. Feldman, *Birth Control in Jewish Law* (New York: NYU Press, 1968), 301. On the lack of consensus regarding abortion at the turn of the 20th century among traditional Jews, see David Schiff, *Abortion in Judaism* (Cambridge: Cambridge University Press, 2002), 116. It would be a mistake to exaggerate the influence of the Catholic hierarchy on European immigrants to the United States in the late 19th century or, for that matter, the role of the Catholic Church in the establishment of the Comstock Act and in the criminalization of contraception and abortion (which movements, led by Comstock, were in large part emphatically Protestant projects). Yet there was a significant difference between the strength and influence of the Catholic hierarchy in America—on which, see Patricia Byrne, "American Ultramontanism," *Theological Studies* 56:2 (1995): 301–26—and the relative absence of authoritative Jewish religious institutions, which will be discussed in chapter 4.
7. Emma Goldman, *Living My Life*, vol. 2 (New York: Dover, 1970), 569.
8. For the targeting of anarchists under obscenity statutes and for an example of Goldman deploring the Comstock Act directly, see Candace Falk, introduction to Falk, ed., *Emma Goldman: A Documentary History of the American Years*, vol. 2, *Making Speech Free, 1902–1909* (Berkeley: University of California Press, 2004), 76; and "Editorial in *Mother Earth*: 'Mother Earth'" (March 1906), in ibid., 177.
9. Margaret Sanger, *Autobiography* (1938; repr., New York: Cooper Square, 1999), 89–92.

10. Ellen Chesler expresses doubt that Sachs existed in *A Woman of Valor: Margaret Sanger and the Birth Control Movement in America* (New York: Simon and Schuster, 2007), 63.
11. Sanger, *Autobiography*, 215.
12. For an appraisal of Liber's career, see Eli Lederhendler, "Guides for the Perplexed: Sex, Manners, and Mores for the Yiddish Reader in America," *Modern Judaism* 11:3 (October 1991): 321–41.
13. Margaret Sanger, *Vos yede maydl darf visn*, trans. K. Teper (New York: Max N. Mayzel, 1916); Auguste Forel, *Di geshlekhts frage*, trans. D. Borukhson (New York: Farlag Zelbst-Bildung, 1920).
14. Ben-Zion Liber, *Dos geshlekts lebn fun man un froy: A populer-visenshafltikh bukh* ([New York?], 1919), 17.
15. Jenna Weissman Joselit, *The Wonders of America: Reinventing Jewish Culture, 1880–1950* (New York: Hill and Wang, 1994), 63–64.
16. See *United States v. One Package of Japanese Pessaries*, 86 F.2d 737 (2nd Cir. 1936).
17. Hasia Diner, *The Jews of the United States: 1654 to 2000* (Berkeley: University of California Press, 2004), 246.
18. Tone, *Devices and Desires*, 50–51, 184–88. For a parallel case in Germany, see Götz Aly and Michael Sontheimer, *Fromms: How Julius Fromm's Condom Empire Fell to the Nazis* (New York: Other, 2009).
19. Russell Viner, "Abraham Jacobi and German Medical Radicalism in Antebellum New York," *Bulletin of the History of Medicine* 72:3 (1998): 434–63 (quote on 436).
20. Abraham Jacobi, introduction to William J. Robinson, *Fewer and Better Babies: The Limitation of Offspring by the Prevention of Conception*, 6th ed. (New York: Critic and Guide, 1916), 13–18 (quote on 18). On Jacobi's role in the birth control movement, see William J. Robinson, *Pioneers of Birth Control in England and America* (New York: Voluntary Parenthood League, 1919), 72–76.
21. On Jacobi's work at Mount Sinai, see Arthur H. Aufses, Jr., and Barbara Niss, *This House of Noble Deeds: The Mount Sinai Hospital, 1852–2002* (New York: NYU Press, 2002). Jacobi was sensitive about the knee-jerk assumption that an individual's Jewishness contributes to his or her conduct. In his review of a book on the German revolution of 1848, in which Jacobi participated as a young man, he criticized the author for referring to two figures not in terms of their revolutionary activities but as Jews. See Jacobi, "The Baden Struggle," in *Miscellaneous Addresses and Writings*, ed. William J. Robinson, Collecteana Jacobi 8 (New York: Critic and Guide, 1909), 507–8.
22. A later case worth considering is that of Gregory Pincus, the Jewish research scientist who led the team that developed the birth control pill, working alongside a Catholic, John Rock, and a Confucian, Min Chueh Chang. As a faithful Catholic, Rock was subject to harsh treatment by Catholics and was eventually alienated from his church after developing the pill, despite his attempts, in *The Time Has Come: A Catholic Doctor's Proposals to End the Battle over Birth Control* (New York: Knopf, 1963) and many public presentations, to argue that chemical

contraception should be acceptable to the Catholic hierarchy. For the details of Pincus, Rock, and Chang's collaboration, see Lara V. Marks, *Sexual Chemistry: A History of the Contraceptive Pill* (New Haven: Yale University Press, 2001); and on Rock's Catholicism, see Loretta McLaughlin, *The Pill, John Rock, and the Church: The Biography of a Revolution* (Boston: Little, Brown, 1982), and, more recently, Margaret S. Marsh and Wanda Ronner, *The Fertility Doctor: John Rock and the Reproductive Revolution* (Baltimore: Johns Hopkins University Press, 2008). While Pincus does not seem to have been a particularly active or religious Jew, his contribution to the invention of the birth control pill did not prevent his funeral services from being held at the Reform Temple Emanuel in Worcester, Massachusetts, after he died in 1967. See "Dr. Pincus, Developer of Birth Control Pill, Dead," *Jewish Telegraphic Agency* (August 24, 1967). Rock, for his part, left Catholicism in the 1960s but began to reconnect with the religion toward the end of his life; he died in 1984, and his family respected his request for a private funeral with a Mass delivered by a priest from whom he had lately, privately, been taking communion. One might say that while Rock's Catholicism did not ultimately prevent him from any of his professional achievements in the field of contraception, it added a degree of emotional turbulence to his career that was likely not a factor for Pincus.

23. Peter C. Engelman, *A History of the Birth Control Movement in America* (New York: Praeger / ABC-CLIO, 2011), 141–80; Linda Gordon, *The Moral Property of Women: A History of Birth Control Politics in America* (Urbana: University of Illinois Press, 2002), 171–242.
24. Alan Ackerman, *Just Words: Lillian Hellman, Mary McCarthy, and the Failure of Public Conversation in America* (New Haven: Yale University Press, 2011), 117–83.
25. Lillian Hellman, *Three* (Boston: Little, Brown, 1979), 48–52.
26. Tess Slesinger, *The Unpossessed* (1934; repr., New York: Feminist, 1984), 345.
27. In that case, Judge Augustus Hand remarked that "statutes . . . [that] suppress immoral articles and obscene literature . . . should so far as possible be construed together and consistently. If this be done, the articles here in question"—pessaries imported from Japan—"ought not to be forfeited when not intended for an immoral purpose." In so doing, he distinguished between birth control prescribed by a doctor and "obscene literature"—though leaving open the question of whether pessaries "intended for an immoral purpose" might fairly be included in the same category as "obscene literature." *United States v. One Package of Japanese Pessaries*, 86 F.2d 737, 739 (2nd Cir. 1936).
28. Charles Dickens himself could not have invented a better name for a Jewish lawyer than "Pilpel." Literally meaning "spice" or "pepper," *pilpul* as applied to Talmud study can be translated as "intellectual sharpness and acumen," though it also carries a connotation of sophistry. See Jeffrey Rubinstein, *The Culture of the Babylonian Talmud* (Baltimore: Johns Hopkins University Press, 2003), 48–51.
29. Samuel Walker, *In Defense of American Liberties: A History of the ACLU* (New York: Oxford University Press, 1990), 301–2, 312.

30. Harriet Fleischl Pilpel, "Is It Legal?," *New York Times* (January 20, 1946): 49.
31. *United States v. 31 Photographs*, 156 F. Supp. 350 (S.D.N.Y. 1957). For Pilpel's account of the case, see "But Can You Do That? Federal Court Makes Important Ruling in Kinsey Case," *Publisher's Weekly* 172 (November 25, 1957): 29–30.
32. See, for example, Pilpel, "But Can You Do That? Some Obscenity Battles Yet to Be Fought in Court," *Publisher's Weekly* 194 (December 30, 1968): 42–43.
33. *New World Writing* 16 (Philadelphia: Lippincott, 1960).
34. Irving Spiegel, "Censors' Foe Sees Need for Limits to Freedom," *New York Times* (January 5, 1970): 46; Charles Rembar, *The End of Obscenity: The Trials of "Lady Chatterley," "Tropic of Cancer," and "Fanny Hill"* (New York: Random House, 1968), 484–85.
35. Harriet Pilpel, *Obscenity and the Constitution* (New York: R. R. Bowker, 1973), 22.
36. Ibid., 23–24.
37. Ibid., 13.
38. Harriet Pilpel Oral History (New York: American Jewish Committee, Oral History Library, 1975), 57, held at the New York Public Library.
39. Ibid., 30–31.
40. For example, Andrew Hoberek has argued that in *The Adventures of Augie March* (1953), Saul Bellow "suggests that Jews are prototypically other-directed Americans but, perhaps even more significantly, that postwar Americans are prototypically Jewish." Hoberek, *The Twilight of the Middle Class: Post–World War II American Fiction and White-Collar Work* (Princeton: Princeton University Press, 2005), 85.
41. Saul Bellow, *The Adventures of Augie March* (New York: Viking, 1953), 294. Further citations of this source are given parenthetically in the text.
42. Theodore Dreiser, *An American Tragedy* (New York: New American Library, 1964), 257. On the attention paid to Dreiser's novel in *Birth Control Review*, see Beth Widmaier Capo, *Textual Contraception: Birth Control and Modern American Fiction* (Columbus: Ohio State University Press, 2007), 64–65.
43. Capo, *Textual Contraception*, 183–88.
44. Philip Roth, *Goodbye Columbus and Five Short Stories* (1959; repr., New York: Bantam, 1963), 95–96. Further citations of this source are given parenthetically in the text.
45. Werner Sollors, *Beyond Ethnicity: Consent and Descent in American Culture* (New York: Oxford University Press, 1986).
46. In the first "Imaginary Conversation with Our Leader," published in the *New York Review of Books* (May 6, 1971), later reprinted in *Our Gang* (New York: Random House, 1971), Roth deals more directly with the political uses of antiabortion rhetoric in the postwar United States, quoting from President Richard Nixon's notoriously calculated rejection of abortion on April 3, 1971, and drawing comedy out of the incoherence of Nixon's positions.
47. An exception is Mary Allen, who notes, "The women in *Letting Go* all let go of their children. . . . They add up to a general malaise affecting the bond between

parent and child." Allen, *The Necessary Blankness: Women in Major American Fiction of the Sixties* (Urbana: University of Illinois Press, 1976), 83.

48. Martha describes her own children as the consequence, precisely, of not aborting those pregnancies: "I got knocked up all right, but I acted like a woman about it. . . . I *had* that child, I didn't have it scraped down some drain somewhere, back in some dark alley. And then I woke up one morning and that son of a bitch was on top of me again, and I didn't have an abortion then either. These are *lives*, for God's sake." Philip Roth, *Letting Go* (1961; repr., New York: Vintage, 1997), 321. Further citations of this source are given parenthetically in the text.
49. Shaye J. D. Cohen's *The Beginnings of Jewishness: Boundaries, Varieties, Uncertainties* (Berkeley: University of California Press, 1999) offers a crucial history of the "matrilineal principle" in Judaism. This principle seems to have gone virtually uncontested by rabbinic authorities of any denomination until the American Reform movement's "Resolution on Patrilineal Descent," issued March 15, 1983.
50. Steven M. Cohen and Arnold Eisen are admirably attentive to the problems caused by conversion and its regulation by the Orthodox in Israel in *The Jew Within: Self, Family, and Community in America* (Bloomington: Indiana University Press, 2000).
51. Irving Feldman, "A Sentimental Education circa 1956," *Commentary* (September 1962): 273–76. James Atlas, "Reconsideration: Philip Roth's 'Letting Go': A Postwar Classic," *New Republic* (June 2, 1982): 28–32.
52. Barbara Melosh, *Strangers and Kin: The American Way of Adoption* (Cambridge: Harvard University Press, 2002), 76–77 (quote on 76, quoting *Revised Code of Delaware*, 1935, 3551 Sec. 4, p. 764).
53. Ibid., 81.
54. Dana Evan Kaplan has succinctly described the transition in the postwar United States from a view of religion "as an ascribed part of identity," which "like one's race . . . was held to be immutable," to one in which "each person needs to embark on her own spiritual journey in order to find her own personal path to the sacred." Kaplan, *Contemporary American Judaism: Transformation and Renewal* (New York: Columbia University Press, 2009), 1–2.
55. On the contemporaneous work of Jewish sociologists to make Americans feel what Libby says here (that "everyone had to have some group identity in the United States"), see Lila Corwin Berman's *Speaking of Jews: Rabbis, Intellectuals, and the Creation of an American Public Identity* (Berkeley: University of California Press, 2009), 93–118 (quote on 117).
56. Indeed, Shaye J. D. Cohen suggests that matrilinearity may have itself developed partly in response to the introduction of a conversion ritual for women (the same ritual, immersion, that Libby engages in a modern version of): once conversion for women was introduced—and it was no longer the case that a non-Jewish woman who married a Jewish husband was automatically considered Jewish—"the gentile woman was now a person whose Jewishness could be determined without reference to her Jewish husband. If she converts to Judaism, the children

she bears to her husband are Jewish; if she does not, they are gentiles, in spite of the Jewishness of her husband" (*Beginnings of Jewishness*, 306). Libby's case asks us to consider how this logic might work in reverse: if Libby's child is Jewish, how can she, its mother, not be?

57. Milton Himmelfarb, "The Vanishing Jews," *Commentary* (September 1963): 249–51.
58. Michael Staub, *Torn at the Roots: The Crisis of Jewish Liberalism in Postwar America* (New York: Columbia University Press, 2004), 241–79. In 1985, citing four studies, one writer claimed that "Jews were 3 to 14 times overrepresented among" prochoice abortion activists. See Raymond J. Adamek, "Abortion Activists: Characteristics, Attitudes and Behavior," *National Right to Life News* (January 31, 1986): 7.
59. Himmelfarb, "Vanishing Jews," 249.
60. See, e.g., Sylvia Barack Fishman, *Double or Nothing? Jewish Families and Mixed Marriage* (Lebanon, NH: Brandeis University Press / University Press of New England, 2004); and Keren R. McGinity, *Still Jewish: A History of Women and Intermarriage in America* (New York: NYU Press, 2009).
61. Tikva Frymer-Kensky, *Reading the Women of the Bible: A New Interpretation of Their Stories* (New York: Schocken Books, 2002), 335. This is even more striking given Shaye J. D. Cohen's reminder that the Tanakh regularly describes non-Jewish women who marry Jews as being automatically, as it were, converted to Judaism (*Beginnings of Jewishness*, 170).
62. See "שֶׁקֶץ," in Reuben Alcalay, *The Complete Hebrew-English Dictionary* (Bridgeport, CT: Prayerbook / Hartmore House, 1974), 2711.
63. English translation from Robert Alter, trans. and ed., *The Five Books of Moses* (New York: Norton, 2004), 569.
64. English translation from *The Soncino Talmud* (Brooklyn, NY: Soncino, 1990).
65. S. Niger, "I. L. Peretz and His Nigun," in *Y. L. Peretz: Ale verk* [The Complete Works of I. L. Peretz], vol. 1 (New York: CYCO, 1947), LIII. For Seymour Levitan's translation of Peretz's 1908 version, see Ruth Wisse, ed., *The I. L. Peretz Reader* (New Haven: Yale University Press, 2002), 3–15.
66. S. Y. Agnon, "The Lady and the Peddler," in Robert Alter, ed., *Modern Hebrew Literature* (New York: Behrman House, 1975), 212. The story was originally published in Jacob Fichman's collection *Ba'sa'ar* [In the Storm] (Tel Aviv: Agudat ha-sofrim ha-Ivrim, 1943).
67. Baruch Kurzweil, "Ha-Adonit v'ha-Rokhel" [The Lady and the Peddler], in *Masot al Sipurav shel Shai Agnon* [Essays on the Stories of S. Y. Agnon] (Jerusalem: Schocken Books, 1962), 125–26; my translation.
68. Robert Alter, introduction to "The Lady and the Peddler," in Alter, *Modern Hebrew Literature*, 198; Kurzweil, "Ha-Adonit v'ha-Rokhel," 128.
69. For the period before World War II, "standard estimates [of Jewish-Christian intermarriage] range from 1.7 percent to 'somewhere below seven percent.' . . . Young Jews and Christians did not interact enough to fall in love."

Jonathan Sarna, *American Judaism: A History* (New Haven: Yale University Press, 2004), 222 (quoting *American Jewish Year Book* 60 [1959]: 9).

70. Frederic Cople Jaher, "The Quest for the Ultimate Shiksa," *American Quarterly* 35:5 (Winter 1983): 518–42; Adam Sol, "Longings and Renunciations: Attitudes toward Intermarriage in Early Twentieth Century Jewish American Novels," *American Jewish History* 89:2 (June 2001): 215–30.
71. An early example of the *shaygets* narrative is Emma Wolf's *Other Things Being Equal* (Chicago: A. C. McClurg, 1892); see also Ann R. Shapiro, "The Ultimate Shaygets and the Fiction of Anzia Yezierska," *MELUS* 21:2 (Summer 1996): 79–88.
72. See Josh Lambert, "Regatta Land," *Nextbook.org* (September 12, 2007); and Kaufmann's novel, *Remember Me to God* (Philadelphia: Lippincott, 1957).
73. Jaher states this effectively: "Belletristic treatment of this subject usually takes the form of an extended metaphor for the problematic existence of the American Jew. The authors who focus on *shiksas* and their attractions to and for Jewish males deploy a variety of traditional perceptions, symbols, stereotypes, and fantasies of Christian women and Jewish men to make interfaith courtship emblemize the experience and concerns of a people long engaged in a desperate struggle for survival" ("Quest for the Ultimate Shiksa," 519).
74. Ezra Brudno, *The Tether* (Philadelphia: Lippincott, 1908), 273.
75. Leslie Fiedler, "Genesis: The American-Jewish Novel through the Twenties," *Midstream* 4:3 (Summer 1958): 27–28.
76. Mary Antin, *The Promised Land* (New York: Penguin, 1997), 196. Isaac Rosenfeld's "Adam and Eve on Delancey Street," *Commentary* 8 (1949): 385–87, articulates the link between kosher taboos and sexual taboos, which was later played out brilliantly in Philip Roth's *Portnoy's Complaint.*
77. Anzia Yezierska, *Salome of the Tenements* (Urbana: University of Illinois Press, 1995), 107.
78. Lewisohn knew the potential consequences of crossing the line of literary obscenity: he claimed that he wrote a novel that was completely destroyed by the NYSSV, on the grounds of obscenity. See Lewisohn, *Upstream: An American Chronicle* (New York: Boni and Liveright, 1922), 145.
79. Lewisohn, *Island Within*, 213.
80. Ibid., 227.
81. Philip Wylie, *Heavy Laden* (New York: Knopf, 1928), 143.
82. Of course, not all such avoidance of explicit sexual description could be blamed on Comstockery or government interference—as chapter 4 will discuss, authors imposed their own standards of modesty on their work. In Agnon's "The Lady and the Peddler," for example, the characters' intimacy is described as follows: "[Joseph] stayed in the lady's room, and slept in her husband's bed, while she waited upon him [משמשת לפניו] as though he were her lord" (204–5). The English translation deemphasizes the sexual implication, but Helen's "wait[ing] upon" Joseph is unmistakably suggestive of sexual relations in the original Hebrew. Agnon plays on the frequent Talmudic use of "משמשת" as a euphemism for

intercourse. Such double-entendres are as far as Agnon was willing to go toward presenting allegorically resonant interracial sex—but not because of any legal threat. Nitsa Ben-Ari argues that obscenity laws were not enforced in Mandate Palestine or early Israel with any real zeal and that "'cleansing' Hebrew formal literature of erotica was more of a self-censorious process." Ben-Ari, *Suppression of the Erotic in Modern Hebrew Literature* (Ottawa: University of Ottawa Press, 2006), 73.

83. Philip Roth, *Portnoy's Complaint* (New York: Random House, 1969), 146. Further citations of this source are given parenthetically in the text.
84. Sam B. Girgus, "Portnoy's Prayer: Philip Roth and the American Unconscious," in Asher Z. Milbauer and Donald G. Watson, eds., *Reading Philip Roth* (London: Macmillan, 1988), 129, 130.
85. John Donne, "Elegy 19: To His Mistress Going to Bed," reprinted in Clay Hunt, *Donne's Poetry: Essays in Literary Analysis* (New Haven: Yale University Press, 1954), 17.
86. Hunt notes that the conceit is "one of the commonplaces of Elizabethan love poetry" but that Donne's particular achievement is that he "works this routine material to sharp concreteness in the treatment of both the metaphor itself and the sexual experience it describes, which is presented with an almost anatomical precision" (*Donne's Poetry*, 20–21). Roth's subtle allusion here was picked up a decade later, for a substantially similar purpose, in the title and epigraph of Johanna Kaplan's novel *O My America!* (New York: Harper and Row, 1980).
87. "Monkey Business, or, the Most Prevalent Form of Degradation in Erotic Life," 56, Box 184, Philip Roth Papers, Library of Congress, Washington, D.C.
88. Estelle Gershgoren Novak, "Strangers in a Strange Land: The Homelessness of Roth's Protagonists," in Milbauer and Watson, *Reading Philip Roth*, 62; Alan Cooper, *Philip Roth and the Jews* (Albany: SUNY Press, 1996), 102.
89. Philip Roth, "How Did You Come to Write That Book, Anyway?," in *Reading Myself and Others* (New York: Farrar, Straus and Giroux, 1975), 39–40.
90. They could have read all about this phenomenon as early as 1959 in Albert Gordon's *Jews in Suburbia* (Boston: Beacon, 1959), 170, where a woman is quoted as saying, "Our husbands do business with them. We see them in the town's shopping area. [But] Jews and Christians do not meet socially even in suburbia." A fairly broad study of the phenomenon was available in "A Study of Religious Discrimination by Social Clubs," reprinted in Raymond W. Mack, ed., *Race, Class and Power*, 2nd ed. (New York: Van Nostrand Reinhold, 1968), 106–14.
91. Jane Gerhard, *Desiring Revolution: Second-Wave Feminism and the Rewriting of American Sexual Thought, 1920 to 1982* (New York: Columbia University Press, 2001), 125. For a compelling alternative reading of "Portnoy's sexual episodes . . . not as erotic in themselves but as occasions of and for resignification," particularly in terms of the novel's complex representations of race, see Dean Franco's "*Portnoy's Complaint*: It's about Race, Not Sex (Even the Sex Is about Race)," *Prooftexts* 29:1 (Winter 2009): 86–115 (quote on 101).

92. Warren Hoffman's sympathetic reading of Portnoy as "queer" emphasizes this point; see Hoffman, *The Passing Game: Queering Jewish American Culture* (Syracuse: Syracuse University Press, 2009), 115.
93. "The Masochistic Plunge," box 185, Philip Roth Papers, Library of Congress, Washington, D.C. The scene, though unfinished and undeveloped, is similar to the one that eventually appeared in *My Life as a Man*, in which Peter Tarnopol is confronted by his wife-to-be, Maureen, with the news that she is two months pregnant. Roth, *My Life as a Man* (New York: Penguin, 1985), 186.
94. This embrace of Zionism was particularly popular among younger Jews: in the wake of the war, the B'nai B'rith Hillel Foundation reported "the most striking expression of Jewish identification and responsibility that ever welled up on university and college campuses," while "some 10,000 American Jewish students had traveled to Israel to fill spots on kibbutzim and in factories left unmanned by the general mobilization." Joshua Michael Zeitz, "'If I Am Not for Myself . . .': The American Jewish Establishment in the Aftermath of the Six Day War," *American Jewish History* 88:2 (2000): 259–60.
95. "Portnoy's Complaint / Jewish Blues Notes," n.p., and untitled note numbered 13 and beginning "The Wailing Wall," Box 188, Philip Roth Papers, Library of Congress, Washington, D.C.
96. Karl Abraham, "On Neurotic Exogamy," in Hilda Abraham, ed., *Clinical Papers and Essays on Psycho-analysis: The Selected Papers of Karl Abraham*, trans. Hilda Abraham and D. R. Elison (New York: Basic Books, 1955), 48–50. Abraham's essay is a stunning anticipation of Portnoy's complaint, in that he diagnoses "neurotic exogamy," which "occurs where a man experiences an insuperable aversion to any close relationship with a woman of his own people or nation. Or, to put it more correctly, of his mother's people" (48–49).
97. Paula Hyman, *Gender and Assimilation in Modern Jewish History: The Roles and Representations of Women* (Seattle: University of Washington Press, 1995), 164.
98. For sources that demonstrate the beginning of this belief in the Jewish mother's responsibility for Jewish continuity in America in the interwar years, see Joselit, *Wonders of America*, 70–73.
99. A sharp and influential statement of this perspective is Thorstein Veblen's "The Intellectual Pre-eminence of Jews in Modern Europe," *Political Science Quarterly* 34:1 (March 1919): 33–42, in which Veblen refers to the Zionist project as "an experiment in isolation and in-breeding" (33). For Freud's essay, see Sigmund Freud, "The Most Prevalent Form of Degradation in Erotic Life" (1912), in *Sexuality and the Psychology of Love* (New York: Collier Books, 1963), 58–70.
100. Maurice Charney, *Sexual Fiction* (London: Methuen, 1981), 119.
101. On Roth's Diasporism, see Sidra DeKoven Ezrahi, "The Grapes of Roth: Diasporism from Portnoy to Shylock," in *Booking Passage: Exile and Homecoming in the Modern Jewish Imagination* (Berkeley: University of California Press, 2000), 221–33; and Ranen Omer-Sherman, "'No Coherence': Philip Roth's Lamentations for Diaspora," in *Diaspora and Zionism in Jewish American Literature: Lazarus,*

Syrkin, Reznikoff, and Roth (Hanover, NH: Brandeis University Press / University Press of New England, 2002), 191–233.

102. Jewish Telegraphic Agency, "Mideast Report," *j.: The Jewish News Weekly of Northern California* (March 21, 2003), http://www.jweekly.com/article/full/19521/mideast-report/.
103. As Michaels deadpans, "intermarriage with Gentiles does not, of course, threaten Jewish survival in the way that the Nazis did. The Nazis threatened Jewish survival because they tried to kill all the Jews; intermarriage hardly kills anyone." Walter Benn Michaels, *Our America: Nativism, Modernism, and Pluralism* (Durham: Duke University Press, 1997), 181n. 242.
104. Sollors, *Beyond Ethnicity*, 165.
105. James B. Twitchell suggests that "we reserve our linguistic wrath for the most abhorrent act: mother-son incest," raising the question of whether mother-son incest is less common because it is more abhorrent or more abhorrent because it is less common. Twitchell, *Forbidden Partners: The Incest Taboo in Modern Culture* (New York: Columbia University Press, 1987), 54. For dates of the appearances in print of the various uses of *motherfucker*, and its near euphemisms, see Jesse Sheidlower's impressive resource, *The F Word* (New York: Random House, 1995), 196–214. Two American Jewish classics, Meyer Levin's *The Old Bunch* (1937) and Norman Mailer's *The Naked and the Dead* (1948), feature prominently among the earliest texts to employ this taboo word's less elaborately euphemized forms.
106. The term "libidinal investment" here is drawn from Fredric Jameson, who offered a famous, if rightly disputed, call for allegorical readings with his statement that "psychology, or more specifically, libidinal investment, is to be read in primarily political and social terms" in fiction of the Third World. Jameson, "Third-World Literature in the Era of Multinational Capitalism," *Social Text* 15 (Autumn 1986): 72. Of course, Jameson's notion of Third World literature is obviously a problem; Aijaz Ahmad's "Jameson's Rhetoric of Otherness and the 'National Allegory,'" *Social Text* 17 (October 1987): 3–25, was the first of many necessary correctives to Jameson's essay.
107. J. M. Kertzer remarks that "reading the novel is itself an unsettling experience" (28), a suggestion quoted, and affirmed, by Marcia Mack. See Kertzer, "Beginnings and Endings: Adele Wiseman's *Crackpot*," *Essays on Canadian Writing* 58 (Spring 1996): 15–35; and Mack, "*The Sacrifice* and *Crackpot*: What a Woman Can Learn by Rewriting a Fairy Tale and Clarifying Its Meaning," *Essays on Canadian Writing* 68 (Summer 1999): 134–58.
108. While the key case in the United States was *Roth v. United States* (1957), in Canada the crucial developments were the emendation of the Criminal Code in 1959 and a case on *Lady Chatterley's Lover*, *Brodie v. The Queen*, [1962] SCR 681. The chapter on *Crackpot* in Ruth Panofsky's study of Wiseman's literary career describes in detail Wiseman's process of drafting and submitting the novel. Panofsky, "Strange, Daring," in *The Force of Vocation: The Literary Career of Adele Wiseman* (Winnipeg: University of Manitoba Press, 2006), 55–94.

109. Panofsky, *Force of Vocation*, 50. A measure of the admiration one influential reader had for Wiseman's debut novel can be glimpsed in letters that Victor Gollancz, Wiseman's British publisher, sent to Robert Giroux in 1956. Wiseman's novel was so "superb," Gollancz wrote, that it might overcome the "immense handicap" of its "subject"—"the immigration of a Jewish family from Russia into Canada"—which he deemed "positively repellent to the British public." Victor Gollancz to Robert Giroux, May 31 and June 7, 1956, box 13, Farrar, Straus & Giroux, Inc., records, Manuscripts and Archives Division, New York Public Library.
110. Panofsky, *Force of Vocation*, 19.
111. Ibid., 79.
112. Adele Wiseman, "From *Crackpot*," in Mordecai Richler, ed., *Canadian Writing Today* (Middlesex, UK: Penguin Books, 1970), 233–45.
113. See letters from Candida Donadio to Adele Wiseman, box 23, folder 19, Adele Wiseman Fonds, York University, Toronto.
114. Panofsky, *Force of Vocation*, 168n. 90.
115. Ruth Panofsky, "From Complicity to Subversion: The Female Subject in Adele Wiseman's Novels," *Canadian Literature* 137 (July 1993): 41–48. Wiseman is paraphrased on this issue in Christl Verduyn, *Lifelines: Marian Engel's Writings* (Montreal: McGill-Queen's University Press, 1995): "Adele Wiseman once reflected upon her successful novel *The Sacrifice* as a book she had written almost by formula for her (male) professor Malcolm Ross. At times, it did not even seem like her book. *Crackpot*, on the other hand, felt entirely hers" (223n. 63).
116. On the lack of real radicalism in Jong, see Susan Rubin Suleiman, *Subversive Intent: Gender, Politics, and the Avant-Garde* (Cambridge: Harvard University Press, 1990), 123. See also Rosalind Coward, "'This Novel Changes Lives': Are Women's Novels Feminist Novels? A Response to Rebecca O'Rourke's Article 'Summer Reading,'" *Feminist Review* 5 (1980): 53–64, in which Coward warns "against any simple designation of" novels such as *Fear of Flying* "as feminist" (60).
117. Isobel McKenna, radio review, December 28, 1975, quoted in Panofsky, *Force of Vocation*, 89–90; Helene Rosenthal, "Comedy of Survival," *Canadian Literature* 64 (Spring 1975): 115.
118. E. G. Mardon, "Revolting Second Novel by Wiseman," *Lethbridge Herald* (November 12, 1974), clipping in box 20 of the Adele Wiseman Fonds, York University, Toronto. Mardon complains about "page after page of revolting and degenerating description," states his belief that "*Crackpot* will deprave or corrupt the reader," and calls it "offensive" and "obscene." He quotes from *Miller v. California* (1973) to suggest that *Crackpot* is "prurient" according to "contemporary community standards," which he claims should be "ascertained . . . through the Herald, and the personal opinions expressed in this review." Rarely has a would-be censor so boldly admitted that when he refers to "community standards," he means no more and no less than his own personal inclinations.

119. Tamara Palmer, "Elements of Jewish Culture in Adele Wiseman's *Crackpot*," *Prairie Forum* 16:2 (1991): 265; Adele Wiseman, *Memoirs of a Book Molesting Childhood and Other Essays* (Toronto: Oxford University Press, 1987), 13.
120. Wiseman, *Memoirs of a Book Molesting Childhood*, 23.
121. Adele Wiseman, *Crackpot* (1974; repr., Toronto: McClelland and Stewart, 1992), 129. Further citations of this source are given parenthetically in the text.
122. For examples of this motif in Yiddish literature, see Isaac Bashevis Singer, "Gimpel the Fool," in *The Collected Stories of Isaac Bashevis Singer* (New York: Farrar, Straus and Giroux, 1982), 3–14; and S. Y. Abramovitsh, "Fishke the Lame," *Tales of Mendele the Book Peddler* (New York: Schocken Books, 1996), 1–298.
123. Theodore Schroeder, *"Obscene Literature" and Constitutional Law: A Forensic Defense of Freedom of the Press* (New York: Privately printed, 1911), 13–14.
124. Wiseman's Pipick seems to bear no relation to "Moshe Pipik" in Philip Roth's *Operation Shylock: A Confession* (New York: Simon and Schuster, 1993).
125. Wiseman could have, but did not, allow Hoda to welcome women as well as men as sexual partners. She privileges heterosexuality in her text in the same way that other feminist novels of the early 1970s did.
126. Wiseman's own statements about her Jewishness are fascinating in their total lack of ambiguity or ambivalence: "The tone of my felt Jewishness is so positive that no alternate model with which life has presented me has ever looked even tempting, in spite of the possible perks attached, and notwithstanding my real affection, and even, in some cases, love, for some alternate model practitioners. Conversely, my sense of myself as a Jew and of the value of that identification has never wavered in spite of the fact that I have occasionally found myself in absolute disagreement with and even enraged by some of the stances, whether considered official or otherwise, taken by other Jews." Wiseman, "Jewishness," unpublished essay, box 16, Adele Wiseman Fonds, York University, Toronto.
127. Twitchell reports that 70% of reported incest is "father-daughter or surrogate father-figure incest," 20% is "brother-sister, including adopted or 'rem' siblings, . . . and the remainder is uncle-niece or in-law activity, and finally in much smaller numbers mother-son" (*Forbidden Partners*, 13).
128. On Jewish mother jokes and their increasing prominence in the years of World War II, see Gladys Rothbell, "The Jewish Mother: Social Construction of a Popular Image," in Steven M. Cohen and Paula E. Hyman, eds., *The Jewish Family: Myths and Reality* (New York: Holmes and Meier, 1986), 118–28. On the Jewish mother as "the nerve center of the Jewish novel of the sixties," see Melvin J. Friedman, "Jewish Mothers and Sons: The Expense of Chutzpah," in Irving Malin, ed., *Contemporary American Jewish Literature: Critical Essays* (Bloomington: Indiana University Press, 1973), 156–74.
129. Peter Thorslev argues brother-sister incest was "made sympathetic" or even "idealized" as "a metaphor for human perfectability" in Byron and Shelley, while Marc Shell reads brother-sister incest more broadly as a sympathetic symbol for the revolutionary ideal of "universal siblinghood." Peter L. Thorslev Jr., "Incest as

Romantic Symbol," *Comparative Literature Studies* 2 (1965): 47; Marc Shell, *The End of Kinship: "Measure for Measure," Incest, and the Idea of Universal Siblinghood* (Stanford: Stanford University Press, 1988). Father-daughter incest has typically provided the counterpoint to such utopian images. See, e.g., Karl F. Zender, "Faulkner and the Politics of Incest," *American Literature* 70:4 (December 1998): 739–65; Anne Dalke, "Original Vice: The Political Implications of Incest in the Early American Novel," *Early American Literature* 23:2 (1988): 188–201.

Rare examples of mother-son incest in literary texts include Stefan Vacano's *Sündige Seligkeit* (Berlin: Fontane, 1909), mentioned by Otto Rank in *The Incest Theme in Literature and Legend: Fundamentals of a Psychology of Literary Creation*, trans. Gregory C. Richter (Baltimore: Johns Hopkins University Press, 1992), 567–69; and the thirtieth story of Marguerite de Navarre's *Heptameron* (trans. George Saintsbury [London: Society of English Bibliophilists, 1894], 3:200–201), discussed by Shell (*End of Kinship*). For a study of the Oedipus myth and modern literature, see Debra Moddelmog, *Readers and Mythic Signs: The Oedipus Myth in Twentieth-Century Fiction* (Carbondale: Southern Illinois University Press, 1993).

130. On the Jewish mother as symbol for Jewish tradition, see Hyman, *Gender and Assimilation*, 160; Riv-Ellen Prell, *Fighting to Become Americans: Jews, Gender, and the Anxiety of Assimilation* (Boston: Beacon, 1999), 150, 163; Zena Smith Blau, "In Defense of the Jewish Mother," *Midstream* 13:2 (February 1967): 44; and Alain Finkielkraut, *The Imaginary Jew*, trans. Kevin O'Neill and David Suchoff (Lincoln: University of Nebraska Press, 1994), 14.
131. It is interesting to consider that the interaction at the root of the chaos in a more recent major novel on Jewish parent-child relations in the 1960s, Roth's *American Pastoral* (1997; repr., New York: Vintage, 1998), is a single erotically charged kiss a father gives his daughter (89–93).
132. Panofsky, "From Complicity to Subversion," 46.
133. Freud, "The Most Prevalent Form," 65.
134. Arthur Waskow, "Judaism and Revolution Today," *Judaism* 20:4 (Fall 1971), reprinted in Jack Nusan Porter and Peter Dreier, eds., *Jewish Radicalism: A Selected Anthology* (New York: Grove, 1973), 15, 18.
135. See Riv-Ellen Prell, *Prayer and Community: The Havurah in American Judaism* (Detroit: Wayne State University Press, 1989), 86–87.
136. Ibid., 71.
137. Michael Greenstein is one of the critics who have noted the "parodic echo of Genesis" in *Crackpot*'s epigraphic opening; Greenstein, *Third Solitudes: Tradition and Discontinuity in Jewish-Canadian Literature* (Montreal: McGill-Queen's University Press, 1989), 110. E. M. Broner's 1978 novel *A Weave of Women* (New York: Holt, Rinehart and Winston) is perhaps the best example of a more widely recognized feminist classic that mimics the syntax and diction of (translations of) Jewish scriptures.

138. Robert Greenblatt, "Out of the Melting Pot, into the Fire," in James A. Sleeper and Alan L. Mintz, eds., *The New Jews* (New York: Vintage, 1971), 47.
139. Lisa Maria Hogeland, *Feminism and Its Fictions: The Consciousness-Raising Novel and the Women's Liberation Movement* (Philadelphia: University of Pennsylvania Press, 1998), 2; Prell, *Prayer and Community*, 92.

Notes to Chapter 4

1. See Edward de Grazia, *Girls Lean Back Everywhere: The Law of Obscenity and the Assault on Genius* (New York: Random House, 1992), 622–88.
2. George H. W. Bush, "Remarks at the University of Michigan Commencement Ceremony in Ann Arbor," May 4, 1991. The case was *John Doe v. University of Michigan*, 721 F. Supp. 852 (E.D. Mich. 1989).
3. Richard Burt, introduction to Burt, ed., *The Administration of Aesthetics: Censorship, Political Criticism, and the Public Sphere* (Minneapolis: University of Minnesota Press, 1994), xii–xiii.
4. Judith Butler, *Excitable Speech: A Politics of the Performative* (New York: Routledge, 1997); Stanley Fish, "There's No Such Thing as Free Speech, and It's a Good Thing, Too," in *There's No Such Thing as Free Speech, and It's a Good Thing, Too* (New York: Oxford University Press, 1994), 102–19.
5. On Freud's use of the analogy of censorship in *The Interpretation of Dreams*, see Michael G. Levine, "Censorship's Self-Administration," *Psychoanalysis in Contemporary Thought* 9 (1986): 605–40; also note William Olmsted's argument that Freud's "central concept of dream censorship develops in response to contemporary antisemitic incidents and policies." Olmsted, "Turning the Tables: Freud's Response to Antisemitism in *The Interpretation of Dreams*," *Leo Baeck Institute Yearbook* 54:1 (2009): 191–216. For Bourdieu's use of censorship, see his "Censorship and the Imposition of Form," in *Language and Symbolic Power*, ed. Gino Raymond and Matthew Adamson, trans. John B. Thompson (Cambridge: Harvard University Press, 1991), 137–59.
6. For Fish, "restriction, in the form of an underlying articulation of the world that necessarily (if silently) negates alternatively possible articulations, is constitutive of expression. Without restriction, without an inbuilt sense of what it would be meaningless to say or wrong to say, there could be no assertion and no reason for asserting it" ("There's No Such Thing as Free Speech," 103).
7. Ibid., 111.
8. Florence Dore, *The Novel and the Obscene: Sexual Subjects in American Modernism* (Stanford: Stanford University Press, 2005), 2.
9. Ibid., ix.
10. Bourdieu, "Censorship," 138. Foucault also distinguishes between censorship and other "negative elements"—that is, mechanisms of suppression—that are "component parts" in the discourse of sexuality he analyzes. Michel Foucault, *History of Sexuality, Volume 1: An Introduction* (New York: Pantheon, 1978), 12.

11. Adorno and Horkheimer noted that "the censors voluntarily maintained by the film factories to avoid greater costs have their counterparts in all other departments. The process to which a literary text is subjected, if not in the automatic foresight of its producer then through the battery of readers, publishers, adapters, and ghost writers inside and outside the editorial office, outdoes any censor in its thoroughness." Max Horkheimer and Theodor W. Adorno, *Dialectic of Enlightenment*, trans. Edmund Jephcott (Stanford: Stanford University Press, 2002), xv.
12. Groups such as the Committee to Protect Journalists, in New York, and Index on Censorship, in London, track and publicize contemporary governmental suppression of writers and artists around the world. The former notes on its website that, at the time of writing, 587 journalists have been "murdered with impunity" since 1992, many of them murdered by governments or by political groups (http://www.cpj.org/).
13. The term *modesty* is, of course, no more impervious to being appropriated and transformed than *censorship* or any other word. Indeed, *modesty* has at times been used as a sickening, Orwellian euphemism for brutal impositions of government-condoned censorship, as in Israel, where so-called modesty patrols roam the streets imposing their beliefs about acceptable norms of dress and behavior through intimidation and violence, with implicit police toleration. See, e.g., "Jewish 'Modesty Patrols' Sow Fear in Israel," Associated Press (October 6, 2008).
14. Jonathan Freedman, *The Temple of Culture: Assimilation and Anti-Semitism in Literary Anglo-America* (New York: Oxford University Press, 2000), 175.
15. Raphael Patai, *The Hebrew Goddess*, 3rd ed. (Detroit: Wayne State University Press, 1990), 26. Patai may overstate the case somewhat in his effort to correct the view of Judaism as a monolithic and unified culture. Recently, David Biale has nuanced Patai's line of argument, describing "a dialectic between, on the one hand, the *idea* of one Jewish people and of a unified Jewish culture, and, on the other, the history of multiple communities and cultures." Biale asserts that "on both the elite and popular levels . . . the Jewish people were, at once, one *and* diverse." Biale, *Cultures of the Jews* (New York: Schocken Books, 2002), xxiii–xxv.
16. Moshe Carmilly-Weinberger, *Censorship and Freedom of Expression in Jewish History* (New York: Sepher-Hermon, with Yeshiva University Press, 1977), 5.
17. The *Shulkhan Arukh* was itself bowdlerized by early modern Catholic censors, not only in its representation of non-Jews but also, in one example, in its discussion of sex. See Amnon Raz-Krakotzkin, *The Censor, the Editor, and the Text: The Catholic Church and the Shaping of the Jewish Canon in the Sixteenth Century*, trans. Jackie Feldman (Philadelphia: University of Pennsylvania Press, 2007), 162.
18. See *Shulkhan Arukh*, Orakh Khayim, 307:16.
19. Carmilly-Weinberger, *Censorship and Freedom of Expression*, 5.
20. *B. Shabbos* 33a.
21. See *Moreh nevuchim* 3:8. Translation from *The Guide of the Perplexed of Maimonides*, vol. 3, trans. Michael Friedlander (London: Trubner, 1885), 29.

22. The towering figure in this area of thought is Yisrael Meir Kagan (1838–1933), known as the Chofetz Chaim. For an introduction to his thought in English, see Rabbi Shimon Finkelman and Rabbi Yitzchak Berkowitz, *Chofetz Chaim: A Lesson a Day: The Concepts and Laws of Proper Speech Arranged for Daily Study* (New York: ArtScroll/Mesorah, 1995).
23. For insight into the community structure that made Spinoza's excommunication possible, see Yosef Kaplan, "The Social Function of the 'Herem' in the Portuguese Jewish Community in Amsterdam in the 17th Century," in Jozeph Michman and Tirtsah Levie, eds., *Dutch Jewish History* (Tel Aviv: Tel Aviv University, 1984), 111–55. Thanks to Hilit Surowitz for pointing me to this source. On "the rehabilitation of Spinoza in Jewish culture," notwithstanding his rejection by the Jewish communal authorities of his own historical moment, see Daniel Schwartz, *The First Modern Jew: Spinoza and the History of an Image* (Princeton: Princeton University Press, 2012) (quote on 3).
24. Jonathan Sarna, *American Judaism: A History* (New Haven: Yale University Press, 2004), 39, 45, 59, 112, 161, 242, 239, 368. For a case study that dramatizes this point, see Arthur A. Goren, *New York Jews and the Quest for Community: The Kehillah Experiment, 1908–1922* (New York: Columbia University Press, 1970).
25. Horace Kallen, *Indecency and the Seven Arts and Other Adventures of a Pragmatist in Aesthetics* (New York: Horace Liveright, 1930), 25.
26. Jonathan Sarna, "In Search of Authentic Anglo-Jewish Poetry: The Debate over A. M. Klein's *Poems* (1944)," in Jacob Neusner, Ernest S. Frerichs, and Nahum M. Sarna, eds., *From Ancient Israel to Modern Judaism—Intellect in Quest of Understanding: Essays in Honor of Marvin Fox*, vol. 4 (Atlanta: Scholars, 1989), 133.
27. "Orthodox Rabbis 'Excommunicate' Author of Prayer Book Though He Is Not a Member," *New York Times* (June 15, 1945): 11.
28. Zachary Silver, "The Excommunication of Mordecai Kaplan," *American Jewish Archives Journal* 62:1 (2010): 21.
29. Rackman was an Orthodox congregational rabbi and scholar with both a law degree and a PhD. He went on to be appointed as provost of Yeshiva University and president of Bar-Ilan University. For a brief personal appreciation, see Deborah Lipstadt's *History on Trial: My Day in Court with David Irving* (New York: Ecco, 2005), 3–4.
30. Philip Roth, "Writing about Jews," *Commentary* 36:6 (December 1963): 446–52; and "Letters from Readers," *Commentary* 37:4 (April 1964): 6–19.
31. Philip Roth to Emanuel Rackman, April 30, 1959, 4, Box 101, Philip Roth Papers, Library of Congress, Washington, D.C.
32. On American Catholics' relationship to the Catholic hierarchy, see Patricia Byrne, "American Ultramontanism," *Theological Studies* 56:2 (1995): 301–26.
33. On the censorship of Yiddish under the czar, see David Fishman, "The Politics of Yiddish in Tsarist Russia," in Neusner, Frerichs, and Sarna, *From Ancient Israel to Modern Judaism*, 4:155–71. For an overview of Yiddish censorship under the Soviets, see David Shneer, *Yiddish and the Creation of Soviet Jewish Culture, 1918–1930*

(Cambridge: Cambridge University Press, 2004), 125–31. On censorship in Israel, see Nitsa Ben-Ari, *Suppression of the Erotic in Modern Hebrew Literature* (Ottawa: University of Ottawa Press, 2006).

34. See "This Book and the Post Office," in Ben-Zion Liber, *Dos geshlekhts lebn*, 4th ed. (New York: Rational Living, 1927), 5; and B. Liber, "Dr. Liber and the Post Office," *New Republic* 20:249 (August 13, 1919): 61.
35. On this case, see Richard Polenberg, *Fighting Faiths: The Abrams Case, the Supreme Court, and Free Speech* (New York: Viking, 1987), and on the belated and questionable translation of the Yiddish leaflet, 51–55.
36. Bruce's biographers love to point out that one of the Los Angeles policemen who arrested him in October 1962 translated his Yiddish taboo words for the court. See Albert Goldman, from the journalism of Lawrence Schiller, *Ladies and Gentlemen, Lenny Bruce!!* (New York: Random House, 1974), 388; and Ronald Collins, *The Trials of Lenny Bruce* (Naperville, IL: Sourcebooks, 2002), 100–101. Bruce responded on his album *Lenny Bruce Is Out Again* (Phillies, 1965), PHLP-4010, contesting the cop's translation: "*Shmuk*! The word *shmuk* is a German word. And it means literally in German a man's decoration." Bruce is a comedian and not a linguist, so it should not be surprising that he gets his facts wrong here—Yiddish linguists agree, contrary to Leo Rosten's popular but unreliable *Joys of Yiddish* (1968) and other such sources, that a German derivation for the Yiddish *shmok* (and not, properly, *shmuck*) is impossible, and they have suggested as more likely sources the Polish *smok*, "dragon," or a corruption of the Yiddish *shtekl*, "little stick," to *shmekl*. Also, despite what Bruce says, most Yiddish lexicographic sources, including many editions of Alexander Harkavy's dictionaries, as well as Nahum Stutchkoff thesaurus, either indicate that it means "penis" or omit it deliberately as vulgarity.
37. Indeed, one of Barth's classic and frequently quoted recorded bits demonstrates her refusal to translate taboo Yiddish words. Responding to a member of her audience who remarks that he has brought his "own interpreter" with him to the show—presumably because he does not speak Yiddish—Barth says, "I'll interpret for you, honey. I'll interpret. There's only two words you need to know in the *Yiddishe* language, and that's *gelt* and *shmuk*: 'cause if a man has no *gelt*, he is." The joke here, of course, is that if you do not already know what *gelt* and *shmuk* mean, Barth's explanation will not help at all. Belle Barth, *If I Embarrass You, Tell Your Friends* (After Hours Records, circa 1960).
38. "Charges against Singer Dismissed," *Los Angeles Times* (February 18, 1961): 3; "Jack Eigen Speaking . . . ," *Chicago Daily Tribune* (December 13, 1958): 16; John Pagones, "For Adults, Belle's Offering a Ball," *Washington Post-Times Herald* (June 22, 1962): B7.
39. While Yiddish speakers to this day tend to hear *shmuk*, for example, as "penis" (or at least as having an equivalent vulgarity as, say, the English *cock* or *prick*), the word circulates now devoid of any controversy whatsoever, even in venues where words such as *fuck*, *shit*, and *cock* would be illegal or shocking—for example, on

broadcast television networks during prime time. The word *shmuk* can be spoken innocently in such contexts, as when it was used by Mary Beth Roe, a devoutly Christian host on the QVC home shopping network. Kathy Levine, *It's Better to Laugh: Life, Good Luck, Bad Hair Days & QVC* (New York: Pocket, 1996), 240–41.

40. Jules Chametzky et al., introduction to "The Great Tide, 1881–1924," in Chametzky et al., eds., *Jewish American Literature: A Norton Anthology* (New York: Norton, 2001), 115.
41. Aviva Taubenfeld, "'Only an "L"': Linguistic Borders and the Immigrant Author in Abraham Cahan's *Yekl* and *Yankl der Yankee*," in Werner Sollors, ed., *Multilingual America: Transnationalism, Ethnicity, and the Languages of American Literature* (New York: NYU Press, 1998), 157–58.
42. Lowell Brentano to Isaac Goldberg, April 2, 1920, box 1, Isaac Goldberg Papers, New York Public Library. See Isaac Goldberg's account of the suppression in "Anomalies of Censorship," *Reflex* 1:2 (August 1927): 56–57.
43. Detailing the earliest controversies, Nina Warnke remarks that "despite the fervent passions on both sides, their fight did not create the public spectacle that the 1923 production would later do, because performance and debate were kept largely within the linguistic realm of Yiddish and the geographical confines of the immigrant quarters—that is, on the periphery of American society." Warnke, "*Got fun nekome*: The 1907 Controversy over Art and Morality," in Nanette Stahl, ed., *Sholem Asch Reconsidered* (New Haven, CT: Beinecke Rare Book and Manuscript Library, 2004), 64. In New York, "the German-Jewish *American Hebrew* . . . called for the New York police commissioner to close down the show" (72), but that suggestion was not followed; and apparently, before one Chicago performance, "the police attempted to keep the audience from entering the hall but eventually gave up" (73). Warren Hoffman argues that the difference between the 1907–8 case and the 1923 one was that "Yiddish audiences were less bothered by the same-sex elements of the play because in 1907 the world in which Yiddish Americans lived was not shaped by modern notions of homosexuality that would paint such relationships in a negative light." Hoffman, *The Passing Game: Queering Jewish American Culture* (Syracuse: Syracuse University Press, 2009), 23. Even if the reasons that Jews and non-Jews objected to the play changed over those years, what bears emphasizing here is that in the earlier controversy, those who wanted the play suppressed and called publicly for police intervention could not convince the state authorities to act as their enforcers, whereas when the play was produced in English, state cooperation could be obtained. Decades later, in London, the government deputized a rabbi to decide which Yiddish plays could and could not be performed, again ending a cultural controversy by giving state support to one party in the debate. See Leonard Prager, "The Censorship of Sholem Asch's *Got fun nekome*, London, 1946," in Joel Berkowitz, ed., *Yiddish Theater: New Approaches* (Portland, OR: Littman Library of Jewish Civilization, 2003), 175–87.
44. My impression is that, with some exceptions, works written in other languages, similar to those in Yiddish, would have usually not been the subject of

censorship especially if written in a non-Roman alphabet that postal censors could not easily read. Indeed, the question of whether it would be constitutional if "matter written in a foreign, non-English tongue be translated into English in order to understand what it means" was raised by Justice Frankfurter during the oral arguments of *Manual Enterprises v. Day* 370 U.S. 478 (1962), and he specifically emphasized materials written "in a foreign script." After pressing the question for a few minutes, Frankfurter remarked that as it "seems to be too difficult a question," he would withdraw it. See Leon Friedman, ed., *Obscenity: The Complete Oral Arguments before the Supreme Court in the Major Obscenity Cases* (New York: Chelsea House, 1970), 137–39. On a particular effort to suppress French erotica in the United States in the mid-1920s, see Paul Boyer, *Purity in Print: The Vice-Society Movement and Book Censorship in America* (New York: Scribner, 1968), 209.

45. Isaac Goldberg, "New York's Yiddish Writers," *Bookman* 46:6 (February 1918): 687.
46. Yankev Glatshteyn, "'*Grobe reyd*' *in literatur*" ["Coarse speech" in literature], *Yidisher kempfer* (December 4, 1964), reprinted in Glatshteyn, *Prost un poshet: Literarishe esayen* (New York: Knight, 1978), 39; my translation.
47. While the terms *pornography* and *pornographic* were bandied about frequently with reference to *shund* in the Yiddish press in both Europe and America, Nathan Cohen's observation about the Polish case, that "the novels in the newspapers were usually far from pornographic, limiting themselves to sporadic hints of eroticism," would seem to apply equally well to the vast majority of American *shund*, too. Cohen, "*Shund* and the Tabloids: Jewish Popular Reading in Inter-war Poland," *Polin* 16 (2003): 205.
48. Robert Darnton, "What Is the History of Books?," in Kenneth E. Carpenter, ed., *Books and Society in History* (New York: Bowker, 1983), 3–26.
49. On the publication of the transcript of the *Madame Bovary* trial, see Elizabeth Ladenson, *Dirt for Art's Sake: Books on Trial from "Madame Bovary" to "Lolita"* (Ithaca: Cornell University Press, 2006), 18. According to Sholem Aleichem's brother, he read Flaubert; see Ken Frieden, *Classic Yiddish Fiction: Abramovitsh, Sholem Aleichem, and Peretz* (Albany: SUNY Press, 1995), 113.
50. Sholem Aleichem, *Shomers mishpet* (Berdichev, Ukraine: Yakov Sheptil, 1888); Sholem Aleichem, "The Judgment of Shomer, or The Jury Trial of All of Shomer's Novels," trans. Justin Cammy, in Justin Cammy, Dara Horn, Alyssa Quint, and Rachel Rubinstein, eds., *Arguing the Modern Jewish Canon: Essays on Literature and Culture in Honor of Ruth R. Wisse* (Cambridge: Harvard University Center for Jewish Studies, 2009), 129–85. See pages 8, 23, 24 in the Yiddish, 135, 142, 143 in the English. On the French trials, see Ladenson, *Dirt for Art's Sake*, 1–77.
51. Z. Reyzin, "Shomer," in *Leksikon fun der yidisher literatur, prese, un filologye*, vol. 4 (Vilna: Kletskin, 1929), translated in Justin Cammy, "Judging *The Judgment of Shomer*: Jewish Literature versus Jewish Reading," in Cammy et al., *Arguing the Modern Jewish Canon*, 103.

52. Ellen Kellman, "Educating 'Moyshe' or Corrupting Him? Polemics around the Novel *Sanin* in the American Yiddish Press circa 1908," Workmen's Circle/Emanuel Patt Lecture, YIVO/Center for Jewish History, March 30, 2009.
53. On this debate, see Ruth Wisse, *A Little Love in Big Manhattan: Two Yiddish Poets* (Cambridge: Harvard University Press, 1988), 125–28; Julian Levinson, "Modernism from Below: Moyshe-Leyb Halpern and the Situation of Yiddish Poetry," *Jewish Social Studies* 10:3 (Spring–Summer 2004): 143–60; and Glatshteyn, "'*Grobe reyd' in literatur*," 39–40.
54. Anita Norich, *Discovering Exile: Yiddish and Jewish American Culture during the Holocaust* (Stanford: Stanford University Press, 2007), 88.
55. See Janet Hadda, *Isaac Bashevis Singer: A Life* (New York: Oxford University Press, 1997), 138.
56. It is emphatically not the case that Yiddish-speaking Americans were somehow more able to resolve these disputes internally because they constituted a more homogeneous community than, say, English-speaking Americans in the 1970s or 2000s. On the contrary, the spectrum of mainstream Yiddish political and cultural opinion in the early 20th century ranged much farther than its postwar American counterpart—mainstream positions ranged from anarchism to religious fundamentalism—and Yiddish-speaking Jews certainly did not typically reach any consensus about what was proper to write, publish, or say. Individuals and groups may have decided to support one party or another in a given dispute, but precisely because so often the upshot of a publishing controversy was the splintering of the Yiddish-speaking population into more and more groups that refused to communicate civilly with one another, it is perhaps more reasonable to regard Yiddish speaking and writing Americans as constituting not a community, per se, but a constellation of what Michael Warner has called publics, or perhaps even counterpublics. See Warner, "Publics and Counterpublics," in *Publics and Counterpublics* (New York: Zone Books, 2005), 65–124.
57. Glatshteyn, "'*Grobe reyd' in literatur*," 39.
58. See, e.g., Yitshak Bashevis, *Sotn in goray un andere dertseylungen* (New York: Matones, 1943), 166. Glatshteyn's novel *Ven Yash iz geforn* (New York: Farlag Inzikh, 1938), for example, contains a number of speeches that include taboo language. The narrator meets a boxer who remarks of his fellow passengers, "entirely in Yiddish: 'Say, what kind of Jewish bastards [*besteds*] are walking around on this ship anyway? They'd eat shit [*drek*] rather than admit that they're Jews'" (19). English translation from Jacob Glatstein, *The Glatstein Chronicles*, ed. Ruth Wisse, trans. Maeir Deshell and Norbert Guterman (New Haven: Yale University Press, 2010), 11.
59. While Michael Warner does not use the term *modesty* in his articulation of "stranger sociability"—which, granted, extends beyond modesty to other aspects of language—he does quote from the 18th-century periodical *The Spectator*, his paradigm for the creation of a public through discourse, as follows: "If I meet with any thing in City, Court, or Country, that shock Modesty or good Manners, I shall

use my utmost Endeavours to make an Example of it" (Joseph Addison, *Spectator* 34 [April 9, 1711], quoted in Warner, "Publics and Counterpublics," 104). And if Warner's paradigm for a counterpublic is the Club of the She-Romps described in *The Spectator* 217 (November 1, 1711), it is fitting that the correspondent who describes that club notes, "We are no sooner come together . . . than we throw off all that Modesty and Reservedness with which our Sex are obliged to disguise themselves in Publick places" (quoted in ibid., 109). "Modesty," in other words, has been one way to think about the limits put on discourse in the formation of a public.

60. Isaac Goldberg, *The New Immorality: A Little Dictionary of Unorthodox Opinion*, Little Blue Book No. 1481 (Girard, KS: Haldeman-Julius, 1929), 25. Thanks to Thomas M. Whitehead of the Special Collections Department at Temple University Libraries for providing me with a copy of this source.
61. Isaac Goldberg, "Index Librorum Prohibitorum," *Panorama* (May 1934): 5. For an example of just how far Goldberg would go to avoid spelling out the taboo words, see Goldberg, "Index Librorum Prohibitorum," *Panorama* (April 1934): 5, in which he refers to them as "the plain Anglo-Saxon words indicative of micturition, eructation, breaking of wind, and other functions of the body beautiful . . . [and] bald reference[s] to phallic phenomena associated with tumescence, not to speak of the vulgar metaphor for testicles."
62. Isaac Goldberg, "Index Librorum Prohibitorum," *Panorama* (April 1934): 5.
63. Irving Howe, with the assistance of Kenneth Libo, *World of Our Fathers* (New York: Harcourt Brace Jovanovich, 1976), 96.
64. So obvious is the notion that modesty varies from place to place and from culture to culture that it can function as an illustration of the basic assumptions of contemporary anthropology. In the afterword to Peter Just and John Monaghan's *Social and Cultural Anthropology: A Very Short Introduction* (New York: Oxford University Press, 2000), the authors explain that when "a student came to Peter with a request to do a course of independent study on the subject of female modesty across cultures . . . without actually investigating the literature he could predict with some confidence what it would show," namely, "that every culture everywhere has some concept that corresponds to our notion of 'modesty' . . . and that its content will vary widely and arbitrarily across time and space; indeed, that what will be regarded as thoroughly immodest in one place will be regarded as quite proper elsewhere." In a sense, the authors continue, this is "what a century of anthropology has taught us" (144–45).
65. Isaac Goldberg, *The Spirit of Yiddish Literature*, Little Blue Book No. 732 (Girard, KS: Haldeman-Julius, 1925), 42–43.
66. Glatshteyn, "'*Grobe reyd*' *in literatur*," 39.
67. For a detailed account of contemporary ultra-Orthodox standards for hair covering, see Rabbi Pesach Eliyahu Falk, *Modesty: An Adornment for Life: Halachos and Attitudes Concerning Tznius of Dress and Conduct* (New York: Feldheim, 1998), 227–66.

68. Isaac Meir Weissenberg, *Gezamelte shriftn* (New York: Literarisher Farlag, 1919), 8–22 (quotes on 12, 14, 19).
69. For comparison's sake, while nudity and discussions of sex were features of the English-language American stage in the 1920s, onstage simulations of sex acts (even aural ones) did not become common in the American theater until the 1960s, and even then they were controversial and frequently subject to censorship. See John H. Houchin, *Censorship of the American Theatre in the Twentieth Century* (Cambridge: Cambridge University Press, 2003), 72–116, 173–224.
70. Sholem Asch, *God of Vengeance*, trans. Isaac Goldberg (Boston: Stratford, 1918), 63; Asch, "Got fun nekome," *Dramatishe shriftn*, vol. 3 (Warsaw: Kultur Lige, 1922), 67–68.
71. As Hoffman remarks, "Where the text most firmly registers is in its silence" (*Passing Game*, 44), by which he means in its avoidance of an explicit and concrete description of the characters' sexual activities. See also Alisa Solomon's reading of the play in *Re-dressing the Canon: Essays on Theater and Gender* (New York: Routledge, 1997), 111–19.
72. Pinski's play has been noted for introducing a new degree of sexual frankness into modern Yiddish theater and literature; in it, the extent of sexual transgression exhibited onstage is just a kiss, and the play concludes with the main character's sincere repentance for his womanizing, celebrating his ability to conquer his sexual desire for the sake of his wife and child. David Pinski, "Yankl der shmid," in *Dramen* (New York: Farlag "Poale Zion," 1919), 7–122.

    On Dropkin, see Kathryn Hellerstein, "The Art of Sex in Yiddish Poems: Celia Dropkin and Her Contemporaries," in Sheila E. Jelen, Michael P. Kramer, and Scott Lerner, eds., *Modern Jewish Literatures: Intersections and Boundaries* (Philadelphia: University of Pennsylvania Press, 2010), 189–212. Sholem Aleichem's story "The Man from Buenos Aires" manages to be about a procurer without ever quite explicitly saying so; it was first published in 1909 and is available in English in Sholem Aleichem, *Tevye the Dairyman and The Railroad Stories*, trans. Hillel Halkin (New York: Schocken Books, 1987), 166–76. On Opatoshu, see Josh Lambert, "Opatoshu's Eroticism, American Obscenity," in Gennady Estraikh, Mikhail Krutikov, and Sabine Koller, eds., *Inventing a Modern Jewish Identity: Joseph Opatoshu, a Yiddish Writer, Thinker and Activist between Europe and America* (Oxford, UK: Legenda, 2013). On Perle, who was shouted down as a "pornographer" during a Day of Yiddish Literature at the YIVO Institute for Jewish Research in Vilna in August 1935, see David Roskies's introduction to the English translation of Perle's novel *Yidn fun a gants yor*, published as *Everyday Jews: Scenes from a Vanished Life* (New Haven: Yale University Press, 2007).
73. Chaim Grade, *Tsemakh Atlas: Di yeshive* (Los Angeles: Yidish natsyonaln arbeter-farband, 1967–68); quotation from Curt Leviant's translation, *The Yeshiva*, 2 vols. (Indianapolis: Bobbs-Merrill, 1976–77), 2:77. Further citations of this source refer to the translated edition and are given parenthetically in the text.

74. On Pitigrilli, see Alexander Stille, *Benevolence and Betrayal: Five Italian Jewish Families under Fascism* (New York: Picador, 2003), 104–17.
75. Manis Friedman, *Doesn't Anyone Blush Anymore? Reclaiming Intimacy, Modesty, and Sexuality* (San Francisco: HarperSanFrancisco, 1990); Shmuley Boteach, *Kosher Sex: A Recipe for Passion and Intimacy* (New York: Doubleday, 1999); Wendy Shalit, *A Return to Modesty: Discovering the Lost Virtue* (New York: Free Press, 2000); Rabbi Pesach Eliyahu Falk, *Modesty: An Adornment for Life* (New York: Feldheim, 1998). Further citations of these sources are given parenthetically in the text. For a modern Orthodox critique of Falk's book, see Rabbi Yehuda Henkin, *Understanding* Tzniut: *Modern Controversies in the Jewish Community* (Jerusalem: Urim, 2008), 72.
76. Among the forthrightly conservative and Christian books that have cited Shalit approvingly are James S. Spiegel, *How to Be Good in a World Gone Bad: Living a Life of Christian Virtue* (Grand Rapids, MI: Kregel, 2004), 138–40; Dinesh D'Souza, *The Enemy at Home: The Cultural Left and Its Responsibility for 9/11* (New York: Broadway, 2007), 145; James C. Dobson, *Bringing Up Girls* (Carol Stream, IL: Tyndale House, 2010); and Chip Ingram, *Love, Sex, and Lasting Relationships* (Grand Rapids, MI: Baker Books, 2003), 194–95. Shalit has also contributed an essay, "Modesty Revisited," to a collection of essays edited by Sandra Boswell and titled *Protocol Matters: Cultivating Social Graces in Christian Homes and Schools* (Moscow, ID: Canon, 2006).
77. See Shalit, *Return to Modesty*, 190, and Falk, *Modesty*, 124.
78. To be fair, if Friedman *did* watch the film, he did not pay much attention. He does not seem to have noticed that it is the single woman who sleeps with the married man who is ultimately punished, by death, in *Fatal Attraction*, while the adulterous married man's greatest loss is damage to his car and the murder of his daughter's pet rabbit. In other words, the film could be read as suggesting that a man can commit adultery without suffering any serious consequences.
79. According to one journalist, the "gleeful discussions of intercourse" in *Kosher Sex* "shocked the British Orthodox community, which forced [Boteach] out of his North London synagogue." Benjamin Soskis, "Who Is Shmuley Boteach?," *Slate* (March 29, 2001).
80. T. Jones, "This book is not G-rated," customer review of Shalit, *A Return to Modesty*, Amazon (September 11, 2007), http://www.amazon.com/reviews/R1BAL1DU02CRBC.
81. Whitney Strub, *Perversion for Profit: The Politics of Pornography and the Rise of the New Right* (New York: Columbia University Press, 2010), 83.
82. Anita Allen, "Disrobed: The Constitution of Modesty," *Villanova Law Review* 51:4 (2006): 841–57.
83. Michael Holquist, "Introduction: Corrupt Originals: The Paradox of Censorship," *PMLA* 109:1 (January 1994): 14.
84. The original article is Wendy Shalit, "The Observant Reader," *New York Times Book Review* (January 30, 2005): F16. Responses to Shalit by Tova Mirvis,

Jonathan Rosen, and Alana Newhouse appeared in the *Times* the following week; see "Letters" (February 27, 2005): F4. A longer response by Mirvis appeared in the *Forward*: "Judging a Book by Its Head Covering," *Jewish Daily Forward* (February 4, 2005). Shalit is invoked in Ezra Cappell's *American Talmud: The Cultural Work of Jewish American Fiction* (Albany: SUNY Press, 2007), 175–76; and Nora Rubel, *Doubting the Devout: The Ultra-Orthodox in the Jewish American Imagination* (New York: Columbia University Press, 2010), 151.

85. Tova Mirvis, *The Outside World* (New York: Knopf, 2004), 124–25. Further citations of this source are given parenthetically in the text.
86. Abraham's *The Romance Reader* (New York: Riverhead, 1995) concerns a teenaged Hasidic woman who is married off to a devout man who has had so little exposure to sex that he is incapable of intercourse; Auslander's *Foreskin's Lament* (New York: Penguin, 2008) recalls the sexual hypocrisy in a supposedly devout but abusive *haredi* family in which everyone secretly enjoys pornography; Brown's *Hush* (New York: Bloomsbury USA, 2010), written under the pseudonym Eishes Chayil ("a woman of valor"), describes child sexual abuse and its toleration by the Hasidic community of Borough Park, Brooklyn.
87. For a sociological study of the *Sports Illustrated* swimsuit issue—that does not, however, frankly discuss the use of the swimsuit issue for masturbation or attend to the long-intertwined history of titillating sexual material and athletics, as in the American "sporting journals" of the 19th century—see Cheryl Davis, *The Swimsuit Issue and Sport: Hegemonic Masculinity in "Sports Illustrated"* (Albany: SUNY Press, 1997).
88. The marketplace position of the novel certainly does not provide an explanation of Mirvis's euphemistic treatments of sex. Whether one compares *The Outside World* to romance best-sellers, such as the novels of Danielle Steele, or to commercially successful fiction of the period, from Lauren Weisberger's *The Devil Wears Prada* (2003) to Sue Monk Kidd's *The Secret Life of Bees* (2002) to Alice Sebold's *The Lovely Bones* (2002), it is difficult to find a mainstream American novel of the period, and especially one that focuses in particular on courtship and marriage, that goes quite as far as Mirvis's in eschewing taboo language and the explicit representations of sex.
89. Ruchama King, *Seven Blessings* (New York: St. Martin's, 2003); Risa Miller, *Welcome to Heavenly Heights* (New York: St. Martin's, 2003) and *My Before and After Life* (New York: St. Martin's, 2010). Orthodox Jewish presses that have recently begun to publish fiction include ArtScroll and Urim; on the former, see Yoel Finkelman, *Strictly Kosher Reading: Popular Literature and the Condition of Contemporary Orthodoxy* (Boston: Academic Studies, 2011). According to Paul C. Gutjahr, it is only since the 1980s that there has been a "noticeable, large-scale commitment on the part of Evangelical-Christian publishing houses to adding Christian fiction titles" to their lists. Gutjahr, "No Longer Left Behind: Amazon.com, Reader-Response, and the Changing Fortunes of the Christian Novel in America," *Book History* 5 (2002): 215.

90. This figure is given on the uncorrected proof distributed to book reviewers.
91. Tova Mirvis, email to the author, March 4, 2010.
92. See, for example, Lucy Fairbourne, *Male Chastity: A Guide for Keyholders* (n.p.: Velluminous, 2007), which explains that "delaying gratification allows more time to linger over the whole experience, and makes the ultimate climax all the more explosive when it comes" (8).
93. Tova Mirvis, email to the author, March 4, 2010.
94. *Board of Education v. Pico*, 457 U.S. 853 (1982). To the degree that *Pico* concentrated on the question of whether a school board has the right to remove books that it finds offensive from a school library, it was still a case about censorship of a sort—but a less pervasive, less effective, and in that sense less pernicious kind of censorship than the ones made possible by obscenity law from the 1890s to the 1960s.

Notes to the Conclusion

1. Matthew Blade, dir., *Nice Jewish Girls* (Dollhouse Digital, 2009).
2. Evelyn Torton Beck, ed., *Nice Jewish Girls: A Lesbian Anthology* (Watertown, MA: Persephone, 1982). There is surprisingly little discussion of pornography in this anthology given the date of its publication. In one essay in the collection, Beck does identify the association of "male lust with violence toward women" as marking a writer's closeness to "the Western pornographic imagination" (Beck, "I. B. Singer's Misogyny," in ibid., 295), suggesting that her perspective on pornography may share elements with the views of antipornography feminists. On the "so-called lesbian or girl/girl number" in hard-core American film pornography, as it developed in the 1970s, see Linda Williams, *Hard Core Power, Pleasure, and the "Frenzy of the Visible,"* expanded paperback ed. (Berkeley: University of California Press, 1999), 97, 127, 140; and also, for a performer's perspective, Sheldon Ranz, "Interview with Nina Hartley," *Shmate* 22 (Spring 1989): 23–24.
3. There is reason to hope that such a comprehensive cultural history will be produced in time not by the Herculean efforts of a single scholar but piecemeal, by groups of interdisciplinary scholars working together—a process begun with collections such as Nathan Abrams, ed., *Jews and Sex* (Nottingham, UK: Five Leaves, 2008).

   A few figures who merit treatment in such studies include the bookseller Frances Steloff; the producers, publishers, and dealers of erotica Ralph Ginzburg, William Mishkin, Irving Klaw, and Marvin Miller; the librarian Judith Krug; such lawyers as Sidney Dickstein, Burton Joseph, Emanuel Redfield, and Victor Kovner; the "impresaria of striptease" Alice Schiller; the gay activist and nudist Rudi Gernreich, who was "inventor of the monokini"; the inventor of the topless bar, Davy Rosenberg; the psychologist and Esalen guru Fritz Perls; the theatrical director Jacques Levy; the prosex feminist critic Ellen Willis; the underground filmmaker Barbara Rubin; artists including Joan Semmel, Martha Edelheit, and Ida Appelbroog; and the recent self-described "Ivy League pornographer" Sam

Benjamin. A few of these figures have already been discussed, at least briefly, in histories of American obscenity and the sexual revolution, but rarely have scholars paid any serious attention to the ways in which Jewishness might have been relevant to their interventions. Such a list does not begin to approach comprehensiveness—its insufficiency is precisely its point—and I offer it here mostly to indicate the variety of the cultural figures whose careers would be relevant to an ongoing discussion.

4. Whitney Strub, *Perversion for Profit: The Politics of Pornography and the Rise of the New Right* (New York: Columbia University Press, 2010). See also Janice Irvine's argument that "the rise of the Right" since the 1960s "did not simply trigger bitter conflicts over sexuality; it was partly accomplished through them." Irvine, *Talk about Sex: The Battles over Sex Education in the United States* (Berkeley: University of California Press, 2002), 2.
5. Like other responsible authors who have written about the history of obscenity and pornography, Strub mentions the Jewishness of figures in his history only rarely and cautiously. For example, Strub notes that one of the recipients of Ralph Ginzburg's mailings, advertising the magazine *Eros* in the early 1960s, returned the mailer with the message "You dirty pornographic Jews!" on it (*Perversion for Profit*, 72). Strub does not mention that Ginzburg was Jewish or otherwise explain why someone might have responded to the *Eros* mailings with this anti-Semitic remark.
6. David Allyn, *Make Love, Not War: The Sexual Revolution: An Unfettered History* (Boston: Little, Brown, 2000).
7. It is well known that the Talmud was censored in early modern Europe—see Amnon Raz-Krakotzkin, *The Censor, the Editor, and the Text: The Catholic Church and the Shaping of the Jewish Canon in the Sixteenth Century*, trans. Jackie Feldman (Philadelphia: University of Pennsylvania Press, 2007), 32–56—but it may be more surprising that the Talmud has also been deemed obscene by Anglo-American observers. At the beginning of the 19th century, John Allen asserted, in his *Modern Judaism; or, A Brief Account of the Opinions, Traditions, Rites, and Ceremonies of the Jews in Modern Times* (London: T. Hamilton, 1816), that "there are multitudes [of traditions] in the Talmud, of which some cannot but disgust by their *filthiness*, and others must excite detestation by their *obscenity*." Not wanting to "offend the chaste reader," Allen quoted a single example, from *Berachot* 62a, in Latin, so that "the filthiness" will be "partly concealed under the veil of a dead language" (144–45). Decades later, the *Century* quoted a Jewish convert to Christianity and missionary to Jews, Alfred Edersheim (1825–1889), to the effect that "if . . . we imagine something containing law reports, a rabbinical 'Hansard,' and notes of a theological debating club—all thoroughly Oriental, full of discussions, anecdotes, quaint sayings, fancies, legends, and too often of what from its profanity, superstition, and even obscenity, could scarcely be quoted—we may form some general idea of what the Talmud is." Richard Wheatly, "The Jews in New York—II," *Century* 43:4 (February 1892): 520. A few years later, Zebulun Baird

Vance, a former governor of North Carolina and U.S. senator, in a lecture on the history and culture of Jews and Judaism, referred to the Talmud as "the most remarkable collection of oriental wisdom, abstruse learning, piety, blasphemy and obscenity ever got together in the world." Vance, *The Scattered Nation* (New York: J. J. Little, 1904), 23. While the suppression of David Pinski's *Temptations* by the NYSSV in 1920, discussed in chapter 4, was essentially a suppression of a loose translation of Talmudic and midrashic narratives, as far as I know, the Talmud itself has never been successfully censored in the United States. One more recent case, *Graydon Snyder v. Chicago Theological Seminary*, 94 L 1423 (Cir. Ct., Cook Co., Ill. 1994), ended with the awarding of damages to a Chicago Theological Seminary professor who had been disciplined for sexual harassment for referring, in class, to a narrative from *B. Yevamot* 54a. See Dirk Johnson, "A Sexual Harassment Case to Test Academic Freedom," *New York Times* (May 11, 1994): D23.

8. Liam Lynch, dir., *Sarah Silverman: Jesus Is Magic* (Interscope Records, 2006).
9. Al Goldstein was profiled by Mike Edison in *Heeb* 2 (2002); the porn performer and entrepreneur Joanna Angel appeared on the cover of *Heeb* 8 (2005); and another porn performer, James Deen, not incidentally the male star of *Nice Jewish Girls*, was featured as one of the "Heeb 100" in 2008.
10. Philip Roth, *Portnoy's Complaint* (New York: Random House, 1969), 153. Portnoy was not alone in noticing this; Norman Mailer noted the year before that he "never felt more like an American than when he was naturally obscene," and Norman Podhoretz, a year before that, described his own "conversational habit of liberally mixing obscenities with the big words." Mailer, *Armies of the Night: History as a Novel, the Novel as History* (New York: New American Library, 1968), 47–48; Podhoretz, *Making It* (New York: Random House, 1967), 188.
11. Robert B. Weide, dir., "The Grand Opening," on *Curb Your Enthusiasm: The Complete Third Season* (Home Box Office, 2005), DVD. Interestingly, Berman published a novelty book in 1966 that lampooned the inanity of obscenity standards. See *Shelley Berman's Cleans and Dirties* (Los Angeles: Price, Stern, Sloan, 1966).
12. Before Weide's work on *Curb*, he was known for writing and directing a well-regarded documentary, *Lenny Bruce: Swear to Tell the Truth* (Home Box Office, 1998).
13. Arthur A. Cohen, "Review: *Discerning the Way: A Theology of the Jewish-Christian Reality*, by Paul van Buren," *Journal of Religion* 62:2 (April 1982): 210
14. The term *dirty Jew* has its own fascinating history, which demonstrates how fluidly a term that was once painful can be recuperated into an icon of pride for some people while still retaining the power to wound others. *Dirty Jew* was a popular anti-Semitic taunt in the 19th century—Isaac Mayer Wise and Sigmund Freud both recalled being insulted with it—but by the time of Zola's "J'accuse!," it was more likely to crop up in the writing of liberals and anti-anti-Semites as a mark of the racism of bigots than in the writing of anti-Semites themselves. American examples include Booth Tarkington's 1923 novel *The Midlander* and Harold Brecht's 1926 short story "Paradise Regained" in *Harper's*. While James

Joyce, Jean Renoir, Leslie Fiedler, and Norman Mailer used it to signal the complexity of Jewish identity and the relations between Jews and non-Jews between the 1930s and 1960s, for more recent writers, including Jacques Derrida and Alain Finkielkraut, it has continued to serve as the epitome of children's anti-Semitic jibes. For Wise, see Arthur Hertzberg, *The Jews in America* (New York: Columbia University Press, 1993), 108; for Freud, see John M. Efron, *Medicine and the German Jews: A History* (New Haven: Yale University Press, 2001), 243; on the term during the Dreyfus Affair and in Zola's famous essay, see Pierre Birnbaum, *The Anti-Semitic Moment: A Tour of France in 1898* (New York: Hill and Wang, 2003), 9, 297; Booth Tarkington, *The Midlander* (New York: Grosset and Dunlap, 1923), 9; Harold W. Brecht, "Paradise Regained," *Harper's* (February 1926): 301–9; for Joyce's use of the epithet, see *Ulysses* (New York: Vintage, 1990), 183; for Renoir's, *La grande illusion* (RAC, 1937); for Fiedler's, "Dirty Ralphy," *Commentary* 4 (1947): 432–34; for Mailer's, *Advertisements for Myself* (New York: New American Library, 1960), 450. Derrida mentions the term in Jacques Derrida and Elisabeth Roudinesco, *For What Tomorrow: A Dialogue*, trans. Jeff Fort (Stanford: Stanford University Press, 2004), 109; and Finkielkraut does in *The Imaginary Jew*, trans. Kevin O'Neill and David Suchoff (Lincoln: University of Nebraska Press, 1997), 4.

15. *Federal Communications Commission v. Fox Television Stations*, 556 U.S. 502 (2009); *Federal Communications Commission v. Fox Television Stations*, 567 U.S. ___ (2012); *Federal Communications Commission v. Pacifica Foundation*, 438 U.S. 726 (1978).
16. For examples, see Dan Kois, "When Do Papers Print the F-Word?," *Slate* (June 25, 2004), http://www.slate.com/articles/news_and_politics/explainer/2004/06/when_do_papers_print_the_fword.html, about newspapers printing and not printing the word "fuck" in a quotation of Vice President Dick Cheney; the innumerable blog posts that spring up every time the *New York Times* tap-dances around printing "shit" or "fuck"; or Ira Glass, speaking as a guest on Dan Savage's podcast *Savage Love*, episode 276 (January 31, 2012), noting how "ridiculous" it is that his critically acclaimed radio show *This American Life* has to warn listeners before even acknowledging the existence of sex.
17. Strub, *Perversion for Profit*, 268–97.
18. While in *New York v. Ferber*, 458 U.S. 747 (1982), *Reno v. ACLU*, 521 U.S. 844 (1997), and *Ashcroft v. Free Speech Coalition*, 535 U.S. 234 (2002) the Supreme Court insisted that the expanded latitude to prosecute purveyors of child pornography rested on the actual harm done to children in the production of such materials, *United States v. Williams*, 553 U.S. 285 (2008) "unmoored this regulation from its originally intended design," Strub writes, "allowing for prosecutions predicated on socially unaccepted desires rather than meaningful child protection." Examples of cases in which people have been convicted or felt enough prosecutorial pressure to plea bargain under this expanding definition of obscenity include a collector of sexually explicit manga (illustrated comic books), a website operator who posted purely textual stories about sexual abuse, and a school official who

pasted photographs of children's faces onto photographs of naked women and was sentenced to five years in prison. See Strub, *Perversion for Profit*, 291–93.

19. On Apple's regulation of the representation of sex in its online App Store, see Brian Chen, *Always On: How the iPhone Unlocked the Anything-Anytime-Anywhere Future—and Locked Us In* (Boston: Da Capo, 2011), 91–94. In February 2012, the website *Gawker* posted Facebook's "community standards" for the representation of sex on that platform and concluded that "when it comes to sex and nudity, Facebook is strictly PG-13, according to the guidelines." Adrian Chen, "Inside Facebook's Outsourced Anti-Porn and Gore Brigade, Where 'Camel Toes' Are More Offensive than 'Crushed Heads,'" *Gawker* (February 16, 2012), http://gawker.com/5885714/inside-facebooks-outsourced-anti+porn-and-gore-brigade-where-camel-toes-are-more-offensive-than-crushed-heads. The absurdity of Facebook's policy was highlighted in a recent incident that Bob Mankoff of the *New Yorker* named "Nipplegate": an Adam and Eve cartoon, tame and standard *New Yorker* fare, led to the magazine's Facebook page being "temporarily banned." Mankoff pointed out, gleefully, that it was just two ink splotches, representing Eve's nipples, that transgressed Facebook's standards. See Robert Mankoff, "Nipplegate," *The Cartoon Bureau* (blog), *New Yorker* (September 10, 2012), http://www.newyorker.com/online/blogs/cartoonists/2012/09/nipplegate-why-the-new-yorker-cartoon-department-is-about-to-be-banned-from-facebook.html.
20. *Bethel School District v. Fraser*, 478 U.S. 675 (1986); *Morse v. Frederick*, 551 U.S. 393 (2007).
21. *Congressional Record* 141 (June 14, 1995): 8329.
22. "The 'Other Woman' Turns Activist," *Register-Guard* (December 2, 1995): 10A; *Congressional Record* 141 (June 14, 1995): 8337–38.
23. On relations between the Christian Right and American Jews, see Naomi Cohen, *Natural Adversaries or Possible Allies? American Jews and the New Christian Right* (New York: American Jewish Committee, 1993); Kenneth D. Wald and Lee Sigelman, "Romancing the Jews: The Christian Right in Search of Strange Bedfellows," in Corwin Smidt and James Penning, eds., *Sojourners in the Wilderness: The Religious Right in Comparative Perspective* (Lanham, MD: Rowman and Littlefield, 1997), 139–68; and Daniel Williams, *God's Own Party: The Making of the Christian Right* (Oxford: Oxford University Press, 2010).
24. At the time of writing, for example, the group Enough Is Enough lists the anti-pornography crusader Judith Reisman on its Internet Safety Council, and the group Morality In Media lists Rabbi Morton Pomerantz, a retired New York State chaplain, on its board of directors.
25. *FCC v. Fox*, 556 U.S. at 758.
26. Telemachus Timayenis, *The American Jew: An Exposé of His Career* (New York: Minerva, 1888), 81, 191. For more of the urbanism ascribed by Timayenis to Jews, see *The Original Mr. Jacobs* (New York: Minerva, 1888) and its tirades against "the modern Jew—a type such as we meet by the thousands in all large cities" (219).
27. See *People v. Viking Press, Inc.*, 147 N.Y. Misc. 813 (Magistrate's Ct. 1933).

28. Janet R. Jakobsen and Ann Pellegrini, *Love the Sin: Sexual Regulation and the Limits of Religious Tolerance* (New York: NYU Press, 2003), 39–41.
29. For an anthropologist's study of the use of taboo language by contemporary road comics, see Susan Seizer, "On the Uses of Obscenity in Live Stand-Up Comedy," *Anthropological Quarterly* 84:1 (2011): 209–34.
30. Clement Virgo, dir., "Old Cases" (originally aired June 23, 2002), on *The Wire: The Complete First Season* (HBO Home Video, 2004), DVD.
31. Studies have proliferated on the subject of children's vulnerability to sexual assault and of the incoherence of the laws protecting them. See James R. Kincaid, *Erotic Innocence: The Culture of Child Molesting* (Durham: Duke University Press, 1998); Philip Jenkins, *Moral Panic: Changing Concepts of the Child Molester in Modern America* (New Haven: Yale University Press, 1998); Marjorie Heins, *Not in Front of the Children: "Indecency," Censorship, and the Innocence of Youth* (New York: Hill and Wang, 2001); and Judith Levine, *Harmful to Minors: The Perils of Protecting Children from Sex* (Minneapolis: University of Minnesota Press, 2002). For a fascinating argument about the relationship between child-pornography laws and child abuse, see Amy Adler, "The Perverse Law of Child Pornography," *Columbia Law Review* 101 (2001): 209–73. No critic has seemed to mention that A. M. Homes's slightly controversial 1996 novel about a pedophile, *The End of Alice* (New York: Scribner, 1996), is set in a Jewish community, though much ink has been spilled lately about child sexual abuse in the ultra-Orthodox community.

INDEX

ABOUT THE AUTHOR

Josh Lambert is Academic Director of the Yiddish Book Center and Visiting Assistant Professor of English at the University of Massachusetts, Amherst.